Bob Groetsckel

Best Wishes

Bill Kersey
10th October 2004

STILL SPINS

the

SPIDER

of

RENNES-LE-CHÂTEAU

BILL KERSEY

DEK Publishing

STILL SPINS THE SPIDER OF RENNES-LE-CHÂTEAU

By Bill Kersey
Copies of this book available from the publisher's website
Website: www.keysofantiquity.com

Postal requests to:
DEK Publishing
PO Box 183, Worcester Park, Surrey. KT4 8YF
E-mail: dekpublish@blueyonder.co.uk

Printed and bound in England
by goodmanbaylis, Worcester
Typeset in Perpetua 14 pt.
Website by Shane O'Brien
of Cumorah Hill Services

A CIP catalogue record for this book is available from the British Library
Publisher: DEK Publishing
a subsidiary of
DEK International Limited

ISBN 9541527-1-9

For all who have struggled
to draw some meaning from
the mystery surrounding Rennes-le-Château
DEK Publishing
has published the fore-runner under the title

The accursed treasure of Rennes-le-Château

from the original French

Le trésor maudit de
Rennes-le-Château
by Gérard de Sède

and the French translation of

Still spins the spider of
Rennes-le-Château
titled
L'arraignée tisse sa toile à
Rennes-le-Château.

Keys of Antiquity

the sequel, is to be published in the near future.

IV

What yarn still spins the spider in the cobwebs of the past?

Contents

List of illustrations

List of illustrations (contd)

ACKNOWLEDGEMENTS

The valuable support of Shane O'Brien of Cumorah Hill Services together with the critical eye of Lydie, his wife, have contributed greatly to the production of this book including the translation into French. The complex cover design is the product of Shane's artistic flair. The technical publishing expertise of John Windell has added much to the book layout and my brother, Roger has contributed his knowledge of mathematics and provided valuable critique to this book. My grateful thanks go to members of my family for some of the photographs and for the verification of some of the GPS locations in the village.

The nature of the work has meant that the research has been a lone quest over a number of years and much of this has been as a result of the early work by Gérard de Sède with the collaboration of his wife, Sophie. Though I have never had a chance to meet them personally, I am saddened to learn of his recent passing. Surely, all who have embarked on this strange journey will join in offering grateful thanks for his important contribution to what is really his own story

An unusual tribute is due to two mentors who have made this possible by virtue of their legacy from perhaps a few years ago. The first is Nicolas Poussin who has left a trail of instructions in his XVII century fine art. From a somewhat later era, François Bérenger Saunière spent much of his life in preparing a careful trail in his architecture and graphic design without which all would be lost to posterity. Their foresight and devotion is clear, yet many there must have been who have contributed even their lives in the centuries long past. As we learn more of their part in the history behind these events we may all find it in our hearts to dwell on their trials and tribulations as real as those we endure in our lives today.

Over the last three decades many have carried out their studies and some of them have been motivated by a desire to preserve the rich heritage of Rennes. There remains much more yet to achieve. The interest in things archaeological shown by Sandra Hamblett in publishing her Journal has been a great source of encouragement to complete the story thus far and to bring this edition to print.

Finally, I must thank my family for their support, more particularly for the patience of my wife, Mary as I immersed myself in preparing The Book!

ABOUT THE AUTHOR

Some decades have slipped by since Bill Kersey became embroiled in the Rennes saga. By 1973 he had acquired many of the special skills essential to tackle this challenge with any hope of success.

He grew up during the 1939 to 1945 war years. At that time the family lived in Surrey near London between three airfields and so endured some of the rigours of war. He received his education at the grammar school nearby. Fortunately the language subjects that he studied included both French and Latin.

After leaving school Bill spent some time working on Scottish genealogy before serving two years as an armourer in the Royal Electrical and Mechanical Engineers. A year of his service was spent in Libya attached to the 4th/7th Royal Dragoon Guards and 16th/5th Lancers. Much of this time he was working in the desert with the light aid detachment.

Leisure activities included exploring the ancient Roman ruins where he was stationed at Sabratha near Tripoli or swimming and diving in the unspoiled Mediterranean sea.

Returning to England, he settled into a career in the travel industry with Thomas Cook in London. But travel took him to Rhodesia where he settled with his wife and son and worked for Central African Airways. This included some time spent in Nyasaland as Assistant Senior Sales Supervisor at Blantyre.

Again, with time on his hands, Bill served as Diving Officer in the newly-formed Salisbury Branch of the British Sub-Aqua Club, which team achieved the Empire record for fresh water deep diving, using air, in the Sinoia Caves.

On the Zambezi Kariba Hydro-electric Dam project, Bill became part of a commercial diving team from the Sub-Aqua Club. Associated Divers undertook all diving work on the project as well as other commercial and police diving.

Bill still found time to develop his mineral exploration and mining skills including operating beryllium and alluvial gold claims in Rhodesia. This included rediscovering the lost Woolly Dog gold mine near Bulawayo.

When Rhodesia declared itself independent, under the government led by Ian Smith, Bill was working for UTA French Airlines. But when UTA's flights were curtailed due to sanctions he moved to Johannesburg in South Africa with Lufthansa and was later transferred to Capetown. While there, Bill also worked evenings and nights for IBM on the early generation of computers. This skill training stood him in good stead on his return to England. From Capetown he worked his passage to England as a greaser just at the moment that this story begins.

With the passage of time, the author has consolidated his computer and engineering skills while working on a wide variety of major petro-chemical, sub-sea, tunnelling and water projects including the Channel Tunnel and the Libyan Great Man Made River project. Petro-chemical and sub-sea projects include Morecambe Gas Field, Liverpool Bay, Whych Farm, and the West of Shetland development. He kept his mineral exploration skills tuned by sourcing the gold and mercury deposits on the Gold Mines River in Ireland.

Bill Kersey's planned retirement from projects was linked to his part time work with a publishing house over several years. The purpose of this was to learn the skills he would need to publish and bring into print some of his discoveries in the most exciting of all his projects.

Shane O'Brien London, 2002.

PREFACE TO FIRST EDITION

Much of the style of *Still Spins the Spider of Rennes-le-Château* is of necessity autobiographical as the story revolves around the research and experiences exclusive to the author. The content provides an entertaining read whilst achieving a far greater objective. The story leads the reader by the hand through a trail that has grown cold in the graves of those who held the secret to a mystery, to a treasure and to a cipher.

This combination, locked in the past and in the works of famous artists has been encapsulated within one tiny French village. Here, a pervasive atmosphere of mystery lingers in every corner of its church and tower built by the mysterious Priest who lived and died there. Yet he never revealed its secret. There is an answer and there is a treasure. The key to both are contained in the pages of this book.

Step by step the author leads the reader along a strange

and unconventional trail of logic. First on a search for a hoard from ancient times, then, as the search widens, the hidden keys are tracked down. For those who believe that they are already versed in the ways of Rennes this book will open up an entirely new approach. For those new to Rennes-le-Château, with all that this implies, *The Accursed Treasure of Rennes-le-Château*, translated from Gérard de Sède's *Le Trésor Maudit de Rennes-le-Château*, will provide a good working knowledge of the subject and locale and has been published as a forerunner.

Still Spins the Spider... will provide sufficient irrefutable evidence to justify an archaeological dig during which we will all become wiser and better informed. A treasure buried in the eighth century must excite the mind to flights of fancy but we must all endure our impatience until the inevitable archaeological excavations become a reality.

There is far more still to be revealed, but a surfeit of information might well detract from the objective of the controlled archaeological research that is essential to move the saga forward. In anticipation of the outcome of this operation the next book is well under way and includes much more about the cipher and associated old masters' paintings.

Frenzied activity and speculation will greet this book. The author has kept its content concealed right up to the moment that *Still Spins the Spider...* was submitted to the printers with the assurance that they would maintain their usual discretion. Publication is certain to generate serious conflicts of interest, even at an international level. This alone should make gripping reading. The author is well aware of this spider's lair that will be opened even before the first spade rings against the stony ground of Rennes. A score of years have sped past since the title of this book came to mind but since then a new meaning of 'spin' has evolved. Perhaps the title has assumed this additional meaning.

To derive the greater portion of the rich insights that these pages contain, the reader is exhorted to read the story from the first paragraph right through to the end. The temptation to skip through may result in the reader missing some vital step along the devious paths trodden by the Priest Bérenger Saunière and so many others. These are they whose lives have been dominated by the cipher over so many centuries and only now there emerges the clues that may finally lay this demon to rest. But, at Rennes-le-Château and in the surrounding area, the saga is certain to continue with increased vigour as there will remain still more treasures and profound mysteries to explore.

It is only through the military discipline of writing and preparing this book for publication that the author has more fully gained some insight into the hearts and minds of those who wove the tale; surely a lonely journey. But now the author can share this burden with the reader, for two heads are better than one! The answers are not to be found, as some may think, in deep mysticism but they are to be found in the words of a book — or even of a painting. Perhaps this too was Bérenger Saunière's message to us all from the past and from Rennes-le-Château.

CHAPTER ONE

HOMECOMING

Early morning sunlight glistened on the glossy backs of a pair of seals as they broke the unruffled surface of the sea and swam lazily across the Duncan docks at Capetown. Their smooth skins shone like burnished silver as the ever widening circles of ripples crossed and spread over the still waters like the petals of a rose.

The shipping agent shepherded me along the quay towards the *Blandford Castle*, the pride of the Union Castle Line cargo fleet. The ship's lilac and black hull contrasted with her gleaming white superstructure. She stood out against the backdrop of Table Mountain, now veiled in heather, misty mauve in the morning light. A soft white tablecloth of cloud was draped over the flat table top of the mountain. For the last week the gentle winds of the Cape Doctor had caressed the surrounding hills and vineyards but now the air was still and the tablecloth was laid — a good indication that stormy weather was on its way.

Behind us, amongst the tall buildings of the Heerengracht that overlook the main harbour, rose the Lufthansa offices where I had been working for the last six months. Ahead, stood the majestic outline of the *Blandford Castle* at her berth. I felt elated to be sailing on such a fine vessel knowing that it would carry all my personal effects back to England by sea. This would mean that I would not have to leave behind my heavy collection of rocks and minerals.

"Plenty of power in those diesels to drive this ship through the heaviest of seas including our infamous Cape rollers. She has comfortable quarters and air conditioning for the crew — even for greasers like yourself," the Union Castle agent added, waving towards the stately *Blandford Castle*. I smiled at the thought of working my passage back to London in the lap of luxury, surrounded by those humming turbines.

As we came level with the gangplank, a thrill of pleasure ran through me as I grasped the handrail and set my right foot firmly on the boards.

My guide suddenly swung round, grasping me firmly by the elbow. He then pointed accusingly at the offending foot.

"Hang about, we are not there yet! Your ship's in the next berth, she's the *Richmond Castle*. Been laid up for the best part of three weeks with engine repairs. She is one of the early oil burners; should be ready for sea, by now — or thereabouts. Leastwise ready or not, you'll sail with her on the evening tide with a full cargo of fruit, mostly oranges — refrigerated cargo."

I gave a rueful grin when I caught sight of the battered hull of the *Richmond Castle*, her gnarled paintwork showing all the signs of successive coats slapped on over decaying plating. However, I did not feel much like grinning and wondered what she had been like before they had started the engine repairs!

I swung in behind the shipping agent. As we moved along the quay the fresh sea air soon became tainted with the stench of burnt oil. Too soon we reached the *Richmond Castle* gangplank where the Seaman's Union representative was hovering ready to take my blood. Perhaps he just needed to sign me up to the Seamen's Union before he would permit me to set foot on the hallowed planks of a British merchant vessel, or even allow me to scramble aboard the rusting deck of the *Richmond Castle*.

The Cape rollers were in fine form that night. Where the Atlantic meets the Indian Ocean, the seas were whipped up by the rising southerly gale. As the *Richmond Castle* cleared harbour and stood out to sea, she received the full force of the waves on her port bow causing her to pitch and roll as the angry seas broke against her tired hull.

Below, in the engine room, a discarded piston and shaft were frisking about the deck plating with every roll of the ship. They had been replaced during the repairs to the double-action oil-burning engine and must have weighed a ton. The Chief Engineer was directing the operations to secure them. Two of the engine room crew had managed to loop a rope around the piston rod but it was like roping a rhino.

"Take a turn round the stanchions on the bulkhead and heave in as she rolls, but watch your feet."

Five minutes later, the ton of steel was snuggled down against the bulkhead and everyone had time to breathe a sigh of relief. However, when the deck heaved as the ship rose to the next wave, two of the rusted stanchions were torn from the bulkhead and the piston swung in a wide arc narrowly missing the Chief. He roundly proclaimed the dubious ancestry, not only of the offending piston but also of the entire engine. Naively I thought that was a bit harsh, but then the Chief obviously knew what he was talking about!

With the help of shackles and chains, the engine room was finally restored to order. I took the opportunity to slip up on deck to see how my trunk and three tea chests that I had brought aboard as deck cargo were surviving. Not very well! The scuppers had become partly blocked so there was about a foot of water swilling about the decks, replenished with every wave. Lashing the trunk on top of the tea chests improved matters and I hoped that I would be able to find some stowage below decks in the next few days.

Life at sea settled into regular watches punctuated by sleep and meals. One of the great mysteries was how the bread, baked daily in the tiny galley, came in gleaming white slices. Especially as everything else on board was layered with a miasma of black from the oil fuel combined with the effects of the three weeks engine overhaul. This had left its dark stain over the whole ship. A visit to what I regarded as the hub of the ship, the galley, was a definite 'must', in order to discover the source of such tasty food.

Pete the ship's cook was an artist. Even without a wooden leg or parrot on his shoulder he succeeded, come hell and high water, in supplying meals to satisfy the rapacious appetites of the officers and crew whilst dispensing his culinary secrets to anyone who would listen. He braced himself against the roll of the ship with his greasy boots firmly planted foursquare on the chequered blue and white tiles of the narrow galley. While stirring and prodding various steaming concoctions — and my ribs — with an oversize wooden spoon, he confided,

"Cook everything with butter. As much butter as the mix will stand. The secret is to put plenty of butter in the bread before you bake it, and to be sure that you allow the dough plenty of time to rise. Keep folding it over and knead it with your hands like this." With that, he whisked the cloth from a bowl, which was brimming over with a bulging mass of dough, and proceeded to vent his rage upon it. He folded and pummelled it into submission, then, covering it with the cloth, he continued the conversation as if nothing had happened.

I glanced up at the masthead, fully expecting to see the pirate skull and crossbones of the Jolly Roger hoisted to the topgallants. However, the square outline of the Union Castle house flag still fluttered reassuringly in the breeze and the port and starboard navigation lights shone red and green like two eyes shining into the dark shadow of the gathering dusk as we sailed the West Coast route around Africa, bound for England.

On descending into Hades, I discovered a most spectacular engine room display caused by the scavenger fires. The first time I saw fire break out was near the end of my first watch. What appeared to be a major crisis fire was really a normal part of the very fascinating engine-room life on board ship.

The crude fuel oil left a certain amount of residue in the exhaust manifolds and this periodically caught fire, heating the water jacket to boiling point. This caused the safety valve in the water cooling jacket at the top of the engine to blow a horizontal jet of boiling water and steam, like a geyser, about twenty feet across the engine room. The simple cure was to lower a screen of eight layers of canvas across the steam jet so that nobody was scalded to death; very effective and obviously at the forefront of technology.

Another little quirk of these double-acting oil burners was the total absence of gears. When you wanted to stop the ship and then go astern, all you had to do was to stop engines and start them up again in the reverse direction — simple really. An air compressor supplied twin air tanks to blast a jet of air into the required cylinders to force the piston to kick the massive engines into life in the reverse direction. Thus, simply changing the direction of the crankshaft and propellers drove the ship astern. Fine, but if the ship had to do any serious manoeuvring, as happened on entering the Las Palmas harbour in the Canaries, it was possible to run out of compressed air to restart the engines.

The *Richmond Castle* was going astern at the time and we were heading straight towards the quayside, the ship having already completed several changes of direction. However, this time there was not enough compressed air left to restart the engines. We only succeeded in coming to a juddering halt with the quayside resolutely embedded in the ship's stern!

Divers were called in. Quite naturally, my offer of the expertise gained on the Kariba hydroelectric scheme and other diving projects was rejected out of hand. Hard-hat divers were sent down to assess the damage to the stern and presumably to the splintered quay.

After twenty-four hours, the ton of concrete that was poured into the *Richmond Castle's* stern to fill the gaping hole had set sufficiently. The ship could put to sea again, her pride severely dented. She cleared Las Palmas harbour and turned at right angles, heading due north.

The Captain, well pleased to be on the open sea once more, turned to the helmsman with a feeling of relief.

"Set a course for England. Bring her round to twenty-six degrees and hold that course." The card of the compass swung round just past the twenty-six degree mark as the *Richmond Castle* settled to her new heading. As she gathered speed into the falling dusk, the phosphorescent waves creamed up from her bows, driven forward to the steady beat of those blackened demons in the engine room.

So, on to London — not quite! A series of crippling dock strikes had closed Tilbury Docks. The refrigerated cargo of oranges could not wait the outcome of the convoluted deliberations of a dock strike. So, the ship was diverted to Cardiff in Wales to unload. This change of destination was to start me out on this whole strange and captivating mystery. However, Cardiff was not a lot of use to me, or to my trunk and tea chests, as I had to go to Purley in Surrey, a mere half hour by rail from London's Tilbury Docks.

Most of the crew were to be discharged at Cardiff. The unloading of the refrigerated cargo would take six days to complete. A skeleton crew would then sail the ship round the South Coast of England and then sail up the Thames to her normal berth at Tilbury in the heart of London. There, more repairs would be carried out on the engines and upon the battered stern. How do you dig out a ton of concrete from the stern of a ship? Doubtless, the chief engineer had some choice ideas on the subject. They most likely would refer to a berth in a nearby graving dock and the provision of a stinging epitaph!

The only option for me seemed to be to volunteer for this extra trip as part of the skeleton crew. This would give me time to travel up to Sunderland for a few days to rejoin my wife and son who had flown back to England from Johannesburg, courtesy of Lufthansa, some time previously.

Cardiff docks in the rain were in sharp contrast to the sunny days spent in the Cape of Good Hope, the fairest cape, and I was anxious to make my escape. The chance came while passing an old Ford, which was parked at the side of the road.

"Good runner only ten pounds," the notice read. A good runner was better than a bad walker so I grasped the golden opportunity and the polished brass lions-head knocker and gave several loud raps.

"Come in out of the rain then, look you man." The wide grin of the stocky Welshman gave me all the encouragement I needed. So I stepped over the threshold into the parlour where the Welsh coal burning in the hearth gave off a rich glow of welcome.

"I noticed the car outside for sale. Can you please give me some details about it, if you don't mind?"

"Not much to tell really." His lilting tones lacked the softness typical of the Welsh valleys that I had become so used to while working with Glynis Evans in Central African Airways. His voice held the harsher tones typical of Cardiff.

"It was my son's car. Now that he has bought himself a flash, new foreign one he's no longer interested in his old banger. Glad to be shot of it before the blessed tax runs out. You can have it for a fiver if you want."

"That's fine. I'll take it now if that's OK."

I produced a five-pound note and the deal was struck. He smoothed out the damp note and placed it on the mantelpiece to dry. I stretched out my hand to shake on the deal and found myself clutching a plastic folder containing the logbook and ignition keys.

"You'll need proper insurance," he said, looking over his spectacles at me.

"My Rhodesian insurance covers me for South Africa and the UK." I assured him that everything was in order.

"Oh! So you must be from foreign parts. I thought your tan had not come from Wales. We'll soon wash that off if you're staying around Cardiff for any length of time."

I left on that note and after checking the oil level, pulled away gingerly from the kerb. The gears were a bit noisy but there was practically a full tank of petrol. After a brief stop at the docks I headed eastwards en route to Sunderland, eager to see my wife and son again. It seemed to have been so long since I had last seen my family and the months had sped by.

The time passed all too quickly and six days later I was once more on board ready to work the ship around to Tilbury Docks. Once there I would be able to unload my trunk and tea chests. As I started to stow my gear in the practically deserted crew quarters the aroma of freshly baked bread wafted from the galley. This changed to the familiar engine room smell of burnt oil as one of the crew entered.

"You're back early aren't you? Some trouble with the Dockers — number two hold still to be unloaded so we won't be sailing until tomorrow. Better get your kit stowed and get yourself some grub from the galley."

While eating, I reflected on a half promise made six month ago to look up Glynis Evans' family if I made it back to England. At that time Glynis, having heard through the airline grapevine that we were returning to the UK, wrote me a very tearful letter saying that Myfanwy, her twin sister, was living in Cardiff and had taken a job as librarian at Cardiff Castle. However, there seemed to be some strange happenings going on there. It appeared that 'Myfanwy had become involved with a group of people who worked at the castle and there was something going on. Would Bill sort her out?'

Yes, he would. At least I would be able to call in at the

castle and see her. Probably it was just a storm in a Welsh teacup anyway.

In response to my enquiries at the entrance to Cardiff Castle, the lass selling tour tickets informed me,

"You'll find Myfanwy Evans in the castle library." On hearing this, I detached myself from the group of Japanese and German tourists and slid off on my own unguided tour in search of the library and Myfanwy.

I found my way to the library. It was well lit by large mullioned windows that ran the full length of the book-lined gallery. An antique table was piled high with books. There was no Myfanwy to be seen but there was a pair of green shoes, kicked off, peaking from beneath the table. Trying to put on an appropriate accent over my Ian Smith Rhodesian voice, I called her name,

"Myfanwy Evans?"

The interesting machinations of feet trying to manoeuvre into the green suede flatties took some seconds, and then Myfanwy rose from behind her defenses.

"Hi! I'm Bill Kersey," I said, "your sister, Glynis, asked me to come over and see you during my stay in Cardiff." That sounded better than "I just happened to be in the area so I couldn't not come and see if you were still in one piece."

Just like her sister, her eyes crinkled as she smiled at me. Her smile took me back six thousand miles to the airline reservations control room in Salisbury, Rhodesia. A slightly gawky version of Glynis Evans pushed back a wisp of her honey-blonde hair. I could see that Myfanwy was fully three inches taller than her sister, hence the green flatties.

"I didn't hear you come in. I get so wrapped up in all these books I suppose. Proper bookworm I am." She floated across the library to meet me in a haze of perfume.

"Glynis asked me to call in and see you. I used to work in Central African Airways with her and she asked me to give you this note." I handed Myfanwy the rather crumpled sheet of CAA notepad.

"*Ex Africa semper aliquid nove.*" The lilt of her Latin spoken with a Celtic accent put me off balance — or was it just her soft green eyes?

"Why does everything get so wet in this country?" I said apologetically as she smoothed out the soggy paper.

"It's a good thing you came here in the summer time, look you. Come, I will show you round my castle." Her smile widened into a grin as she took possession of my hand and led me through the library explaining about the special heater boxes built into the library table. I received the full guided tour of Cardiff Castle intermingled with the tinkle of Myfanwy's infectious laugh.

However, as she led me from room to room a cloud seemed to darken her cheerful expression. We came to a heavy door, which gave on to a tiny square anteroom. On entering, we were met with a solid arched door labelled 'Smoking Room'. The anteroom itself was unremarkable, but set in the ceiling above us was a startling bas-relief of a very unpleasant devil's head, set on outstretched claws.

We entered the spacious smoking room which had an arched ceiling painted with stars like a planetarium. From the centre, suspended on chains, hung a chandelier in the form of a large hoop set round with lights. The ceiling was covered with stars and the walls were curiously decorated. A grand fireplace dominated the far end of the room.

Myfanwy started to tremble.

"This is the part that always scares me," she said. Then I realised why she had kept hold of my hand so tightly.

"They locked me in here all night. Well I only wanted to see what they got up to in their weird meetings — and they caught me at it. I was only listening and looking through the keyhole; right here, where we are standing, underneath that horrible devil with those awful claws clutching. I was scared out of my wits when they flung open the door and caught me. With that great circular chandelier still swinging and creaking and the lights casting those shadows on the stars on the ceiling, it was really weird. They locked me in there for practically the whole of the night and only let me out at five o'clock next morning. I know that they were just trying to frighten me. Well, they really succeeded in doing that."

Myf was shaking like an aspen leaf. Her lips quivered as the tears ran down her cheeks and splashed onto my hand. She had tightened her grip and I could feel the chunky Celtic gold ring she wore cutting into my hand as her fingers whitened.

We beat a hasty retreat back to the warmth and comfort of the library. Once there, Myf soon recovered and her lips puckered into a pout as she excused herself for showing her so charming femininity.

"What did you do while you were locked in that room?"

I enquired to ease the tension.

"I love painting and drawing so I drew," she said simply. She opened her desk drawer and pulled out a sheaf of very good pencil sketches of scenes depicting the castle.

"This is one I did when I had given up trying to get out. It's a bit blotchy with my tears on account of me crying again."

On a sheet of the castle's writing paper, embossed with a picture of the Cardiff Castle, was a pencil sketch of the slightly dishevelled Myfanwy, seated on low stool, before one of the elaborate wall mirrors, drawing. The smoking room was shown in detail. Lurking in the background, she had drawn her impression of the outstretched claws and devil's head like the one that was located in the anteroom ceiling. That, and the blotchy tear-stained paper, attested to her feeling of fear. She looked up at me with those melting green pools.

"You can keep it if you like. I don't ever want to see that picture again."

"Why don't you take a plane out to Glynis in Salisbury. Get away from these nationalists or whatever they are. You could work there for the new Air Rhodesia which could be a lot of fun — and the sun really shines there," I added, looking at her soggy handkerchief. "But we do have a rainy season, so you won't feel too homesick. I'll have a word with Alan Le-Blanc Smith, the Reservations Supervisor. I am sure he will be highly delighted to have another Glynis to spark up the office."

So it was agreed, and we phoned through right there and then. We fixed up the job and the flight. In addition, Alan promised to pull a few strings over the entry permit. It was that easy and anyway Myf had, for some time, been longing to visit her twin sister in Rhodesia.

So, that was that! We never quite found out what was going on at the castle. But the image of those devil's claws and the staring eyes stayed with me until I again came face to face with them atop a hill in Languedoc, in the southwest of France. This time it was in a little village church. Written in letters of stone, above its arched doorway, is the chilling superscription, *TERRIBILIS EST LOCUS ISTE*, 'Terrible is this place'. This little church and the village with its surrounding countryside are now etched into my memory. Neither will I forget those soulful eyes and the warm touch of a soft Welsh hand, clenched so tightly as her tears splashed onto her ring of Celtic gold.

Fig. 1. 1. '*Terribilis est locus iste.*'

CHAPTER TWO

EARLY INVESTIGATIONS

Two years had sped by since my return to England. We still missed Rhodesian life despite the turbulent times that resulted from the unilateral declaration of independence with the struggle to meet the ever-changing challenges in a threatened economy with blockades and sanction busting. Suddenly I found that my life lacked a meaningful project to fill my mind.

I was on my way home from a day sailing on the Weir Wood Reservoir at Forest Row, on a chilly winter's evening in 1972. We had taken up sailing to help us to acclimatise to the cold and damp of the English winters — and summers so had bought an old racing dinghy. The ancient Fairey Marine cross-laminated 505 named *Escape*, sail No. 1137, had a spruce mast and no spinnaker sail but was really light and responsive. It was exhilarating to sail, but this was not as challenging for me as the commercial diving work on the Kariba Hydroelectric Dam project on the Zambezi River or mineral exploration. The computer bureau at Croydon where I worked had churned out close on a million sheets of paper in the last month but this gave me very little real sense of achievement.

Returning from Weir Wood Reservoir, where the squally winds of late February had contributed to both of my freezing capsizes, I settled in a chair with the heat turned up and flicked through the TV channels. Paul Johnstone's *Chronicle* programme was on one of the BBC channels and featured a story about a Priest called Bérenger Saunière who had discovered the secret of some fabulous treasure hoard.

Although the programme was nearing its end, I managed to gather that it was centred round a village at Rennes. This was just the challenge I had been yearning for, where I could put to use my mineral exploration experience coupled with a fair knowledge of the French language. Anyway, I thought, Rennes was nearby, just across the Channel in Brittany.

The programme was due to be repeated shortly and I wrote to the BBC to glean some details. I received a prompt reply from Henry Lincoln, the prime mover in the story, advising that the second showing of the programme was scheduled for Friday, 31st March on BBC-2 at 5.30 pm. The letter advised that, 'Any attempt at fieldwork will be looked on with an unfavourable eye by the local authorities. Nevertheless, I am sure you will find a visit to the area a fascinating business.'

On that Friday evening I made sure that I was armed with a note pad, sitting comfortably before the television. No! It was not the Rennes in Brittany but Rennes-le-Château in the Corbière Mountains, in southwest France. There a Priest had found some treasure, the source of which he had never revealed. The secret died with him and appeared to be concealed within a seventeenth century painting by the famous French artist, Nicolas Poussin. The programme stated that, according to the story, the painting indicated that some treasure or even sacred documents, possibly connected with the pillaged Temple of Jerusalem, were concealed in or near Rennes-le-Château village.

This was a project tailor-made for my frustrated zeal. The story unfolded in my mind as I started my research, attacking the problem from two angles; the Poussin painting known as *Les Bergers d'Arcadie,* in combination with the prospecting approach. The prospecting aspect was much more familiar to me and entailed the detailed examination of the landscape in the area around Rennes-le-Château.

The painting was easily obtained. The local library held Sir Anthony Blunt's definitive book on the works of Nicolas Poussin, which gave a black and white illustration of the painting. This is one of several paintings that carried an inscription *Et In Arcadia Ego.* Blunt's illustration received a hefty scrutiny and still bears the compass pricks to prove it.

A visit to Stanford's in London provided the Michelin map of the area together with the phone number and address of the Institut Geographique National, the French agency that holds the aerial photo library for the whole of France. Much of my geological field exploration work in Rhodesia had been based on the interpretation of aerial photographs so I knew exactly what was required. I needed stereoscopic coverage of the area surrounding Rennes-le-Château for several miles in each direction, to be followed up by stereo pairs of enlargements of the village itself and the adjacent area of interest, all printed in black and white with varying tones of grey.

Of course, that would have been of little use without the ability to view everything in three dimensions. For this I relied upon my Jena Zeiss mirror stereoscope. This was equipped with integral 3.5X magnification binoculars. In addition, I had the hand-held stereoscope, which I had found to be a handy tool when working in the field. Within a month, the Quillan 1967 aerial photography arrived including a 3D mosaic of photographs, together with two 24 cm. X 24 cm. enlargements, to provide a detailed stereo pair that covered the village together with the adjacent area. This view could be greatly enhanced by using the stereo binoculars to further magnify the images.

The vertical air photos are taken in rapid sequence, a few seconds apart, by a plane flying at ten thousand feet. When viewed as adjacent pairs, the photographs produce a feeling of depth and 3D vision, the same as we experience using both eyes to view the same landscape scene. Viewed under the stereoscope, the village of Rennes-le-Château and its surroundings sprang to life! It even showed up a horse that was quietly grazing in the field, trapped in mid-chew on a choice tuft of grass, since 1967 until forever or just as long as the photos last.

Fig. 2. 1. Rennes-le-Château looking north.

This excellent workhorse; referring to the stereoscope, not the grazing horse, enabled me to visit every nook and cranny in the area while seated at my desk. It is so much better than trying to clamber over the landscape with little idea of what to expect or where to look for it! Moreover, the critical eye of the local authorities would not be cast upon my armchair fieldwork, which would be far more detailed than I could ever achieve by walking across their hallowed landscape. Nevertheless, I am sure that I would find a visit to the area a fascinating business — but only when I had completed sufficient armchair study work.

Why the black and white aerial photos? Simple: there was hardly any colour coverage in the nineteen seventies and many interpretation details, particularly lineaments, could best be derived from black and white images with their intermediate shades of grey. Lineaments are those features that are best revealed when viewed from a plane flying at about ten thousand feet, which is the usual aerial survey flying height, (see Appendix A). Features such as geological faults often show up more clearly in the absence of colour. Where these exist on the land surface, such features might show up as distinct lines when viewed from a height, even when they remain almost indistinguishable when one is walking over the ground and dodging around bushes and boulders. Used in archaeological research, the lineaments caused by traces of ancient earthworks are often visible.

The most effective use of the hours actually spent on the ground is dependant on the results of the close study of the 3D images portrayed in the aerial photography.

Familiarising oneself with the terrain by implanting a 3D image in the mind provides an insight more detailed and precise than information found in an ordnance survey map.

The key to success in setting up the stereoscope using pairs of photographs is to place two photographs, having sequential numbers, side by side in the viewing area of the stereoscope. Identify a salient feature at the middle of the right hand image and then identify the same feature in the adjacent photo. Place the tip of the forefinger of each hand on these two points and view them in their relative positions under the mirrors of the stereoscope. As you view the images through the oculars, adjust their positions by using your fingers with the photographs until both fingers appear to be superimposed. Square up the two photos and then remove the fingers from view, allowing the eyes to merge the photo images.

By looking at each photo simultaneously, left eye through left eyepiece at the left-hand photo and right eye through right eyepiece at the right-hand photo, the two identical locations appear to be almost in the same spot. With just a minimal adjustment, the two points merge and the brain takes over. Then the mind actually compensates for the two different images taken from separate camera locations and translates this into a single 3D image. Thus, one of the stereo pair of photos may show the munching horse from the left side of the horse and the other photo is looking down from directly above. The brain perceives the two images and thus creates the impression of a 3D horse with a rounded paunch replete with succulent grass.

Adjustments to the angles of the two mirrors moves the perception of the two images wider apart or closer together causing an apparent change to the heights of buildings, trees and mountains. The normal view gives the impression of slopes and heights being somewhat steeper or higher than on the ground. To highlight anomalies, or identify any unusual features, a very useful technique is to reverse the images, left film under right eyepiece and vice-versa. What would you hope to see? Ouch! A frightening transformation takes place before your very eyes! The river valleys rise up and appear as sharp ridges, while the hills and mountains shrink down into the abyss.

This topsy-turvy world clearly displays the Aude River running along the top of a mountain peak while the village of Rennes-le-Château now lies in a deep valley. We are able to interpret what we see rather than having the mind busy rationalising its interpretation of some hills and valleys with a gentle river flowing through pleasant pastures. It is what one might expect to see when looking upwards at the fragile skin of the earth from the subterranean depths, give or take a few rocks in the way. Scary! But this technique does have a name; pseudoscopic viewing.

Back to the normal view: peering through the oculars without the binoculars provides a wider field of view and implants a sensation of moving through the 3D landscape, merging the rocks and thorns of the physical features under foot with the mental picture of the whole tapestry of this rugged countryside. This study provided that immediacy of experience that is such a stimulus in the search for mineral deposits or archeological clues. This is vital in order to

Fig. 2. 2. Jena Zeiss mirror stereoscope and field stereoscope.

induce the land to yield up its innermost secrets: secrets of hidden ore deposits dormant for aeons, or mysteries laid in the earth but a few centuries ago.

Bérenger Saunière, our Priest, built the road that winds steeply from the village of Couiza up past the white ridge of the Roc Fumade. As the road enters the village, it snakes between the houses past the old Château with its collapsed roof. Even if the roof of the château were since repaired, it would still appear to us as on the day that the photos were taken by the plane flying ten thousand feet above, and the horse would forever graze in the lush meadow. Our studies must therefore be based on the landscape that was recorded at that precise instant in the history of Rennes-le-Chateau.

The road continues through the village past the Church of St Madeleine to the summit where the vista opens onto what was Saunière's domain. Here the square tower of the Tour Magdala, flanked by its round *échauguette,* rises from the ramparts of the belvedere, with its commanding view across the wild terrain.

I cannot pretend that familiarisation with the landscape through the stereoscope was achieved in a few minutes but gradually I became familiar with the various landmarks and geological features. I picked out a distinct line where an earlier landscape had been eroded away, to be replaced by later deposits in an era where river gravel laid down a wide band having the appearance of a conglomerate of sand and pebbles, solid as concrete. Peaks rose on every side, yet the marks of man were always in evidence.

The stereoscopic image revealed the ruins of Coustaussa, the Sentinel, overlooking the Sals River. A sentry on its walls would command a view across the river to the lofty peak on which stands the village of Rennes-le-Château. An ancient wall surrounds the château and village to the north and this has been extended by Saunière to include his domain as far as his tower on the south western extremity. The outline of the ancient fortifications is faintly visible, yet many of the stones from the original fortified tower must have been taken to furnish materials for more peaceful dwellings in the village.

Settled comfortably at the stereoscope, using the photo pair of enlargements combined with the binocular optics, it is easy to pick out the features of the village and identify the square shape of the Tour Magdala flanked by its round *échauguette*. This marks the limit of the sheer wall, which stands as two sides of a square with a sweeping curved corner surmounted by the ramparts of the belvedere. The walkway of the belvedere finally terminates in the glazed orangery at the north-eastern extremity, providing a sweeping view from the grandiose promenade. Saunière's designed and constructed this belvedere to traverse the full extent of his ramparts. It encompasses his formal garden accessed by the ornate arcs of a stairway.

A conical, glazed spire rises to flank the orangery mimicking the layout of the tower with its *échauguette*. I later discovered that below the orangery spire there is also a spiral staircase leading down to the far end of a gallery that extends beneath the belvedere. Was the orangery just built for his garden pot-plants? No, perhaps not!

I tried to imagine the view from the belvedere. The panorama would be seen to extend out from Rennes-le-

Château and indeed must have included Rhedae, its ruined Visigothic predecessor, that once covered the surrounding area. There are still significant ruins some distance to the north. The rugged terrain slopes down to the Aude and Sals river valleys below. Much of this land is only fit for grazing. On the northern side of the village below the castle, there is a level cultivated area and a small vineyard, on a narrow strip of land enclosed on two sides by a drystone walls to form a flatter strip of ground that stretches like an extended arm and hand clutching at the steep hillside.

Various other interesting features could be resolved only by a visit to the site. For this sort of detailed study I would certainly have to wade through a mass of brambles and burn off some energy clambering over the rough country. In practice, most of this would probably be poor use of any available time spent in the field; an expensive commodity. However, for now I would have to content myself with examining the aerial photographs. An extensive study of the geological map gave me to a feel for the whole area.

With the objective of locating the mythical site of some fabulous or fabled treasure, I felt that any mining sites were best left out of the equation as they would probably not yield a likely hiding hole that could be detected without a complete mine survey. One of the striking geological features was a series of circular lineaments that could hardly be described as ring complexes; also, there was a geological evidence of erosion and deposition where the upper sedimentary strata lay unconformably on the lower strata indicating a long interim period of erosion. The terrain was rugged and many of the hills and peaks rose steeply.

The photographs also showed a square feature on a hillside at one point, as if a series of stones had been meticulously laid out by hand. From my experience while placing beacons on the ground in Rhodesia to mark out mining claims, I had learned that a degree of dedication and purpose would have been required to achieve this amount of accuracy.

Fortunately, at that time, I had no knowledge of the book entitled *Le trésor maudit de Rennes-le-Château* by Gérard de Sède or I might have been greatly distracted from my studies.

* * *

In *Still Spins The Spider …* we can share an insight into the life and conflicts of a formidable man. The Abbé François Bérenger Saunière was commanding of stature. His tall, powerful frame carried well the broad temples and striking features fronting the penetrating brain of this man of thought and action. He had developed a high degree of tenacity in his early years as he struggled to survive. He had learned to care for his flock on the paltry stipend that he received. Despite his poverty, he was able to find the funds to undertake repairs to his dilapidated church.

Being so dependent upon his keen eye and steady hand he bagged the occasional red-legged partridge and other game for the pot to supplement his diet and that of his house-keeper Marie Denarnaud. This much prized bird with its bright plumage receives its name, 'the rare game' from its tendency to live in the higher and more inaccessible regions. Perhaps Saunière used an old Prelat percussion lock, muzzle loading fowling piece with its acrid clouds of smoke from the black powder. In his youth, our resourceful Priest would have acquired his skill with the rod and line in the nearby Aude River, or perhaps on the River Rhône while fishing for the shadowy *ombre*.

It would appear that the local Priests held the secret of the ancient mystery that surrounded the village and church of Rennes-le-Château and possibly included the nearby village of Rennes-les-Bains. Once Bérenger Saunière became privy to this hidden knowledge, he succeeded in incorporating elaborate clues into the refurbishment he carried out on his little Church of St Madeleine at Rennes-le-Château.

Now we can see the work of Bérenger Saunière's hand, an enterprise on which he must have lavished unlimited time and money. He extended the clues to involve additional building work within his domain. All his labours were accomplished with precision and what appears excessive attention to detail. Some might claim that the devil is in the detail. Though we may not comprehend every aspect of Saunière's meaning, yet in the detail lies the crux of the whole matter.

To define and resolve the puzzle I needed to look beyond the stereo images of mountainous terrain and study the figure at the centre of the mystery, the Priest, Bérenger Saunière. The only hope of success was to tread the maze that he has constructed for some future generation. The generation of which we now form a significant part.

The location was critical. It must not be within the ancient town of Rhedae itself, in case of capture. Even the rumoured existence of a buried treasure was sufficient reason to lay siege to that important city. If the hoard had been so well concealed that no invader would know of its existence, many problems would have been avoided; but people have long memories. Thus, it needed to be kept under surveillance from the city walls. The chances of marauders pillaging on a dark and stormy night must be taken into consideration. Yet, to approach from the rear and retrieve the contents, given enough labour and pack mules, would be important to the vanquished, should the city fall into unhallowed hands with little prospect of its recapture.

The chance of such a vault being of natural construction, such as a limestone cave, seemed unlikely. The implication was that some potentate had time, resources and determination sufficient to create for himself, his own bank — literally. One wonders what became of the work force. Those involved must have been very special, trustworthy men bound by a peculiar loyalty or oath, or a team that was entirely expendable once the work had been completed.

* * *

It looked as though a field trip would shortly be required. First I had to familiarise myself with two of the Poussin paintings featured in the *Chronicle* films. The earlier of the two was *The Arcadian Shepherds*, painted about 1637, now in the late Duke of Devonshire's collection at Bakewell. This painting depicts shepherds grouped round a tomb on which is placed a human skull. *Les Bergers d'Arcadia*, was the later painting with the same theme, also painted by Poussin. This was the one I had seen in the Anthony Blunt book and the painting that I intended to examine during my visit to the

Fig. 2. 3. The arm feature related to the ground layout.

Fig. 2. 4. The arm in both Poussin's *Arcadian Shepherds* paintings.

Louvre in Paris on my way down to Rennes-le-Château.

The Arcadian Shepherds painting is hung at Chatsworth, the stately residence of the late Duke and Duchess of Devonshire. The Chatsworth Curator, Peter Wragge, kindly replied to my request for the photographs by sending me some 35mm transparencies in a most helpful letter detailing the history of the painting. As I studied The Arcadian Shepherds in relation to the landscape, certain similarities in the painting struck me. Some of the physical features that existed in the rugged landscape surrounding Rennes-le-Château bore a marked resemblance to features included in the actual painting.

The torso, head and arm of the shepherd whose hand is pointing to the inscription on the tomb were so similar to certain aspects of the landscape just to the north of the village, that it was possible to relate the terrain to parts of the painting and to adjacent features bearing a likeness and a similar positional relationship. The shape of a cultivated area of land had strikingly similar markings to those on the arm in the Poussin painting. The pointing finger tended to draw the eye to focus on that particular portion where the finger of a shepherd traces out the letters on the tomb. The particular strip of cultivated land shaped like an elongated horseshoe was clearly replicated in the Arcadian Shepherds painting.

This similarity was also apparent in Les Bergers d'Arcadie but here that distinctive shape was not visible on the arm of the kneeling shepherd pointing to the tomb inscription. There again the arm was placed almost centrally in the painting. The enlarged stereo pair images, when viewed through the magnifying binoculars reinforced this effect and revealed that an area on the ground on the arm appeared slightly lighter in hue. On careful examination it seemed likely that this was due to a difference in the appearance of the vegetation at that location on the ground. This seemed to extend across the arm between the two drystone walls at this specific point.

Certain dry patches of the ground vegetation were clearly visible. Typically, these could occur over a rock just below the surface, or be due to the presence of a concealed cavern, which would have the effect of reducing the water retention locally. An oval-shaped hollow structure, created between the two drystone walls, was a distinct possibility and would require further investigation. This would entail a visit to the site, when I had completed sufficient preliminary work to fully justify a visit.

Fieldwork is expensive. Every hour spent poring over maps and photographs — and paintings — would represent a saving of time and effort on the ground. Without sufficient study and preparation, fieldwork could be completely abortive. Certain other features on the land bore a marked similarity to parts of the two Poussin paintings. One needs caution in applying this type of technique, which could be construed as being the result of staring too long at both the paintings and the aerial photography. I found myself dozing off as I gazed through half-closed eyelids at *The Arcadian Shepherds* painting with the skull set on the top of the tomb.

The theme, *Et in Arcadia Ego,* suddenly sprang to life, or to death. 'I too, (death) am in Arcadia.' I found myself staring at a skull cleverly concealed to the left of the large tree in the painting; the two eye sockets being formed by the head of the shepherdess and that of the adjacent shepherd.

I studied this image for a while, but when I moved the painting around, changing the angle, I discovered that the skull image merged into an even larger skull, which filled the centre of the top third of the painting. Those yellow-brown hues exactly matched the colours one associates with skulls. This was a truly ingenious work of art by a truly extraordinary artist. But, too much speculation could lead one away from the main issue, what ever that might be. This was the time to accelerate my armchair investigations and put my preliminary findings to the test, in the field. Was there a real solution to the enigma that surrounded Rennes-le-Château and would the challenge really prove as exciting as the TV programme had portrayed?

CHAPTER THREE

RENNES ON A SHOESTRING

In the preparations for my first visit to Rennes-le-Château in the autumn of 1972, everything was on a shoestring budget. The project did not warrant any great expenditure at that early stage. Bérenger Saunière had been able to make his early discovery without great expense, so perhaps I could as well. Having reached Couiza by some devious route, I branched off the main Carcassonne highway and set out on foot to the village of Rennes-le-Château. The steep Tarmac road stretched before me and I inwardly thanked Bérenger Saunière for using some of his wealth to replace the original dirt track with this road to enable his distinguished visitors and his beloved parishioners to travel in comfort. Perhaps he intended that one day someone would use his road in the recovery of his treasure.

In the mistaken hope that the steepness of the hill was just a quirk of the aerial photography, I set off expecting to see the village around the next bend. Though I could not see the village perched above me, I imagined it just as shown in the aerial photographs. Before setting out, I had imprinted a vivid 3D image of the landscape on my mind. This was achieved by poring over the aerial photograph stereo pairs that I had laid out to show the landscape as an overlapping mosaic. My mirror stereoscope had served me well with its X3.5 binocular attachment. Now my desk study could be tested in the field. Would the experience I had gained over the years serve me well or was I doomed to be met with an ignominious failure? Certainly, the steep road that stretched before me was not a little hill to be skipped up.

The October evening was warm with the buzzing of the insects lulling me into a reflective mood. I noticed a smooth rock at the roadside inviting me to sit a while and view the scenery. Behind me rose the white crest of Roc Fumade. Ahead, the ribbon of road snaked up towards the village, but I was looking for a particular point where the road swept round in a sharp bend. There I would strike off to the right following a distinctive ridge and gully. As I left the road, following the gully that led upwards towards the hilltop village, I found the terrain more rugged than I had imagined.

Dense thorn bushes hemmed me in as I struggled to find a way to scramble up the steep eastern slope of the gully. That way I would be able to see the terrain rather than being swallowed up in it. My first encounter with the thorns of Rennes made some impression but provided a lesson that I never seemed to learn.

I climbed to a point from which I could determine my exact location. There, I opened my rucksack and pulled out my aerial photos together with my pocket stereoscope and sat down on a rock where I could lay out the photos. The grey tones of the photos sprang to life as the different shades of green and brown mingled with all the other hues that go to make up the pastoral scene of rock and river, flower and fern. I imagined the shepherds of Arcadia grazing their flocks in the meadows.

The terrain revealed the effects of the over zealous grazing of sheep over the centuries. The soil, deprived of its protective grassy mantle, had fallen victim to erosion. In places, the bare rocks poked through like gaunt knees on a threadbare and patched garment. However, this endowed the ancient land of Roussillon with a certain rugged charm and attested to its chequered past. Ruled by Celts, Merovingians, Visigoths, Albigensians and Knights Templar to name but a few, the land and people had cried out for freedom, the right to raise their families and flocks and moreover, the freedom to think and express their religious convictions.

The next two hours of intimate acquaintance with the local thorn bushes gave me a feeling for the terrain as I familiarised myself with the finer points of the flora and landscape. But I was no botanist. Some of the level areas had been cultivated but the more uneven parts would have benefited from a small herd of goats that would have cleared the scrub and provided natural manure to sweeten the land.

I found a grassy bank close to where I wanted to be.

Fig. 3. 1. The ivy mantled château stands dark and menacing.

Fig. 3. 2. The ruins of Coustaussa, guardian through the centuries.

There, the ground was almost level, and a flattish outcrop of rock provided me with a comfortable seat. Sitting there, I had a commanding view of many of the features of Poussin's painting, including a symmetrical round hill. However, driven by auto-suggestion and wishful thinking, it is easy to imagine similarities where none exist. At that time, I knew little about the painting but later I developed a burning desire to unlock its powerful secrets.

While the daylight lasted, I needed to select a suitable place where I could set out my sleeping bag and lay my head for the night. Where I was seated provided an ideal view and seemed to be the very spot where Nicolas Poussin might have sat while making his sketches centuries before, so I named it the 'Poussin Seat'.

Looking south, the menacing walls of the ivy-covered château stood outlined against the blue sky. To the north, the afternoon sunlight picked out the Sals River winding in a silver streak through the valley below, where the sentinel ruins of Coustaussa guarded the high ground across the river. Before me and to the west, the white curves of rock of Roc Fumade rose in an arch like the back of some mythical beast crouching beneath a few wispy clouds.

My gaze focused directly below me where a spring oozed from the red soil like tears splashing down from Mary Magdalene's penitent eyes. Tears that seemed to fall from the little Church dedicated to her name in the village above. They welled up from the red soil of Rennes to trickle down towards the raised ridge of ground supported on either side by drystone walls some seven feet high. There, a field of stunted grape vines clung to the ground in desperation. The ridge extended downward in the direction of the road built by Saunière many years before. At one point the drystone walls appeared to have a curved ridge slightly raised on either side of the level area. Opposite where I sat, a thick covering of bushes masked the wall and I felt an urge to scramble behind there to examine the ground more closely.

The evening sky reddened and the sun dipped behind Roc Fumade as I spread my bedroll to overlook this Arcadian scene. A tin of sausages and beans heated on my little portable burner renewed my strength. The effects of my energetic day soon brought me peaceful sleep *à la belle étoile* with no fear of scorpions, snakes or jackals, yet my sleep was still somewhat troubled by the subconscious impression of the dark shadow of the ancient château of Rennes, which stood out against the night sky like some immense lurking spider. When I awoke briefly during the night, snug in my sleeping bag, it still hung like a huge bat hovering in the half-light of those dark hours before the dawn.

* * *

The first rays of the rising sun awoke me. The heavy morning dew may have encrusted the gossamer of spiders' webs with diamonds as the sun rose but it had also heavily bedewed my bedding. I sprang lightly from my sleeping bag? No! I lay dozing for some time while I contemplated the pastoral scene, part of which I had now become. I related it, in my mind, to the aerial photography that I had studied with such care.

The early morning would be the best time for me to

Fig. 3. 3. Roadway to Rennes-le-Château looking east.

Fig. 3. 4. The village of Rennes-le-Château viewed from the east.

study the site — these things were best undertaken while the village was yet abed. I needed to have a look at the wall behind the dense shrubbery, also I wanted to check out the possibility of the *souterrain* or underground cavern, which was outlined by the difference in vegetation and ground shading as shown on the aerial photos. I wanted to assess the possible causes of the apparent lack of moisture or thin topsoil over what might possibly be the arched roof of a subterranean cavern. It had to be there or my whole hypothesis would go up in smoke like some long forgotten pipe dream. Yet I had every confidence in the accuracy of my interpretation of the aerial photographs linked with the supporting chain of logic that had led me to this idyllic corner steeped in a forgotten history.

Below me lay the vineyard wall. The particular portion of land that held my attention was covered by a dense foliage of tangled undergrowth. Where I had laid out my bedroll was an ideal spot for an artist to sit and sketch the surrounding countryside; perhaps even while capturing his impression of the scenery relating to the Duke of Devonshire's *Arcadian Shepherds,* I mused.

Quite likely, this could have been the source of some of the vignettes, which were included in the Louvre version of *Les Bergers d'Arcadie.* It is unlikely that any actual painting would have taken place amidst that rugged landscape. The logistics of carrying the equipment on the back of a mule would present problems and Poussin needed all the facilities of his studio to meet the challenges of his commission. Sketches would provide sufficient detail to supplement the impressions that would remain with the Master Artist.

I found the vineyard had once been planted in neat rows but looked as though it had expressed its own will over the years. The drystone walls that struggled to retain the level cultivated area looked as if they had striven to maintain their position for many centuries. I followed the nearest drystone wall until I came to its northern extremity.

Traversing the width of the vineyard, I walked the length of the western wall, which overlooked a ravine separating this ridge from Roc Fumade. This brought me to the southern extremity, which was overlooked by the ramparts of Rennes-le-Château some hundred metres above.

One feature of the paintings that now appeared on this landscape was the marking in the shape of an elongated horseshoe on the arm shown in the centre of the painting. This feature was clearly repeated on the ground as the vineyard area, just as it appeared when viewed in the aerial photos or anciently from the walls of the fortified village on the hilltop. Another striking feature was the high curved ridge of Roc Fumade, cleverly mimicked by the highlighted ogee curve on the corner of the tomb in the *Arcadian Shepherds*. The location relative to the 'arm of the shepherd' was also replicated on the ground.

Below me to the north-east, I could see the dead straight line made by the roadway that had been meticulously designed and laid out by Saunière to line up exactly with this arm feature. To the south rose the skyline of the village. Comparing this with the painting of *Les Bergers d'Arcadie* reveals the old château with its distinctive roof outline joined to a prominent tower that has two faintly discernable windows and what appear to be the battlements of a round tower. However, at first glance it does bear some resemblance to Roco Negro or some other similar outcrop of rock. The varnish, darkened through time, did not lend itself to instant recognition of this feature. The similarity to the château is more apparent when one is lying sleepless on the rough ground beneath its forbidding outline on a windy night with the dark clouds scudding across the moon, as I discovered many years later.

The arm of the vineyard terminated in what resembled a clenched fist, comparable to the shepherd's hand in Poussin's paintings. Returning to the vineyard, I was able to walk across the dry area using my hazel twig (see Appendix B). In fact, the generic term 'hazel twig' refers to any forked stick. Hazel has some superior qualities, which include strength and resilience. Most forked sticks have a tendency to split in two or quickly lose their spring. Of course, most sites never seem to have a convenient hazel tree so any forked stick must serve. Failing that, a piece of bent copper wire or even a wire coat hanger works. I cut a couple of suitable branches from the shrub that so conveniently shrouded the drystone wall, obscuring where the front entrance to the suspected cavern might lie.

Tucking the spare stick into my belt, I grasped the twin prongs of the fork in both hands, palms upward, with the point of the ' Y ' to the fore and applied a little tension. I started to work my way across the area some distance from the particular point that I was interested in. I hoped that any prying eye would think that I was just a casual stroller. True to form, the point of the forked stick dipped obligingly at the boundary of the exact area. It stayed firmly pointing towards the ground until I reached the other side of what I believed to be the area of the underground cavern. The point of the stick then rose, returning to the horizontal.

I then started walking from the drystone wall, across the width of the vineyard, east to west. The branch dipped when a metre and a half from the eastern drystone wall and remained pointing firmly towards the ground until about three metres from the other wall. This indicated a difference in the level of the electrostatic charge, similar to that found in the plates of a condenser. Usually this may be caused by the variations in the electromagnetic field of the earth at that point on the ground. This technique I had used with unerring accuracy while tracing stockworks of mineral veins together with other geological features such as fault lines or boundaries.

The next part of the routine was to zigzag along the edges of the suspected area, crossing and re-crossing the approximate line of the perimeter. This causes the point of the stick to dip and rise successively, thus defining the exact outline of the electrical anomaly. This could be interpreted as indicating that there was a clearly defined oval area about nine paces wide by twenty paces long for most of the width between the drystone walls. It is not practical to use a tape measure while holding a stick with both hands.

If I had been equipped with the sophisticated ground search instruments now recently invented, or had set up a series of wires and measured the earth's resistivity, I am sure

I would be able to analyse the approximate location of
something or other. Perhaps I could have measured the P
and S waves resulting from a series of seismic explosions and
thus deduced the possible existence of some anomaly. If
portable computers had been developed in the early 1970's,
I would have had an answer within just a few hours — the
whole village of Rennes-le-Château and I, that is. I, being a
Philistine, preferred to use the more discreet, cost effective
and well tried hazel twig.

It appeared that, despite the lie of the land lending itself to
the design and construction of the vineyard area, somebody
had to make a monumental effort to create this man-made
feature. No person undertakes more work than is required
to achieve an objective. It would be difficult today to construct
a hiding place that would be sufficiently large to contain the
hoard and be able to withstand the ravages of time while still
blending into the surrounding landscape.

In the distant past, using manual workers and hand tools,
the task would require much effort and some justification.
The cut and fill method would reduce the excavation work
to a minimum. There were plenty of stones around for the
construction work; sufficient to build the vault along with
the drystone walls at either end of the vault. The arched
cavern would need to withstand both the weight of overburden
and the weight of its own structure, despite the relentless
passage of time.

My next step would be to determine a possible means of
entry. From the steeper, western drystone wall there was
no possibility of entry without undertaking an organised

and equipped excavation exercise. From the eastern side, the movement of the forked stick had indicated that I would still need to excavate for over a metre in order to expose the entrance to the passage. For a mining operation, this would not be too difficult with the right tools. My mind slipped easily back to my mineral exploration and mining days as I found myself working out where to drill the holes and how many sticks of gelignite would be required to do a clean job without causing too much damage including a cave-in.

"Think archaeology," I reminded myself sternly. In an archaeological excavation, clearing a few feet of rock and earth can be a week's work. A top entry could lead to a cave-in and the certain danger of an unsupported roof, with a consequent rock-fall. Even a royal arch when without its keystone cannot stand. This was not a task to be taken lightly without more information and thought.

Finally, I spent some time in checking the external dimensions of the cavern, the probable depth and the layout. The thick covering of bushes masking the eastern wall may have been placed there centuries ago in order to hide the rocks and any special markings. The western, or back wall was higher and the ground fell away sharply to the ravine that boarded the high ridge of Roc Fumade. To examine the front end of what I now referred to, in my own mind, as the cavern needed some gymnastics. It was almost impossible to squeeze behind the thick bushes at the front or eastern end. Nevertheless, I did succeed, with plenty of scratches, twigs in my hair and torn shirt in achieving the necessary contortions. Wedged tight against the rock face, there appeared nothing special to see apart from several large stones.

I expected to see some definite indication that this was the correct location. Perhaps there would be some peculiar marks. At that time, I could not discern anything that appeared significant. Forcing a passage between the stones and the shrubbery was no easy matter and did not reveal any quick solution to the problem of gaining entry. There was no door to swing back on rusting hinges, just some hefty stones strategically placed to bar access. Clearly, the builders did not intend to make it easy.

Having completed my survey I returned to my pack, well pleased that I had turned my hypothesis into a theoretical possibility, with real dimensions and a real subterranean site roughly as predicted. Certainly, it was a lot easier than prospecting for gold. I was able to verify the likely presence of a subterranean void exactly at the point where the aerial photos had suggested. This consisted of a narrow passage wide enough for a man. After about a metre and a half, it widened out into an oval shaped cavity that extended for almost the entire width of the ground between the drystone walls. There was no indication that a passage at the far end of the subterranean chamber existed.

Food was now uppermost in my thoughts and after I had demolishing a baguette and a good portion of Camembert, I risked a drink from the spring that emerged nearby. It tasted a bit high in lime, but it slaked my thirst. If these were the tears of Magdala, which moistened her repentant cheeks as she sorrowed over the departed glory of Rennes-le-

Château, perhaps they ought at least to taste salty! If the spring water had originated from the village, I should be contented with the chalky flavour.

I had done all I could at the vineyard and felt well pleased with what I had achieved that morning. I wandered around the immediate area to familiarise myself with the layout, the paths, and any significant features such as prominent marker stones. What I really lacked was a good camera to record everything, rather than relying solely on my memory.

Before retrieving my rucksack from where I had left it in the bushes near the vineyard, I lay back upon the flowery bank. As I relaxed, enjoying the quiet of the scene, I became aware of the many sounds that broke the silence while enhancing the tranquillity of the morning air. Grasshoppers sawed endlessly with their bows, competing with the high-pitched song of the larks above. A brace of the rare red-legged partridge wandered across the landscape; I thought how gladly the poverty-stricken Priest would have bagged them for his pot before opulence and power overtook him.

I was keen to complete all the fieldwork before visiting the village church in order to distance the geological aspects from the mass of confusion I knew awaited me there. The mingled desires to reveal yet conceal, which drove the Priest of Rennes to adorn so strangely the Church of St Madeleine, would certainly confuse my reasoning. Most likely, I would quickly become one of those who had passed within those hallowed walls to emerge instructed to distraction. At least it would surely cloud the clarity of my mind. Still deep in thought, I collected my pack and directed my footsteps up the steep slope, joining the path that led to the village.

With the ivy-mantled château looming above me, I climbed the worn steps leading to the ancient well that was the source of water for the village. Here I could feel the faded opulence of the late nineteenth and early twentieth centuries, brought to a sudden end when the clock stopped on the 22nd January 1917. This date marked the passing of a Priest, the end of an *empire extraordinaire* as it returned to become just a sleepy village nestling amongst the Corbière Mountains.

With the death of François Bérenger Saunière, the hopes and aspirations of the entire village did not wither and die but lay dormant, as if forever entombed. In many respects, this tiny community appeared indistinguishable from many others in that part of the Languedoc. Isolated from mainstream France by language, tradition and a sense of identity, this corner of France held itself separate from *La République*.

To Marie Denarnaud the passing of a Priest meant much more. She had kept house, shared his hardships in those early days, and joined in his triumphs later. She had learned some of the ways of Rennes with its many puns. That sentence plucked from the manuscript Bérenger had found, took on a new meaning.

Il est la mort: 'It is death'; 'it is there, death'; 'he is there, dead'. 'It is a death's head and it is there!'

As she cast her eyes upwards, catching sight of the pattern of blood red hearts in the stained glass window above the door of the Villa Bethania, which property she would now own, perhaps there was a metaphor more cruel to bear than them all. The stark reality of Death had come to Arcadia; this little village set in the very heart of Languedoc where even the shepherd had been taken from his flock. The empty eye sockets of the death's head replaced the kindly watchful eyes of the Priest. However, perhaps it had always been like that in Rennes-le-Château.

The villagers knew that within their grasp lay the means of obtaining their release from poverty and from their banal daily grind. All the clues were there to be read. Surely, their beloved Priest would not have abandoned them in their hour of need?

"Why hast thou forsaken me," would have been the lament on every lip. At his funeral, all paths led to the little church restored in such an unusual manner. François Bérenger Saunière was laid to rest in the tiny graveyard next to the Church that he had made his monument. He could watch over his secret hoard concealed in the cavern beneath the vineyard. Yet, those grapes of success, so sweet when ripe, would never reach fruition, remaining forever sour in his sacramental chalice.

The irony of this came to me while I stood on the belvedere that Saunière had constructed during his life and upon which he sat in state after his death. His corpse was draped with a red, tasselled robe. In accordance with an ancient Cathar funerary custom, the mourners preserve some memento of the departed such as a lock of hair or a piece of the cloth from the body. As the mourning villagers filed past his body, each plucked a tassel from his robe in

Fig. 3. 5. Asmodeus cowering beneath the angelic presence.

Fig. 3. 6. Some of the decorations in the Church of St Madeleine.

remembrance of him and the region's Cathar heritage.

Above the doorway to the little Church of St Madeleine the inscription *Terribilis Est Locus Iste* warned of what I would encounter as I entered. There crouched the plaster figure of Asmodeus, fabled keeper of Solomon's treasure, supporting the stoup of holy water, overshadowed by four angels. My mind jerked back to Cardiff Castle and to Myfanwy Evans with those tearful eyes as she recounted her fears. The tears that splashed onto her whitened knuckles with her ring of Celtic gold reminded me of the little spring I had just used to quench my thirst: the tears of Magdala.

Bérenger Saunière took care to include in his decoration within the Church, the image of a possible treasure. Before me, I saw the painting, which shows Christ standing upon a flower-covered hill. A leathern bag of money, lying upon the hillside, bore a slit to show the gold coins bursting out. I saw that the tie ribbons of the bag had the same form as the paths leading to the site on the hillside that I had just visited. The similarity was so obvious that no wonder none has noticed it. The most effective concealment is in the obvious, when surrounded by a surfeit of information. Later I learned that it was on land once owned by a Monsieur Fleury. This could be punned to refer to the *terrain Fleury* or a terrain covered with flowers, just like that flowery bank below the village of Rennes, where I had spent the previous night. All this, of course, would remain pure speculation until I had achieved a full investigation of the site.

A strange and interesting painting, reputedly by the hand of Bérenger Saunière himself holds centre stage in the Church. It shows a young girl, presumably Mary

Magdalene, sitting in what appears to be a cave. In her lap, the intertwined fingers of her hands rests upon her heart-shaped apron. An open book and a human skull lie on the ground before her yet she gazes fixedly at a rough wooden cross. I looked for some reference to the vaulted cavern I had been investigating. Far-fetched, it was! However, as I began to walk in the ways of Rennes I found that the language of Rennes is not only langue d'oc, or the language of *Oc* where that is the word used for 'yes', as opposed to langue d'ouil that uses *Oui*.

The language of Rennes is also Punic — not the Punic tongue of the ancient Carthaginians, but the Punic that was introduced by the Abbé Boudet, the language of puns, sometimes crossed between two languages. This Punic language is ever present in the ways of Rennes. This results in a double take that becomes endemic within the usage. Thus, in the reasoning of Rennes, there was a bag of money situated in the field once owned by M. Fleury.

How easily the unwary can interpret every impression or image received in this strange place of worship or in this web of fantasy woven with half-truths and *double entendres*. A variety of interpretations may be placed on any one of the threads to draw one ever closer to a supposed truth only to find oneself caught in a silken snare of half-truths. One would be left clutching at tenuous drawstrings of an elusive bag of money as deceptive and destructive as the spider's webs that glistened like jewels in the *terrain Fleury*.

Having allowed myself sufficient time to become totally confused by the immense amount of detail and overt clues scattered for all to see, I emerged from the church, my mind

Fig. 3. 7. Saunière's painting holds centre stage in his church.

Fig. 3. 8. The rugged hillside looking south towards the village.

engorged with a glut of information and strange images. There was so much information but so little knowledge or comprehension; this was, surely, the way of Rennes. What a brilliant means of concealment!

What of the original clues mingled with those added over the centuries? Lengthy excursions into the surrounding terrain resulted in a pile of stones collected by the Priest — perhaps these were markers left by the Visigoths and Templars. Clearly many had taken great pains in the past to preserve a trail for the initiates of the future. Now we were left with a complex and intriguing set of signposts that might or might not be based on the original system. Had he removed all the signs? Perhaps he had not. At least he had not removed the main treasure. Saunière certainly had laid his hand on some loot, but not all. He would not have expended such great efforts to guard an empty tomb.

After spending some time at the other sites of interest, I visited the glass conservatory to gaze down at the hillside area that I had visited and investigated before climbing up to the village. This would have presented me with a fine view to reassure me that all was as I had left it but trees and foliage now obstructed a clear line of sight to the vineyard from the orangery.

I had detected an unexplained square lineament on the aerial photos in the locality. Perhaps this could have been a marker laid down hundreds of years ago or just a square 'something'? Who knows, but I could at least check out the markings on the land and be just that bit more informed. I retraced my footsteps past the ancient village pump next to the steps that led to the steep path to the countryside in order to look for my square, which was marked by the lines of stones. I located the four lines of stones neatly laid out on the hillside in dead straight lines. This was no coincidence. I wondered about one of the cornerstone that I immediately recognised as being ironstone while all of the others that made up the square were normal local rock. Perhaps these stones had no relevance or Bérenger Saunière had slipped up, lost his bearings, or just lost interest. The stones may still be there now, three decades later, or they may have fallen victim to the recent mechanical scrub clearing exercise. This marker could possibly be useful corroboration if I only understood how it fitted into the pattern. Perhaps it was just another blind alley. It is doubtful that the wily Saunière or someone from the past put them there to confuse!

Was there some evidence, possibly documentary, that was being preserved for some reason? It seemed unlikely that such a large cavern would be required just to conceal a few documents. Could this great secret present an imagined threat to the religious status quo of the Judeo-Christian faiths?

Religious groups have tended to lose without trace those things that they considered to be undesirable; even the truth. Many of the ancient prophets of Israel had been stoned to death for declaring unsavoury judgements or daring to suggest that God's Chosen People, chosen, as was Abraham, would send their Messiah to His death. The mere suggestion that their nation would be required to make Him a sacrificial lamb, in the similitude of the sacrifice by

Abraham, of his son, Isaac, could not be countenanced. Yet, every prophet from Abraham to Zenos had foretold this.

The possibility existed that the hoard comprised some of the temple ornaments, including the Menorah, from Jerusalem's Temple. That would be sufficient reason for successive generations to preserve the location of the treasure, as the Jewish nation still had no homeland and was out of favour with the established church. Now, of course, since 1948 this nation has been gathering to its historic homeland.

The bankers of Europe, the Templars, had secreted hoards of treasure at different sites around Europe before and during the great purge of Friday, 13th October 1307 and these have never been fully recovered. This could be because they may have used a complicated key known only to a few. Even if it were to be extracted by torture, it was either too complex or too dependent on local knowledge to allow recovery of the wealth. The secret of the key might be known but its application would prove to be too difficult. The secret would be so closely guarded that eventually, even perhaps after just a few generations, it would be lost.

"Guard it with your life!" Yet life in those days was such a fragile thing. *Mort épée* — death in the flash of a blade could cause the secret to be lost forever in a pool of blood. This last possibility is worthy of consideration. One could discuss it interminably, while exercising the mind with an endless list of theories, variations and scenarios. It is as vital to find where the truth lies, as to find where the truth does not lie.

CHAPTER FOUR

WITH THE BBC — GOLGOTHA

No site to conceal a treasure appeared to be more favourably located than the one that my hypothesis had indicated. It was where a leader in possession of a valuable hoard of a bulky nature might well hide it. The site was near enough to the village, but concealed so that marauders had failed to find it when the battlements were stormed and the village ransacked in the fourteenth century. The anecdotal evidence present in the paintings supported the possibility of this site. But still it was just an hypothesis.

My exploration work had been successful so far. Of course, there might never have been a treasure, but I felt it was worth further investigation. The only way forward was through the BBC, then situated in Kensington House, Richmond Way, which was located twenty miles from home.

I contacted Henry Lincoln, the principle player, and he was rather dubious, especially when I could present no hard evidence such as a hidden trap door or a fistful of gleaming gold coins. Doubtless, many had come forward with theories and many are the solutions that have been offered since. However, the excuse that my proposition could provided a reason to produce another *Chronicle* programme on the subject of Rennes was too good to pass-up. Paul Johnstone, the Senior Producer of the BBC Archaeology and History Unit, finally gave permission to proceed with the project at the beginning of May 1973.

Preparations were made for the BBC to work together with the French TV Company, Telacia, on the project. Paul Johnstone was the Executive Producer in charge of the BBC contingent with Roy Davies as the Director. I was required to apply for permission through my solicitor, to carry out the excavation. The influence of the Telacia management must have played an important role in obtaining this.

A simplification was that there was no actual archaeological evidence so no permission was required, apart from that of the Maire of Rennes-le-Château. The Maire graciously consented, as the village would derive valuable publicity and revenue from the combined productions. Dates were agreed and the machinery was set in motion. I submitted to the BBC detailed drawings of the method of excavating together with an inventory of the equipment needed on site. My detailed plans were made to cover every conceivable eventuality, but there is always the unforeseen event that can scupper the best-laid schemes.

By September 1973, details were finalised. My flight to Paris was arranged for Friday, 12th October. From there, I would catch the Wagon-Lits sleeper at 22.59 from the Gare de Lyon to arrive at Carcassonne on the Saturday at 08.02. The S.N.C.F. French Railways gave me a smooth ride. The first class sleeper booked for me provided single occupancy of my own compartment. I slept right through until I awoke at dawn as the sleeping car slowed and rattled over some points. I washed, shaved and dressed hurriedly as I had to change compartments at Narbonne and used the remaining few minutes to check that I had all my possessions packed.

The dialect of Languedoc immediately struck a chord in my memory as I stepped down to the platform at Carcassonne. The first time that I encountered this dialect was on a visit to Paris when I was working for UTA French Airlines. I had flown from Bulawayo for a sales conference. The Regional Director for Southern Africa spoke with a strong Languedocian accent. Unfortunately, he usually talked with his rosewood pipe firmly clenched between his teeth. It was then that I realised that my French was not as good as it might have been. Now my memories of the sales conference are limited to an image of the pipe and the Director's admonition that *"Les pipes d'Algerie sont les mieux."* Therefore, if you are rashly thinking of taking up pipe smoking, you must settle for nothing less than an Algerian rosewood masterpiece.

At Carcassonne, I took the local train for Quillan. It wound south through the valley of the River Aude via Limoux, closely following the course of the River. The train finally reached the point where the Sals River flows in from the east.   Here, at the confluence of the Aude and Sals Rivers, is situated the twin towns of Couiza and Montazels, where Saunière was born. Leaving the train there, I stepped out into the fresh morning air, feeling the warmth of the sun on my back though it was still early. Shouldering my pack, I followed the now familiar streets of Couiza towards the steep winding Tarmac road that leads to the village of Rennes-le-Château.   Indeed, I set off once more on that winding road of metaphors and mystery, riddled with cul-de-sacs and blind alleys that have trapped even the wariest of travellers in their search for the ways of Rennes. I was rescued from my reverie and my hike as the BBC car pulled up beside me and a sweet voice said,

"You are Bill Kersey, aren't you?" How could I deny it?

Leaving Couiza, I travelled in comfort up that steep winding road, while I was briefed on how the filming was progressing. It so happened that the anniversary of Friday 13th October 1307 fell at midnight, the previous evening. The film crew had accompanied a group of enthusiasts who assembled at the summit of the mountain at Bézu, once the site of a Knights Templar commanderie. They all stood around to commemorate that fateful day in Templar history six hundred and sixty-six years ago, when Philip The Fair arrested many of the Knights Templar on a pretext. Then they all trooped down from the mountain and everyone retired to their beds. The tortured screams echoing down the centuries from the inquisition failed to disturb their deep slumber and the camera crew awoke refreshed, ready

Fig. 4. 1. The view from the belvedere across the Sals River valley.

for a hard day's filming of the sequel to the Chronicle *Temple Treasure,* on the sunny ramparts of Rennes-le-Château.

The car carried me through the village depositing me at the Villa Bethania, where I was to stay. The film crew were already at work making the best use of the clear early morning light.

On arriving at the ramparts, I found that the filming crew were fully occupied. Eddie Best and Colin March, two of the cameramen, were shooting a scene next to the orangery with Henry Lincoln. I stood watching, listening to Henry Lincoln's heavily accented tones as he unfolded the story of the manuscript. He had highlighted the raised letters and spelled out the cryptic message he had discovered in one of the manuscripts that the Priest had found while renovating the church of St Madeleine. The manuscript started with *Et factum est eum in sabbato secundo primo*. The message was about King Dagobert II. The ancient king reputably, was murdered on 23rd December AD 679.

> The raised letters clearly spelt out the following text:
> A DAGOBERT II ROI ET A SION EST CE TRESOR
> ET IL EST LA MORT.
> Henry Lincoln gave his translation:
> TO DAGOBERT II KING AND AT SION IS THIS
> TREASURE AND IT IS DEATH.
> Interestingly *la morte* takes the feminine gender and the '*là*' must be translated as 'there' assuming the inclusion of a grave accent, as in Henry Lincoln's translation. Admittedly, these are at least two possibilities. Once we stand within the walls of Rennes, everything seems to have acquired at least two possible meanings. If you find only one it is because the others remain hidden.

I watched with interest as the filming proceeded and awoke from my speculation as the camera team reached the end of a shooting sequence. Henry Lincoln was still deep in his presentation so I spoke to the Director, Roy Davies to let him know that I was there. The main party had arrived previously, but I could not leave England to accompany them as I had a night shift to complete at the computer bureau where I worked.

The ramparts of the belvedere overlooked the magnificent view across the steep slopes and rough country that stretched as far as the distant mountain peaks. I wanted to gaze down over the hillside further to the north to reassure myself that all was well in Zion. At least I needed to make sure that the treasure of Rennes-le-Château continued to lie peacefully, still undisturbed.

My sleeping arrangements had been well taken care of and I had been allocated a room in the Villa Bethania, built by Saunière. It turned out to be Bérenger Saunière's own bedroom and I felt it rather an honour to be using it, though Saunière probably lived mainly in the old presbytery. Perhaps he spent many nights lying awake; his peaceful sleep disturbed by thoughts of the awesome responsibility the treasure had placed upon his broad shoulders.

An American Indian saying sprang to mind, 'To know a man you must first walk in his moccasins.' However, to sleep in his room must surely give me some insight into how Bérenger Saunière lived and felt at the turn of the century. Perhaps I would experience some empathy with Saunière awakening with the morning light streaming into his room, just as he must have done every day all those years ago.

In one way it did seem fitting, as of course I planned to excavate his treasure in the next few days, given the tools.

The tools had been a sore point. Without disclosing the exact location, I had submitted a detailed excavation plan, together with sketches and the list of tools required to achieve a successful dig. I had an expectation of at least the basics being acquired and shipped out to France with the team. Just a few days before departure I had been advised that there would be adequate equipment on site. The basic requirements were a couple of mining shovels, the ones with the pointed blade, a steel bar to use as a lever and some form of wheelbarrow to remove the spoil. The television crew would of course supply lights.

Doubtless, as soon as we were to uncover anything of value, the authorities would swoop upon us, to take control from that point. On the basis that the inhabitants of the village had been rooting around the area for years they must have a good supply of picks and shovels together with other excavation equipment. Perhaps, though, the locals might not want to co-operate with those who came to dig up their own personal treasure.

In order to undertake the excavation work I would need those picks and shovels, steel bar and wheelbarrow. With two assistants, I could complete the initial excavation within a reasonable time scale. The combined French and English television team had received the written permission to proceed with the excavation work, though, strictly speaking, it would not be an archaeological dig because there was no evidence to support the theory that there was anything that could be considered archaeological at the site.

I asked Roy Davies whether the tools were organised on site. I was advised that the loan of a long-handled mattock had been arranged. The special arrangements for an excavation team had been set up with me in charge but no work force. To be fair, of course, the BBC was here to make films and not to dig holes. I should have been more aware of this and arranged for some local volunteers or brought my own team down with me. I moved across to the ramparts to where I could look down upon my intended excavation site, which lay below me.

The morning was already well advanced and the sun was burning down upon the scene. I collected the mattock. At least I had brought my folding entrenching tool and prospecting pick with me as a precaution. On the way down to the hillside below, I wondered just how it was going to be possible to achieve such a major exercise with so limited resources available.

"Nevertheless all things are possible," I thought to myself.

Everything was as I had left it on my previous visit. The bushes in front of the excavation sites were as thick as ever. My first task was to clear them so that I could get access to the face of the drystone wall. I took up my entrenching tool, the blade of which I had sharpened for just this purpose. I slashed away lustily at the undergrowth and soon had the bulk of the branches cleared. This had taken me a full half hour and I needed a break to plan my next attack.

I walked back up the slope to where I had laid out my sleeping bag on the first visit. Sitting down on the flat rock, I wiped the sweat from my face with my sleeve and realised

that this was going to be no easy task. I had not even taken
one shovel full of earth yet. Glancing at my watch, I found
that the morning was already spent and I could feel the
heat of sun at its zenith, scorching down on my shoulders.
Gazing across at the site I tried to estimate the work ahead.
I stared blankly at the rocks I had so rudely denuded of their
foliage. I felt it was important, from an archaeological
perspective, to record the layout of the rocks before they
were disturbed. I made a rough sketch of the positions of
the different rocks in the denuded area and stared at them
deciding on my best approach to begin the actual digging as
it was already midday, and hot!

I though of Nicolas Poussin making sketches there all
those centuries ago and wondered how he had envisaged
that scene. As I stared down at the rocks, the rocks stared
back with unseeing eyes as they had done for centuries past.
It was at that moment that I realised that I was not going to
be able to complete the excavation on that occasion. It was
clear that I had insufficient time and resources at my disposal
to proceed with a worthwhile excavation. I resolved to
return to the site when the next opportunity presented
itself. Meanwhile, I needed to arm myself with a much
deeper understanding of the whole mystery. There was so
much work yet to be done and so much that I did not know.

The effect that my decision to abandon the dig would
have upon the filming programme could be catastrophic.
Anyway, I would soon find out. The swinging gait and
chunky build was unmistakable as Roy Davies moved all too
rapidly down the path towards the scar on the landscape

where the shrubbery had been. I moved across to where I had been laying waste the vegetation. I felt that I was about to be crucified — this was to be my Golgotha, right here on that hillside.

"You've made good progress so far." He greeted me warmly as he eyed the scene of devastation.

"I thought we could have a little chat about when you would be ready for the film crew so we could start shooting some footage."

If anyone was going to be shot in the foot, it was going to be me. This was my big chance to ruin his day. Mine had already been irrevocably changed.

"Yes, I have been at it for less than an hour and I have already cleared the bushes around the site." Rather a dumb remark as anyone could see what I had been doing.

"When do you think you will have anything to film? The French team are particularly keen to see some action," he added brightly.

"Well," I said, clawing for time and the right words, "I've had a good look now the bushes have gone and I expected to find something quite different. In fact, I am not sure that I should carry on digging here."

"I thought it all sounded a bit too easy. You always seemed very confident though."

"The trouble is that …" I groped for the *mot juste,* but none came to mind.

"…I came here ill prepared, both as regards tools and also as regards being certain that I should be excavating here and not somewhere over the other side of the vineyard, by the other dry-stone wall." I indicated the location of the rear end of the subterranean cavern that my hazel twig had delineated. "I feel I need to put in a lot more research before I can be certain, and that is going to take some time." I breathed a sigh, which, for me, was a sigh of relief but for Roy Davies, I hoped it sounded like a sigh of deep contrition.

Roy seemed to have the message. Everything that he heard was quite true. It would take me more time — quite a lot of time. Roy's face had fallen.

"Oh!" he exclaimed flatly.

"Where do we go from here?" My words must have echoed his thoughts.

"Well, all it not lost!" he replied. "We have put together a pretty heavy filming schedule and as you know we have a combined effort with the French team. The time scale is going to be tight. We have scheduled most of the filming around the church and in the village. Henry has a full repertoire of points he is anxious to include. We can miss out the excavation bit, if you are O.K. with that. It looks like there may not be much to film down here."

Now I knew why he is considered such a great Director.

"What about the French team?"

"They wanted some shots of you," he replied.

"After I tell them the bad news about the dig it will be a different sort of shots they will want of me. They may even want to use the mattock afterwards."

"Henry will keep them all occupied."

"I do hope they keep a sharp blade handy for Madame Guillotine."

"I don't think we could film that," he reassured me, as we climbed up towards the village. As it turned out they did take some shots of me up in the village talking about the failed dig but they were never used. I do not think they thought my French was quite good enough and the notion of anyone, other than a Frenchman, digging their land was not good public relations. The 13th of October had not been a propitious day, being that same black date in 1307 when the Knights Templar were arrested throughout France as well as the day their treasure failed to see the light of day.

That evening we all met up for dinner in the restaurant once owned by the Corbu family who had so kindly bought all the property from Marie Denarnaud in her declining years after Bérenger Saunière had passed from his earthly ministry. This purchase at least gave the ageing Marie an income and meant that she would be able to remain in the Villa Bethania throughout her life. Sadly for all concerned, all of the income derived through Bérenger Saunière ceased on his death despite the great plans he had at that time in 1917 to start anew an extensive building programme.

The restaurant extended for the full length of the belvedere wall below the ramparts that connected the Tour Magdala. The four round windows, now shone out across the landscape; a row of glistening white teeth. What must it have been like in that exotic era with the whole of Bérenger Saunière's domain a blaze of light? Humble pie was on the menu for me that night as I confessed my failure. Perhaps I had provided an excuse to take this second bite of the cake; the reason for the team to revisit Rennes for a sequel to the original Chronicle film. The meal was excellent and the film crew were most conciliatory over my excavation disaster.

My eye rested long upon the row of lights set into the ceiling. The coloured glass photographic transparencies, which covered the lights, were each about two and a half inches square and all depicted old masters' paintings. Perhaps our good Priest had compiled this collection?

That night, I packed my bags and slept well in Saunière's room. He could rest easy in his grave knowing that we were not about to pillage his treasure for a while. In the morning, I thanked Roy Davies, made my excuses and set off through the village to the steps leading down through the castle wall past the well. Following the path down to the excavation site, I stopped to gaze at the devastation I had wrought and to replant the roots I had torn out. While replacing the cut branches as best I could, I offered a silent prayer for their speedy growth to hide my embarrassment.

I continued down the steep overgrown path to the road and made my way down to Couiza. Here I caught the train to the *Ville Lumière* as Saunière had done towards the close of the nineteenth century. I too would visit St Sulpice and look once more at *Les Bergers d'Arcadie* in the Louvre before returning to England, not entirely dissatisfied with the eventful trip. Henry Lincoln, with great forbearance, treated the incident with only moderate disdain in his book *Key to the Sacred Pattern*. His description of events provided me with welcome anonymity by assigning me the *soubriquet* 'Mr. A', for which I was most grateful.

CHAPTER FIVE

ET IN ARCADIA EGO

A Prelate in Rome, Cardinal Giulio Rospigliosi, who later became Pope Clement VII, may well have had his fortunes determined by his involvement with a certain key, the key to the mystery of Rennes-le-Château. The possibility of some form of key to the riddle is intriguing. The tendency is to assume that there exists some underlying system to the mass of conflicting images presented to the mind. Human logic rebels against the affront that the whole of Bérenger Saunière's architecture is little more than an expensive hoax.

The tale of the parchments implies code with a solution based on manipulation of the letters to produce some lucid text. The method used to solve this may be regarded as an aspect of the key. Further complications appear when that meaningful text fails to satisfy our minds. References to Poussin's paintings lead the inquisitive to search for a pattern in those paintings. A unified system common to every related painting fits comfortably within our tidy logic. We must assume that such a key exists. Therefore we must search for its origins and authors. Details of this complex system that has baffled the mind of the experts for centuries may perhaps have been extracted from ancient inquisition documents or Vatican archives. Because of its nature, it needed to be preserved but kept well concealed. Cardinal Rospigliosi had been set a difficult task.

The idea of a key secreted in a painting excites the mind with innumerable possibilities. Few had access to books in those early days. Even religious books were not readily available to the masses and few there were who could read Latin, so the churches were full of religious paintings and icons upon which the congregation could gaze. From these images, the faithful could learn, while attending to their devotions at Church. The services were conducted mainly in Latin, the language of the liturgy, which inspired a sense of reverence but did little to instruct.

The works of the artists were divided into two categories, sacred and profane, or religious and secular. Profane was used in its broadest sense, referring to all those works of art that did not contain a religious theme. The ability to have a steady source of paintings and artefacts that would decorate the drawing rooms and salons of the wealthy was crucial. These would provide adornment; moreover, they would be a rich source of conversation and would generate that vital commodity — social status.

Patronage towards the arts and artists formed an essential constituent of the mediaeval structure. The future Pope Clement VII may be considered as a likely sponsor for the ET IN ARCADIA EGO paintings, and if he had known what was involved I am sure he would feel flattered to be considered for the rôle. Therefore, we shall include him in the story.

To achieve the particular result that Cardinal Rospigliosi envisaged would entail all the genius of an artist who was also discreet. The artistic skills could be determined. The discretion of the artist would require the offer of a suitable reward such as the promise of continued patronage that would guarantee financial security. The direct threat of loss of patronage when combined with the veiled threat that the artist would be unable to continue to paint upon the rich canvas of life would surely secure his undying loyalty.

Giovanni Francesco Barbieri was first chosen as the man for the job. He was advised as to the theme and format of the painting and warned of the dire consequences to his immortal soul, not to mention the future patronage of the Vatican and his future well being, should he be indiscreet.

Barbieri retired to his workshop and produced *Et In Arcadia Ego*. This painting might appear to the casual eye to be a rather banal representation of two shepherds gazing at a skull on a tomb that bears the title inscription. The only other noticeable object is a goldfinch sitting on a branch. A more informed examination, at a later stage, might well reveal a grotesque representation of a face disfigured by a squint. Perhaps this was intended as wry humour by the artist who is better known as 'El Guerchino', 'The Squint'.

The Cardinal may not have been too delighted with the result, for he then approached the best expert that he could find. There was one painter, with a reputation for great attention to detail and pictorial design. He was an accomplished French artist who had moved to Italy despite pressure from his King. He was Nicolas Poussin.

Born at Les Andelys in Normandy in 1594, he had gone to Italy to develop his talents despite pressure brought to bear by the French court. The courtiers were desirous that he should remain in Paris where all coveted his work, yet few would pay to support the struggling young artist of unkempt appearance. His early self-portrait clearly depicts his unimposing figure; he drew and painted what he saw!

Nicolas Poussin's early self-portrait sketches the vision he held of himself in his early years as a struggling artist. He portrays himself as a rather scruffy peasant, which of course he may well have been. By the end of his career, his powerful self-portraits depict him in his rôle as the self-assured master of his craft. His rugged features had been mellowed by the passage of the years yet were still clearly recognisable. Most of his work was executed personally rather than by the more usual practice of having a substantial part of his work undertaken by his pupils as part of their training. He was a lone artist and perhaps would have lost patience with any fumbling incompetence displayed by lesser men. He was meticulous in his work. When asked how he achieved his high standards he stated that he left nothing to chance.

In his later years, he had to contend with what must have been his greatest source of frustration; himself! Ill health affected the steadiness of his hand and limited his ability to maintain the high standards he had set himself. He had left his mark upon the world of art yet his greatest secret was to lie hidden, concealed within those masterful brush strokes; a combination of design and colour. His balance of composition and the visual harmony could be attributed to a self-imposed discipline.

This was the discipline of the golden ratio. It remained concealed yet self-evident in his greatest works. Here lay the reason that the key was safe in his hands. He used that key to create paintings with such a wonderful balance of design, the mark of his genius.

To understand the artist we must look to the source of his strength. He was his own man. This enviable characteristic gave him great stature yet may have inhibited his career path. It was with extreme reluctance that he agreed to work in France, and then only by response to royal decree. It is likely that he received the key to his rigorous discipline from some other source, although he could have acquired this knowledge from the analysis of the work of other artists.

The likelihood was that Nicolas Poussin received his commission to construct a painting on the theme of *Et In Arcadia Ego* from Cardinal Rospigliosi, but it could equally as well have been from another person. It might have been Poussin's best patron and friend in Rome, the lawyer Cassiano dal Pozzo. We have no conclusive evidence to establish the sponsor and Poussin may have created the paintings to satisfy his desire to express knowledge that he had acquired during his artistic career. The sponsor would certainly have required an artist who was capable of giving great attention to accuracy and detail.

The painting delivers a striking message about the frailty of human existence. The theme relates to the ever-present spectre of death, even in the idyllic surroundings of Arcadia, that Utopian land where peace and tranquillity reign and there is naught to make afraid. The real Arcadia still forms a part of Greece that is known particularly for the ancient temple at Tega.

The mind might associate Tega with temples designed and constructed with due deference to the use of the golden mean, as were many of the temples of antiquity. Alternatively, one might be drawn to the common house spider, the *tegenaria domestica*. One might consider that such aberrations are etymological rather than entomological and best left to monumental masons such as a certain Antoine Bigou, Curé of Rennes-le-Château from 1774 to 1790.

The cold stones of the Arcadian tomb invoke the image of the skull and other skeletal remains, perhaps of some shepherdess from a bygone age. The tomb portrayed in Nicolas Poussin's painting has remained closed since around 1645 and the grisly contents were subject only to the vivid imagination of four centuries of the peoples of France, of Europe and eventually of the World in the search for their hidden meaning.

The earlier commission, which was granted to El Guerchino from the same source, had indeed produced a clever painting that may not have met the expectations of its patron. Perhaps the sponsor considered that it fell short of

Fig. 5. 1. *Les Bergers d'Arcadie* as it appears in The Louvre.

This painting hangs in the Richlieu Gallery under the enigmatic gaze of Nicolas Poussin.

portraying the message that must perpetuate the key encoded in its geometric pattern. Perhaps those who understood the purpose and hidden message of the painting would feel constantly confronted with the unpleasant image of a skull fleshed out as the grotesque squinting death mask of El Guerchino, rather than that of two young shepherds gazing at a skull on a tomb. The outcome was that the patronage was bestowed upon Nicolas Poussin, who was known to display such excellent qualities of precision and detail in his workmanship.

However, it appears that a more onerous commission was involved. The geometric key had not only to be self-generating but it also had to be capable of demonstrating its practical application. Ideally the painting should be explicit yet still remain innocuous, it should be enigmatic yet benign. To be explicit, the painting must be capable of being dissected to produce the geometric pattern that was to be the key to the precise location of the ancient treasure buried near Rennes-le-Château, deep in the heart of southwest France.

The key must indicate its own method of construction and system of operation, while remaining inscrutable to all but the chosen few. The patron would need to supply the format of the key together with the exact location to be portrayed. Certainly, this was a challenge worthy of so great an artist. The key was to become the discipline and driving force that was to transform Nicolas Poussin into one of the most skilled draughtsmen and artisans of his time. He used the key in many of his paintings, including his imposing self-portrait executed towards the end of his brilliant career that revealed him as a man of such remarkable stature.

The title *Et In Arcadia Ego* is in itself enigmatic. One could enter into mental and etymological gymnastics to produce a variety of possible interpretations but, at this stage, I had insufficient data to distinguish any two likely meanings. There is still plenty of scope for the reader to enjoy the luxury of some speculation, particularly in the light of the various skulls concealed in *The Arcadian Shepherds*.

It is interesting to dwell on the need to produce a work displaying the key geometry alone. By Poussin's era the Flemish artist, David Teniers the younger, includes the system in his paintings, specifically in those paintings that relate to Saint Anthony the hermit. It is likely that Teniers received the key system from his father of the same name. Nevertheless, the great clarity of Poussin's work added much to the earlier masters. It is quite possible that David Teniers and his son were fully aware of the cipher beforehand; as the key was within the domain of artists over the centuries and it is possible that Poussin had himself received it from other artists. It could well be that both Poussin and Teniers knew about the location of the hoard of Rennes from the same source. Nevertheless, it seems likely that Poussin did produce the two *Arcadian Shepherds* paintings because of a specific commission.

Nicolas Poussin had tended to turn his back on France and clearly preferred to work in Rome. Accomplished artist as he was, he could not have undertaken the paintings unless he had travelled up from Italy to the Rennes-le-Château area to execute at least the outline sketches of the first painting, though Poussin may have taken a second visit to complete sketches for *Les Bergers d'Arcadie*.

The *Arcadian Shepherds* painting from the late Duke of Devonshire's collection, kept at his Bakewell estate in Derbyshire, has already yielded one possible location of the probable treasure hoard in the exploration work already accomplished in conjunction with the aerial photography. Yet, the excavation had not proceeded as planned. Surely, it should be possible to learn the secret of the paintings if indeed there was anything to be revealed.

The most likely subject for detailed study must surely be Poussin's *Les Bergers d'Arcadie*, now hanging in the Louvre in Paris. This appears to be the painting acquired by Bérenger Saunière when he first started out on his journey of discovery. To hope to learn the secrets of the painting in just a few minutes would be unrealistic but this journey of discovery is well worth the effort.

If we gaze one more time with fresh eyes at *Les Bergers d'Arcadie*, we will discern that centrally placed in the painting the shadow cast resembles the head and shoulders of the grim reaper with his curved scythe. Poussin's message 'ET IN ARCADIA EGO' has surely been changed into the message and the example of the Priest to his congregation and indeed to the world. The architecture within the little church of St Madeleine conveys so much yet it is expressed in the words,

"Come unto Jesus all ye who are heavy laden."

Perhaps Saunière would have wished to change the theme from 'ET IN ARCADIA EGO' to 'AMOR VINCIT OMNIA'?

Reflecting upon my abortive filming exploit that had reached its ignominious conclusion, I could see the need for much more background knowledge about the treasure location and access to it. My philosophy was that anything lying in the ground for hundreds of years could remain undisturbed for a bit longer, and should not be allowed to disrupt my family life.

The transparency of *Les Bergers d'Arcadie* arrived, after a long wait. It seemed that everything was conspiring to delay that moment when I would be able to grapple with the secrets contained within the painting. While I awaited its arrival, I had time to dwell on the inscription ET IN ARCADIA EGO; 'I too, am in Arcadia'. The accepted implication is that this inscription on the tomb refers to the lurking presence of death, as depicted by a tomb and often by a human skull, existing even in the idyllic world of Arcadia. Though this interpretation has not been entirely satisfactory, it certainly invokes a tantalising flavour of enigma. Perhaps the only word that appears unambiguous at first glance might be 'ET'— 'and'!

What struck me was the perfection of design and the rich passages of colour that mark Poussin's composition. If the inscription on the tomb were not partially obscured, we might glance fleetingly at the words and pass on. However, we are drawn to puzzle out each letter and can hardly avoid mimicking the shepherd who points to a letter as he studies the words.

Les Bergers d'Arcadie is classified as being in his *deseigno* period, but Poussin's deployment of colour in *The Arcadian Shepherds*, concealing the image of the skulls amongst those drab yellow and brown tones displays a masterly use of paint.

Later he was able to afford the more expensive pigments for his work and moved into his *colore* era. Though Poussin's reputation rose, he preferred the accolade of connoisseurs of art in Rome and Florence with their patronage, rather than the somewhat empty praise of the courtiers of Paris and France. His brother in law followed his example in the arts and even executed his own *Et In Arcadia Ego* painting, but he lacked the finesse and flare for composition displayed by Nicolas Poussin.

It was customary for many of the renaissance Masters to run a school where talented young artists performed much of the more mundane work while the Master would add the signature and a few final changes. It is likely that his 'brother', as he was called, executed some of Nicolas' work. Yet, Nicolas Poussin differed from the main stream. He set himself apart with the unusual characteristic that he would retire to his studio and work away alone and in secret until the day that he would finally reveal the finished masterpiece. Such an artist would not have been satisfied with less than perfection and suffered great frustration and anguish in his declining years. Then, ill health cruelly robbed him of the ability to match the shaky hand and failing eyesight of a Past Master to the accumulated skill and finesse of his many years experience. Yet, who amongst us could detect anything less than perfection in his work?

The challenge of the *Et In Arcadia Ego* theme brought Nicolas Poussin to Rennes-le-Château, perhaps to that very spot on the hillside where I slept on my first visit to the village and which I called The Poussin Seat. He would have visited various locations and prepared sketches for what is regarded as one of his great accomplishments. Perhaps the true measure of his expertise could never have been fully comprehended.

Experts have been studying his painting since the mid-seventeenth century, more particularly during the last twenty years, and have finally conceded that there is no concealed geometry therein apart from a pentagram with a five-pointed star in a circle relating the overall dimensions of the painting to the geometry of the pentagram as described by Professor Cornford. Fortunately, the experts had not reached their conclusions by the time I returned from my first visit to Rennes-le-Château.

I had looked at a black and white print of the painting and had read most of Sir Anthony Blunt's book on the artist. Blunt had specialised in the works and life of Nicolas Poussin and was the Curator of the Queen's paintings; truly an expert on art. At the time, he was held in high regard, being a cornerstone of the establishment and had an unimpeachable reputation in the world of art. Accordingly I spoke by phone to Sir Anthony. I asked him about the possibility that Nicolas Poussin had visited the Rennes area during that era when the two paintings would have been created. This is thought to be between 1630 and 1645. He was adamant that Poussin had not visited that area during this period, though he did travel to Paris. Sir Anthony was less than polite about the suggestion. In fact one could say that he was rather blunt.

To be fair, his health had been poor at that time and his mind was probably fully preoccupied with those allegations of treason, which were to follow shortly thereafter. These caused the downfall of Sir Anthony a few weeks later. The accusations sent a shock wave through the Establishment and rocked the world of fine art but could not detract from Blunt's expertise in that field, particularly with regard to Nicolas Poussin.

The rich talents possessed by Nicolas Poussin could well conceal a complete layer of ingenuity suspected yet lost to the art experts of our time. Yet to lose sight of this for ever would be a tragedy for art, limiting our comprehension of the work of this great artist and others who shared his insight. The gauntlet had been cast down and it would have been churlish not to take up the challenge.

CHAPTER SIX

THE BLUE APPLES OF RENNES

Returning after my first visit to Rennes, I decided to break my journey at Paris to visit the Church of St Sulpice. This was where Bérenger Saunière was reputed to have gleaned some vital information whilst endeavouring to find experts who were able to decipher some encoded manuscripts. These manuscripts were the ones that he is said to have discovered when he first started to refurbish the chapel at Rennes-le-Château. While in Paris, I spent some time at the Louvre Museum where *Les Bergers d'Arcadie* is on display and I made a particular point of studying the painting in its distinguished surroundings. At the Louvre, I was able to buy half a dozen postcards of the painting together with some 35 mm colour transparencies.

I needed a copy of Gérard de Sède's paperback edition of *Le Trésor Maudit de Rennes-le-Château*, as it was the book that triggered so much interest in the mystery surrounding the Priest and his little church. I finally bought a copy at Hachettes in London on my return. Gérard de Sède had included a lot of background information and illustrations of the various manuscripts. These are the same manuscripts that featured in the BBC Chronicle programme on the subject.

De Sède's book proved a handy reference for the mystery of the village set against the backdrop of a wild countryside with a wilder history. I read it avidly and found it to be a comprehensive study providing much valuable information. I now felt more familiar with the landscape and pictured the pastoral scene in my mind as I studied the cipher that Saunière had composed in his notebook.

As in Saunière's day, not far from Rennes, at the mouth of the River Rhône, anglers would be launching their boats to seek out the fish lurking in the deep pools. The rebus cipher mentions 'no fish upon the griddle'; their prize catch swam in the murky depths of the river for the taking. Once hooked, the Ombre, that shadowy fish common at the mouth of the Rhône, would be better placed on a griddle over the glowing embers of a fire. Reminiscent of the expression used by the skilled French code breakers at the turn of the twentieth century and particularly during the 1914-18 war, 'a fish upon the griddle' referred to cipher text to be subjected to scrutiny by placing it on a matrix, or vigenère table, enabling letter substitution to be performed during code breaking. This system was named after Blaise de Vigenère, a French Diplomat born in 1523, who wrote

Traicté des Chiffres. However, Leon Battista Alberti, born in 1404, originated this system of encryption. *(The Code Book,* by Simon Singh, pages 45 & 51). Code breaking methods often depend on the frequency with which certain letters occur and upon word and letter patterns. For instance, the most common letter 'E' occurs in text generally about twelve percent of the time while the next most frequent occurrence is the letter 'T' usually at about nine percent of the letters used in the average text.

This may seem Greek to you at the present. In the rich language of Rennes-le-Château Punic is the *lingua franca* and is the language of concealment. This versatile language of puns can involve Greek, Latin, French and even English.

Taking but a brief glance at the cipher displayed in Saunière's notebook and reproduced in *The Accursed Treasure* ... page 50 we might review the text as a rebus. For an example of such a cryptic message in rebus form current in Saunière's era there is much truth in this little ditty:

Too wise you are,

Too wise you be,

I see you are too wise for me.

Expressed as a rebus one might write:

YY UR YY UB IC UR YY ME ME ME ME.

Like all things connected with the story Saunière's rebus is likely to contain a more profound hidden meaning or two that could be so easily overlooked at a first casual glance.

Y E N S Z N U M G L N

Y Y R F V H E N M Z F P ● S O T + P E C H E

U R + A + L ' E M B Z

V O U C H U R E + D U + R H O N E , S O N Z

U P O I S S O N + S U R + L E + G R I L + F

What if Saunière's cipher text is referring to the painting of a famous French artist? In the Poussin painting, *Les Bergers d'Arcadie*, the shepherd's finger points to the curved shadow, *un ombre*. As we are looking for a starting point to unravel the secrets that might be contained therein, this would at least provide a possible entry. The scythe shadow is cast by the shepherd's arm yet the sun is painted centrally on the horizon so would not cast such a shadow. There seems to be this pun with *un ombre*, a shadow and *un nombre*, a number. This should be borne in mind. These insignificant details might prove to be relevant, even important. Everything is significant. Significant despite the confusion spread by so much information. However, lurking there somewhere is a meaning. I was still lacking some spark of comprehension to kindle a flame of understanding. From the distant past the first wreath of smoke was rising from the tinder but the Ombre still lay chilled upon the griddle.

Another point of interest that struck me was that Henry Lincoln's image of the coded manuscript that the camera team were shooting in the film sequence at Rennes-le-Château that morning was not the same as the illustration in Gérard de Sède's book. In *Le Trésor Maudit de Rennes-le-Château*, the little 'P - S' logo, in the bottom right hand corner of the Manuscript II, had been omitted from the illustration in my copy of the book I had just bought. As the logo also appeared in the Stublein illustration of Marie de

Nègre d'Hautpoul de Blanchefort's tombstone in the same book, was the omission careless or was it intentional? Bérenger Saunière expended time and energy defacing the tombstone bearing the logo and if he considered it a threat, it would be unwise to dismiss it out of hand. I have recently verified that the 'P - S' logo was included in the first case-bound edition.

Having studied de Sède's book, I then focused my whole attention upon the Poussin paintings that had served me so well. Thus far, it had proved possible to establish the connection between the relevant Poussin paintings and a group of vignettes representing parts of the landscape around Rennes-le-Château. Already established was that one of the vignettes represented the strip of land that runs from the Couiza road half the way up the hill towards the village of Rennes-le-Château. This represented the arm and fist, lying between the drystone walls on the land that had been a cultivated area until just a score of years ago (as shown in Fig. 2.3. and 2.4.). The drystone wall on either side defines the outline of the arm.

A flight of fancy perhaps, yet the outline of the cultivated land was similar to the mark clearly painted on the forearm in Poussin's earlier *The Arcadian Shepherd* painting in the late Duke of Devonshire's collection at Chatsworth. If the main issue were only to define the precise resting place of a treasure hoard, it would seem that this method of representation could well have served its purpose. But one could not escape the certainty that not a few layers of hidden meaning still remained undisclosed.

Bérenger Saunière did and said many things while his
mind must have been focused on his need to conceal yet
reveal. When asked about the treasure, he was reputed to
have said in the Languedoc tongue,

"Me l'han donat, l'hay panat, l'hay parat é bé le téni", which,
using Gérard de Sède's interpretation, may be translated as:

"It has been shown to me, I put my hand upon it, I have
worked it all out and I am holding it firmly."

Could Saunière have been aware that the treasure lay
within the clenched fist clawing at the landscape? On such
flimsy evidence, it would be folly to proceed. Yet, to
develop an hypothesis is a way forward. Whether to destroy
it or to enhance it is immaterial; the analysis of information
within the discipline of an hypothesis, based on the original
data will often lead to an improved theory or at least hook a
shadowy fish lurking in a murky river.

It is true that both of the paintings by Nicholas Poussin,
The Arcadian Shepherds and *Les Bergers d'Arcadie* contain some
vignettes of the area around Rennes-le-Château. Perhaps all
that was required was the correct key. My father, who had
a good knowledge of French, set about making a careful
translation of de Sède's book. Later the BBC requested a
copy, which may have assisted them in future programmes.
From information in the BBC Chronicle programmes, I
learned that X-rays of the painting, *Les Bergers d'Arcadie,*
showed that the positions of all three shepherds' staffs were
established as the initial step in the painting's composition
The other snippet of information was that the artist had
experienced problems in painting the head of the shepherd

on the right, holding the long staff. We can refer to him as the 'Red Shepherd', as M. Poussin has attired each shepherd in distinctive colours.

Henry Lincoln, the driving force behind the BBC productions, received, via de Sède, an explanation of the cipher contained in one of the manuscripts. The cipher when broken yields the following text:

BERGERE PAS DE TENTATION QUE POUSSIN TENIERS GARDENT LA CLEF PAX DCLXXXI PAR LA CROIX ET CE CHEVAL DE DIEU J'ACHEVE CE DAEMON DE GARDIEN A MIDI POMMES BLEUES

Each word may be considered on its own merits and might lose one or more of its true meanings within the context of a sentence. The words could be strung together to give the following approximate interpretation:

Shepherdess without (*pas de*) temptation (or feet or steps of temptation) that Poussin Teniers guard the key peace 681 by the cross and this horse of God I overcome this demon of a guardian at midday, (or, in the Midi region, at the middle or centre), blue apples.

Henry Lincoln defines the method that de Sède, or his informants, have given to elucidate the original cipher of 140 letters in Appendix One of his book *The Holy Place*.

The *bergere pas de tentation* … is an anagram of the PS PRAE-CUM plus the letters appearing on the headstone of the Marie de Nègre tomb. It may also be achieved by setting out the letters into two square blocks of sixty-four letters separated by the words AD GENESARETH. This phrase is discarded out of hand. The remaining letters are shifted

Fig. 6.1 *Les Bergers d'Arcadie* (Scala)

one place down the alphabet, then passed over a table of Vigenère using MORT EPEE as the key. The resulting letters are again passed over a further table of Vigenère using the contents of the Marie de Nègre headstone plus PS PRAE-CUM in reverse, or mirrored. Again, there is a one-letter shift down the alphabet before setting out the letters in two square blocks like two chessboards. The final move is to pick out the letters in the sequence of a chess knights tour, one block being a mirror image of the other.

I concluded that the object of describing these complex machinations was not merely to play with the letters, but to identify a pattern, which may serve some useful purpose that might later become apparent.

However, what does it all mean? Bearing in mind, that one of the functions of any cipher is to confuse the enemy it must be agreed that this is certainly an excellent cipher. Awarding marks out of ten, we must give it at least twelve. Considering that the *Arcadian Shepherds* painting suggested a location of a treasure and *Les Bergers d'Arcadie* was executed after the Chatsworth painting it certainly was worth tackling the later version, now in the Louvre. The added confusion provided by the decoded cipher gave a strong argument for further detailed study of the painting.

On reviewing *Les Bergers d'Arcadie,* there seemed to be no discernable relationship linking the three staffs, two crooked at one end, one of them having a distinct bend. Every effort to identify a geometric pattern such as a triangle, pentagram, or circle met with little success. Several possibilities almost fitted yet in every case it was necessary to cheat to produce any semblance of a conventional geometric figure. Like most drawings or paintings, it consisted of a mixture of straight lines and arcs. Extending the straight lines on one of my postcards of the painting had produced nothing of any discernible interest so I started work on the curves.

No arc extended into a complete circle so I started afresh on another of the postcards that I had purchased from the Louvre. It was slow work, as I had to find the centre point of each arc before I could construct its full circle. Where should I start? Heads were a possibility especially as Poussin had suffered difficulty with the Red Shepherd's head. Then I continued with the blue cloak, which seemed to have some nice swirls to work upon.

As I progressed, I produced a wondrous tangle of lines, some of which were construction lines. As I kept working on the picture the circles became smaller and smaller and the card became covered in compass point pricks. There seemed to be some sort of a pattern emerging producing triangles on the bare back of the Blue Shepherd. The circles were moving down to the left onto the shepherd's blue cloak. I eventually ended up with two sets of converging circles that intersected on the left side of the blue cloak. These lines were cut by other circles in such a manner that I found myself staring at a blue apple. Not only that, but it had a short stalk with a leaf coming from the stalk — just the way you would pluck it from an apple tree. Except, one must concede that very few trees produce genuine blue apples. Perhaps one may be found!

This was certainly one of the blue apples referred to in

the manuscript cipher. However, it still seemed to lack meaning. It did confirm that Nicholas Poussin was a clever artist. Yet more important it gave me the assurance that the key could be discovered in the painting. Even more vital was the obvious conclusion that this artist of such sombre appearance had a great sense of humour. He had a joke, which he was very willing to share with anyone who would endeavour to match his effort if not his skill, line by line.

I was keen to discuss this with my father who was busy with the translation of *Le Trésor Maudit*… After gazing at the postcard for some time he looked up and said,

"*Pommes bleues*, blue apples."

"Yes," I replied, "But it's still all Greek to me, just like the shepherds in Arcadia."

"Yes and it's all Greek, or at least Latin, to me too. So is *helis pomata!*"

My father explained that this is the term used to refer to an apple-shaped geometrical figure comprising two matching helices. He went on to explain that the apple shape is known by the term *helis pomata*. This geometric figure may be produced by progressive mathematical curves resulting from a series of numbers such as the series of square roots represented by geometry. When the mirror image of the h*elis pomata* is superimposed adjacent to the original figure, they do indeed form a shape exactly like that of a heart or an apple, which M. Nicholas Poussin had so carefully concealed, except from my prying eye. My father reminded me that many mathematical formulae may be equally well expressed geometrically and many problems in mathematics can be solved with pure geometry.

Helis is also a pun relating to the colour blue as in
heliotrope. Some research into the twelve ancient volumes
of our family etymological dictionary shed further light on the
subject. Heliotrope is a plant, commonly having distinctive
blue flowers and the name is derived from two Greek
words, *helios*, the sun and *tropos*, turning. Hence, it could be
designated as *pommes bleues* or blue apples. There is also the
Helix Pomatia Linnaeus. This creature, which some consider
to be a delicacy had its common habitat in orchards whence
it received part of its Latin name, *pomatia*. *Helix* refers to the
spiral shape of the shell of what is now commonly known as
the Roman Snail, being somewhat larger and lighter in
colour than the garden snail

Though scientific references to the oddity, the *helis
pomata* as a mathematical fruit seems to have faded into
obscurity, fortunately it had not yet vanished from living
memory. Perhaps this name was once an ancient Greek or
Roman pun as well. Vital clues disappearing from human
memory seems to be a problem endemic to the ways of
Rennes. This is what makes the quest so challenging. We
have to rediscover those truths along with the rules that
were used to govern them. Our investigations were moving
forward, albeit at a snail's pace.

Finding the helix of *helis pomata* was indeed a great leap
forward. We were in the business of solutions to problems.
A sudden flashback to the tombstone of Marie de Nègre in
the village graveyard conjured up the LIXLIXL inscription
on the gravestone. Saunière took such pain to obliterate it,

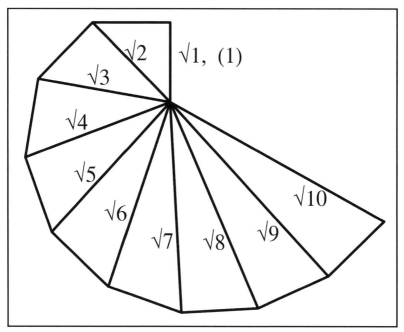

Fig. 6. 2. Geometric figure to give the roots of numbers.

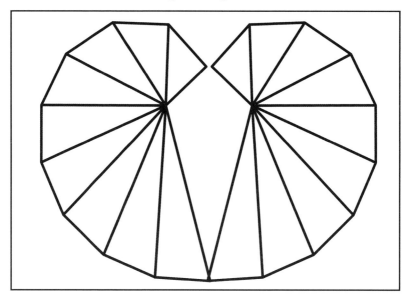

Fig. 6. 3. Rather indigestible roots forming a goodly apple.

and with good reason. I thought of him working with the
stonemason's tools muttering to himself over and over
LIXLIXLIX. It was a treasure in the spoken word, truly a
trésor mot dit.

We set about drawing various examples of the double helix
required to form an apple shape. We hoped to hit upon the
correct mathematical curve. We started with progressive
roots of whole numbers. That is the number which, when
multiplied by itself produces the desired whole number.
Thus, root one is one, easy really. The root of four is easy;
two times two equals four and three times three is nine so
root four is two and root nine is three.

This must seem like teaching your grandmother to suck
grapes. So, what is root two? A number, which when
multiplied by itself, equals two exactly. Perhaps grandma
might put down the grapes and give you a hand with that
one. They did not have calculators in Nicholas Poussin's era,
unless you count Sir Isaac Newton as a calculator — he was
also pretty good with apples. First, construct a figure as
shown in Fig.6.2. on the previous page using one as the unit
for the length of the first two sides keeping the first angle as
a right angle. Then join up the third side to form a right
angle triangle. The third side is actually root two if you care
to measure it. Draw another right angle, still keeping the
length of that line equal to one and draw in the third side
of the new triangle, which must be equal in length to root
three. In addition, the next right angle triangle produces a
line exactly two units in length because it is root four. As
we now have all become mathematical geniuses, draw three
more, which must give you root five, root six and root

seven. Copy this figure in the opposite direction as a mirror image and you have made the double helix or *helis pomata*. Yet we have not introduced any curved lines into the figure.

Clearly, this was not the answer, what is needed is the geometric progression that produces the correct helis pomata spiral to match the curves on *Les Bergers d'Arcadie*. Yet, if, as stated in the cipher rendering, both Poussin and David Teniers had the key then perhaps there would be some merit in examining the paintings of both David Teniers the younger and of his father of the same name. Later paintings could be expected to reflect more expertise than perhaps did the earlier ones.

The cipher phrase *pas de tentation* could indicate that those paintings depicting St Anthony the hermit undergoing various forms of temptation should be ruled out, on the basis that *pas de tentation* meant without temptation. On examining several of the paintings, it became clear that the artist generally depicted those evil tempters with fowl feet — ugly chicken's talons. On this basis all paintings showing the goodly saint being tempted would be likely candidates — such are the ways of Rennes!

The *Temptation of St Anthony* theme must have proved to be popular, also financially rewarding for the painters. Numerous versions may be found within the art galleries of the World. It would be profitable for the searcher to look for similarities that can be found in most of these paintings.

First, let us consider the three main *Et In Arcadia Ego* paintings discussed so far. Staffs normally appear, skulls rate high on the list, people are certainly depicted including their feet, foul or otherwise. What has St Anthony to offer? Well, he was renowned for being able to resist temptation. He was religious and practically all the paintings depict a cross. In fact, he had his own particular cross, for the Tau cross is much like the capital letter 'T'. This is derived from the Greek letter *Tau*. St Anthony is usually shown with the Tau cross embroidered into the right sleeve at the shoulder of his robe. Now this could prove significant because the letter Tau is the mathematical symbol for the Golden Section.

We need to familiarise ourselves with some aspects of the Golden Section or Golden Mean to define how this relates to the geometry that was emerging from the paintings and to provide some interesting background information on Rennes. The Golden Mean represents the mathematical division of a line in proportions aesthetically pleasing to the eye. This has particular relevance when considering the composition of a drawing, painting or sculpture. Artists consider that this division is best achieved by dividing a line in the ratio of 1 to 1.618 approximately.

This ratio has some interesting properties. The practical application of this is best understood by considering, or drawing a rectangle. Now imagine the rectangle such that when a line is drawn across the rectangle it forms a square and an additional portion. Now the extra piece will again be a rectangle, probably similar in proportions to the first rectangle drawn. If it is exactly the same shape, only smaller, then you must have started out with a Golden Rectangle and have just produced a smaller Golden Rectangle which can itself be divided into a square leaving an even smaller Golden Rectangle. In other words, you have divided the long sides of the rectangle in the Golden Mean.

1 Divide the rectangle into a square and a rectangle.

2. The sides of the rectangle will be in the Golden Ratio.

3. This rule applies only if the original rectangle sides were in the Golden Ratio.

4. If the ratio between the shorter sides of the rectangle longer sides is 1 to 1.618 this rule applies.

1 Divide the rectangle into a square and a rectangle.

2. The sides of the rectangle will be in the Golden Ratio.

3. This rule applies only if the original rectangle sides were in the Golden Ratio.

4. If the ratio between the shorter sides of the rectangle& longer side is 1to 1.618.

1 Divide the rectangle into a square and a rectangle.

2. The rectangle will be in the Golden Ratio.

1 Divide the rectangle into a square and a rectangle.

2. The rectangle will be in the Golden Ratio.

Fig. 6. 4. Reducing the size of the Golden Rectangle.

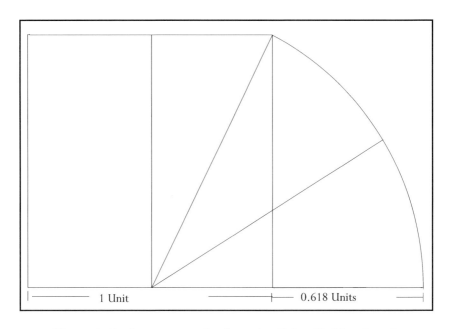

1 Unit   0.618 Units

Fig. 6. 5. Increasing the length of the Golden baseline.

You can think in units of miles, kilometres, feet, inches or centimetres and the same rule always applies. This was very popular amongst Greek temple builders and artists, as designs based upon the Golden Ratio are reputed to produce balance and to give an aesthetically pleasing result. It was even given religious significance by some, though it is still just a number. Perhaps a visit to the famous Greek temple at Tega in that part of Greece that was once known as Arcadia, would be instructive.

So far, we have been able to reduce the size of the Golden Rectangle by dividing it. It must surely be possible to increase the length of a short line to generate the Golden Ratio in order to produce this mathematical oddity by means of a geometric construction. What had St Anthony to do with all this? Teniers did depict him wearing the Greek Tau symbol for the Golden Ratio on his robe. St Anthony probably had time on his hands, so in between temptations he might have taken a sheet of parchment and drawn a square, dividing it into two equal rectangles by joining the two opposite mid-points. Sitting in his cave, with only the dim religious light from a guttering candle, St Anthony could draw a diagonal from the mid-point on the baseline to the top corner of the rectangle. Using a pair of compasses from his fine collection of writing instruments, he would describe an arc centred on the baseline. The radius must be equal to the diagonal, to intersect the baseline (Fig. 6.5.). This would extend the baseline to equal the length of the new Golden Ratio. In so doing, St Anthony would have designed a new Tau cross to stitch to his robe, just in time for his next temptation. This would be recorded by David Teniers (the younger, of course) as he painted St Anthony's portrait, while surrounded by all manner of foul creatures reeking with the sulphurous odours of the pit. Such is the life of a devoted artist or of a saintly hermit.

Considering the deep interest that artists express in the Golden Mean, it is reasonably likely that Nicholas Poussin may have integrated this system in his ET IN ARCADIA paintings. On searching for evidence of this in *Les Bergers d'Arcadie*, the Red Shepherd's staff presents itself to the eye as the main unit of measurement. The Golden Ratio exists between the length of the Red Shepherd's staff and the full width of the painting. This relationship is incidentally the same as distance between the fingertip resting on the 'R' and our one-legged Red Shepherd's sandal-loop or toe. Here the Golden Ratio is not 1: 1.618 but 1: 2.618 or, 1:1.618: 2.618, being two steps along the Golden Ratio path, thus more difficult to detect. Matches occur and the toes and sandal-loops do seem to feature among the *pas de tentation,* in the steps along the tricky path of understanding.

Meanwhile, the paintings mentioned so far all have some attributes in common and these should be borne in mind though Poussin's *Les Bergers d'Arcadie*, being the later work, seems crucial. Confirmation of any system discovered may be sought in the other paintings. Of course, as the paintings were all different sizes it would be necessary to use either different scales for the measurement for each painting or else enlarge each painting to fit the standard scale, which must be based on the Red Shepherd's staff.

For the paintings by David Teniers, I would prefer to use one that depicted St Anthony the hermit bearing the Tau cross on his shoulder. I wanted one of the Teniers paintings that showed all, or some of the significant features such as the crucifixion, the skull, open books, a staff and possibly some *pas de tentation*, either steps of temptation, footsteps of temptation or in contrast, without temptation.

This solution found in the *pommes bleues* cipher fulfils the Rennes criteria by referring to the works of one of the Teniers family or to Poussin's *Les Bergers d'Arcadie*, or even some additional feature yet to be discovered. The beauty of the quest is its never-ending nature. Teniers depicts the personified temptations of St Anthony the hermit as those personages or creatures whose true nature is revealed by their feet. The various elements will have their distinctive uses and may not appear in every painting; one of the less complicated being *St Anthony Tempted by Drunkenness*.

It was an achievement to identify the meaning of *helis pomata*. However, it was not an answer so much as a further challenge. I still needed to create the correct mathematical model by trial and error and error and error. The method of construction shown in Figs. 6.4 and 6.5 does produce the golden ratio but fails to generate a series of arcs linked to the straight lines in my attempts to satisfy the mathematics. Poussin was giving it a definite 'thumbs down'. However, despite this, it was exhilarating to find myself sitting at the feet of such a Master.

Like so much of the puzzle, it was a matter of inventing a new method. The old methods were long forgotten except by those who still clutched them in their untimely graves.

Fig.   6. 6.   *St Anthony being tempted by drunkenness.*

This painting by David Teniers the younger contains the elements
typical of the St Anthony temptation series and shows the 'T'.

It was essential to form a figure that would generate two continuous arcs that increase in size to form a *pomme bleue* figure. I have to approach this problem with an open mind. Every construction line could be moved. Eventually the half section of the baseline was rotated in line with the diagonal, as in Fig. 6.7. This retained the increase in length to the diagonal required to produce the Golden Ratio proportional to the original square. To extend the arc for the subsequent step it was necessary to construct a square upon the new baseline. One might expect that this square would naturally be constructed on the uncluttered side of the baseline but this was fruitless. No blue apple appeared. The solution was to construct the square then to divide the baseline into two equal rectangles as shown in Fig. 6.7. The diagonal is then drawn and extended through the baseline to intersect an arc, centred at the mid-point of the baseline, with radius equal to half the baseline. This arc extends between the nearest corner and the extended diagonal. The extended diagonal then becomes the new baseline. Using this new baseline, we next construct a square over the existing figure rather than on the uncongested side of that baseline.

As shown in Fig. 6.8, the new square is divided into two rectangles. The diagonal is constructed and extended through the baseline mid-point to intersect the new arc. This arc forms a continuation of the existing arc to the new extended diagonal but with a larger radius having its centre at the mid-point of the new baseline and continuing the existing arc. This construction thus generates the new Golden Ratio line and completes the step using the only

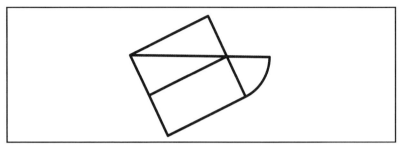

Fig. 6. 7. First step drawing the Tau arc.

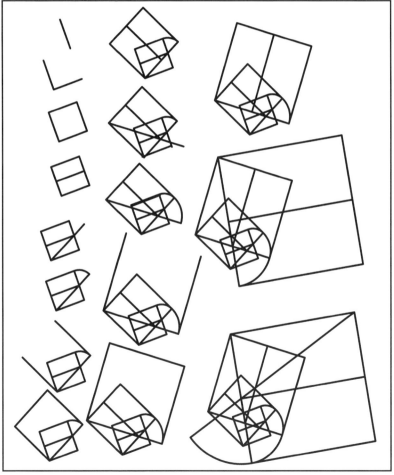

Fig. 6. 8. Rotation of baseline produces the Golden Ratio.

method possible that provides an elegant solution to the problem. One is tempted to repeat each step though the key figure becomes more convoluted as it progresses.

By constructing this new square on the reverse side of the newly formed Golden Ratio line, a suitable progression of curves, linking the straight lines is produced. This gives a series of squares, each divided in two halves, linked by a series of arcs, resulting in the theoretically perfect solution to the problem, and constitutes the sort-after key required to give some meaning to Poussin's enigma.

Refer once more to Figs. 6.7 and 6.8 in order to become fully conversant with this method, allowing it to sink into your mind. This exercise, though complex, is vital in order to comprehend the way forward as you follow the winding paths of Rennes. The mathematical figure can be calculated without generating the square construction lines. But these construction lines form an essential part of what has become a portion of the key. This is but half an apple and yet even Eve had to reserve a portion to offer to Adam. The two halves would need to be combined at some stage. But to yield to temptation and rush headlong into confusion before mastering this first breakthrough and becoming conversant with the mechanics of the key would be folly.

The prototype key, consisting of a spiral and a series of squares still did not quite fit the curves on the painting. The relative scale of the key had to be matched to that of the illustration under examination. In those early days, this was achieved by trial and error using a photocopier that had an enlarger. The first attempts involved measuring the length of the staff and then constructing a drawing from that first measurement. I had become familiar with the use of tracing linen to draw my mining maps and this fine waxed linen was suitable but not perfect, being reasonably transparent.

There were, of course, no personal computers in 1973, certainly nothing capable of producing computer graphics. Modern graphics and CAD packages were what I dreamt of for many years in those early days, working on steam-powered mainframe computers of the early seventies when there were no disks and no keyboards.

When I first produced the key on a transparent sheet, I remember fitting one side of the square with the staff on the painting and seeing that nothing matched. This is because each line of a square can be superimposed on the painting in either of two directions, or four if one takes account of the mirror image. There is also the middle line in each square. After some juggling of the key, the following encouraging match is achieved, as shown in Fig. 6.9. As I applied the key, it was exciting to see Poussin's handiwork as he intended it to be used, with his accuracy and attention to detail. When examining the painting in an earlier analysis, I had extended the two long staffs to intersect at a point below the painting. I had noted that the included angle was the same as that made by the diagonal of a half square.

The Blue Shepherd's staff is curved at the lower end, which would seem to eliminate it as a measure. However when matched with the quadrant, as shown, the staff fits exactly with the curved portion of the arc, the top of the staff being at the arc centre. Poussin was meticulous and has divided the width of each staff by a straight line of shadow enabling the narrow lines of the key to be positioned with great precision. When the key matched, it was gratifying to see that the angle between the two staffs matched the lines of the relevant squares. This is how Nicholas Poussin had intended it to be. I was surprised and a little disappointed to note that the match did not extend to fit the lengths of both staffs at the same time. M. Poussin still had some tricks up the sleeve of his shepherdess. This was a good time to sleep on the progress thus far.

Having achieved a portion of this demon of a guardian at the correct scale, it was possible to familiarise myself with the numerous matches of curves and squares. Two of these are illustrated in Fig. 6.9.

We now have a key that was to be used in a particular manner. The manner of using the key was a bigger problem than so far encountered. Poussin would have given clear instructions on how to produce the key, and on how to use it. To differentiate between these two essential functions, both to construct and to use, might not be easy. Nothing at Rennes was ever easy.

The earlier analysis of *Les Bergers d'Arcadie* revealed some anomalies, particularly with regard to the shadows that the suns cast. There appeared to be two suns, one central in the picture and one further to the right, neither of which cast any shadows in the foreground. These shadows fall as if another sun was shining from behind the artist. Thus, the shadow of a shepherd's arm falls upon the side of the tomb in the shape of a scythe. The paintings portray the idyllic Arcadian landscape where carefree shepherds disport with

their partners until suddenly confronted with the realities of
life — death, the tomb,the skull and the scythe of The Grim
Reaper.

The shepherd's right index finger points to the letter 'R'
and is positioned right at the top of the scythe shadow. The
pointing fingers cry out to trace the outline of the shadow.
As I had been working with the large transparencies, this
was not difficult to achieve by holding up two transparencies
to the light and moving the image of the fingers down either
side of the curved portion of the shadow from its origin at
the 'R'. This kneading motion of bread-making brings one
of the transparencies down in a curving motion until the
Red Shepherd's left index finger is arrested at the point of
the shadow's elbow. The Blue Shepherd's right index finger
is brought to rest in the crook of the shadow's elbow.

The two pictures have now merged to produce a new
image. The Red Shepherd's left knee coincides precisely
with one of his heads and the Blue Shepherd is wearing a
white hat. The angle of rotation is, of course, equal to that
of the half square diagonal. The subtlety of this great work
of technical perfection is beginning to be revealed as the
bright line of the 'R' matches the corresponding portion of
the small triangular shadow only when the paintings are
exactly superimposed. It will be noted that the 'R' is more
akin to a straight line adjacent to a curved line thus inviting
the index finger to traverse betwixt them.

The centre of rotation is defined by a chevron on the Blue
Shepherd's cloak. This discreet mark would be identified
only when the rotation has been done in confirmation; M.
Poussin does not relinquish his secrets lightly. The right

Fig. 6. 9. The key applied to shepherd's staffs.

hand edge of the painting is divided at the exact length of the staff allowing the next largest Tau square to align with the top edge of the superimposed painting, which is set at the 26.565 degree angle, the angle of the diagonal to the half square or at least as precisely as it can be measured on a painting. The opposite top left edge of the painting is divided at a point equal to the staff length thus providing an elegant confirmation of the steps so far. The White Shepherd's hand now bears the prominent 'T' mark found central in the painting. There seemed to be so many things matching that it was difficult to take it all in. But what gripped me the most was to see that the whole front of the tomb had swung open like the door of an ancient crypt to reveal its macabre contents, or was it just a grim figment of the fertile mind of Nicholas Poussin from beyond his grave?

Here we must return briefly to the cipher BERGERE PAS DE… in Parchment II and refer to the cipher decoding, provided via Gérard de Sède. To achieve the decoding, as discussed earlier, twelve letters, AD GENES ARET H were so casually discarded. When translated into the Punic, from a mixture of Latin and French, the letters read TO THE KNEE STOP H. This first step has now been completed. Perhaps the 'H' looks similar to the two squares, one upon the other, as set out in these first steps of the solution to the cipher as leaked by de Sède.

Taking stock of the overlay paintings, the head of the Red Shepherd superimposed on his knee can rotate on its own axis as in Fig. 6.10. The positions of the crossing staffs must be noted and compared with portions of the key. There are two directions to proceed. A rotating and sliding motion, while continuing to trace the outline of the shadow is the obvious next step. The alternative is to rotate the head on the knee of the Red Shepherd. This time the pictures are rotated on the knee in the reverse direction until the head lies horizontal on the knee. Though this contortion might appear to be slightly uncomfortable, it has its uses. Now the index fingers are moving towards the white sandal lace and finally the left index finger homes in on the lace loop.

The final counter-clockwise angle is 36.87 degrees being the arc angle of one segment, 63.435 degrees, equal to 90 degrees less 26.565 degrees. Deducting the original clockwise rotation produces this final figure of 36.87 degrees. These two movements demonstrated the method that Poussin defined in order to produce the new golden ratio. First, the half square diagonal line created by a rotation of 26.565 degrees, followed by describing an arc, having a radius equal to half the length of the square, completes the extension of the diagonal to make the new length: $(1 + \sqrt{5}$ divided by 2).

These rotations are reflected in the angles and lengths of the staffs as they cross each other. The two index fingers seek the loop and ankle band on the white sandal of the Red Shepherd to define the limit of rotation. The two opposing rotations follow the key construction method by moving a corner of the square to the midpoint, which become the centre for rotation. The key centred on the hand of the White Shepherd with the curve running down the back of the Shepherdess does provide a good match to this rotation move of the paintings. These rotations replicate the system on the legs of the spider shown on the tombstone of Marie de Nègre measured from the spider eyes to the dots, being approximately 36.87 degrees. This is enough to make ones head spin but M. Poussin's shepherds have had to endure this exercise since the middle of the seventeenth century.

Perhaps the ET IN ARC CARDIA EGO theme may assume greater relevance if we consider the Latin, *arca dia* referring the sun's movement across the sky. This creates an image or idea related to CHEVAL DE DIEU or even to 'heliotrope'. We cannot ignore the Latin noun *cardo - inis*, which the Oxford Latin Dictionary defines as door-hinge; pole, axis; chief point *or* circumstance. The Punic would then be, ET (which many have considered to be of so little relevance) in an arc, one must use the ego or head as an axis. The skull, or head should rotate upon its own axis. That concept is easy to absorb, having just followed this specific instruction with the transparencies. These two movements are somewhat similar to the letter 'R', having the diagonal line rotating in a semi-circle to produce a longer vertical line. For, *Et in 'R' cardia ego.*

The most difficult part, and one that has been nocturnally thought provoking, is to define exactly what three meanings should be attributed to 'ET'. The Oxford Latin Dictionary defines the conjunction 'ET' as: and; also; moreover; et …et …both …and… (where the conjunction is repeated). Nicholas Poussin has incorporated both the 'E' and the 'T' in graphic form within his *Arcadian Shepherd* and *Bergers d'Arcadie* paintings and made it clear that the fingers and knuckle are often given the appearance of an 'E'. Teniers,

Fig. 6.10. The clockwise and counter-clockwise rotations.

father and son, also uses the Greek Tau symbol in relation to St Anthony and his famous cross. In the *St Anthony* paintings, Teniers always draws the cross of Christ as viewed obliquely such that the angle of the cross bar is at the precise angle used in the key. The 26.565 degrees angle variation from the horizontal is always present in every case that I have met so far except one that will be discussed later.

After the initial movement the key matches in various positions and after the counter rotation there are more matches as might be expected. However there remains the imperative to slide the key parallel to the staff.

As we have already mentioned the *Shepherds in Arcady*, it seems an appropriate moment to superimpose a couple of key figures onto that painting to bring it into line with progress thus far. The presence of the two additional skull can be seen as well as the relationship of the small skull to the double curve of the ogee shaped tomb mimicking Roc Fumade in the field adjacent to the pointing finger feature.

Nicole Poussin's works of art have been divided into two catagories reflecting the changes in emphasis. For a struggling painter the availability of materials somewhat limited his style. His early works have been placed in his *deseigno* period. As Poussin was able to avail himself of a wider range of more costly pigments, his paintings developed richer hues in what is referred to as his *colore* period.

There has been a marked emphasis on the design side of *Les Bergeres d'Arcadie* so far, but of great significance is the part played by Poussin's skillful use of colour. The blue of the apple has featured strongly so far. But the requirement to overlay copies of the painting has entailed using paler shades in the top layer underlain by the richer tones. This in itself required great skill and precision following complex design work after first conceiving the whole concept in his mind.

The practical difficulties of achieving this in the first half of the seventeenth century were daunting but mirrors the camera obscura and optical lenses were not unknown amongst artists at that time. The technique of projecting an image of a person or object onto a canvas was utilised to facilitate portrait painting. This has resulted in paintings where the left and right side of the subject are reversed such that a known right-handed person is painted writing with his left hand.

As an example of the particular use of red in *Les Bergers d'Arcadie*, place a reversed sinister key with the arc centred on the shepherds' hands with the mid line of the square aligned on the Red Shepherd's staff. The key then matches his red robe, particularly the triangular portion draped over his knee. At no time can Poussin's use of colour be treated lightly.

*   *   *

Running in parallel with the study of the painting, the Marie de Nègre d'Ablas tombstone illustrated on page twenty three of *The Accursed Treasure* ... must display a certain relevance. The Greek aspect is emphasised by the presence of the Greek characters on the gravestone and the Et In Arcadia Ego inscription. Perhaps we should refer to the P - S logo as the *Rho Sigma* logo using the Greek alphabet terms.

So where is the requisite skull, one might enquire? Certainly the logo has some resemblance to the blue apple curve but it doesn't look like the real thing. But we have neglected to *redis bles* the image of the gravestone, thereby producing two transparencies.

If one of the transparency is slid to the left until the top of the 'A' just touches the dash in the P -S logo we have the word PAS and a copy of the logo is above the E. This might suggest that one image is rotated 26.565 degrees counter-clockwise around the 'E' until the arrow is points to the top

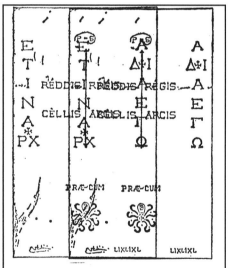 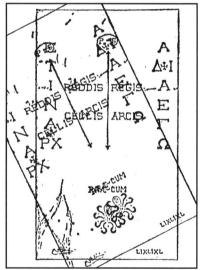

Fig. 6.11. The gravestone. of Fig. 6.12. The skull appears.
the 'T'.

The triangle of the Greek 'D' aligns with the other logo to create the skull with a little dot for the eye cavity. The poor fellow also has a cross in the centre of his cranium. The Omega now lies on the 'S' and two dots align on the spider.

The P - S logo in the top left hand corner contains the 'E' to read the Latin 'PES' or French 'PAS' meaning 'foot'. To follow Boudet through from Alpha to Omega would drive the mind into a spin and would be a diverting pastime. Suffice it to say that Boudet was a man of hidden talents, some of which could remain that way for a considerable time. Similarly, the mind needs time to assimilate the steps taken thus far in the gardens of Rennes.

CHAPTER SEVEN

SAUNIÈRE'S DOMAIN —
HISTORICAL REFLECTIONS

Charged with the new responsibilities that followed his discoveries, Bérenger Saunière's lifestyle changed dramatically. His first step must surely have been to obscure the earlier paths of temptation so that those who would follow would stumble into a thicket of confusion. Saunière's first priority was to render it very difficult for anyone to discover the great secret. It was crucial for him to maintain his position as sole keeper of the hoard and its key specifically applied to his village. Only then could he lie easy in his bed.

The first priority must be to remove any markers on the ground. The dolmens and stone squares, so carefully laid out, were there for all. Though, where it would lead them without the key all may judge.

Our Priest set out with his little Madonna and scoured the countryside for stones to build his grotto in the precincts of the church. The stones would need to be harvested from those carefully laid out in bygone ages to mark the devious route to a hoard. In this enterprise he succeeded but the stones he used for his grotto were quarried elsewhere.

Others might never be able to follow in the footsteps of the good shepherd, though his flock would all be eager to try. Saunière's path as a shepherd *'pas de tentation'* that led to his sudden riches would be tempting to all. This knowledge was the preserve of the priesthood to ensure the survival of the main secret and sacred hoard. It seems that the lesser trophies encountered en route were available only to a few elite Priests, to be disposed of as the conscience dictated. It would indeed be unfortunate if control of this should fall into the hands of the flock and every effort would have been made to ensure that this didn't happen. Despite this, there must be a pathway for future generations to follow, else the secret hoard and its key could be lost forever.

A great source of concern to our rock-hound Priest was the glaringly obvious headstone and tombstone carved by Abbé Bigou. The Marie de Nègre d'Ablas tombstone (page 23 of *The Accursed Treasure* ...) must display some relevance as the Greek connection is emphasised by virtue of the Greek characters displayed on the tombstone, providing the oblique reference to Arcadia. The original resting place for the mortal remains of Marie de Nègre was at one end of the tiny graveyard attached to the church. The markings on these stones were such a source of embarrassment to our

Priest that he first moved the stones to the other end of the graveyard, and then erased the engraving on the tombstone, toiling diligently with the stonemason's tools.

He did not stint his efforts to deface the Latin text, which incorporated some Greek characters, the equivalent of *Et in Arcadia ego,* together with the other strange symbols that were carved on the tombstone. The cracked remains of the stone lie there silenced and still, the empty skull never more to utter words from the past, the spider insignia never to spin its web of intrigue. Yet, even now, across the valley above the ruins of Coustaussa, there are ancient earthworks that manifest their presence on the aerial photos as letters laid out upon the hillside similar to some of those on the tombstone. Certainly these would have been more than a match for our energetic Priest.

After some months of labour Bérenger could feel secure in the knowledge that the secret was vested in him alone, and those previous clues had been rendered inscrutable to the masses. He could take stock and prepare those things that he would need in order to develop a nice little earner. A good camera and darkroom were high on his shopping list. He must have improvised a camera obscura to meet his needs as regards the copies of the Poussin painting that he had acquired from the Louvre in Paris. However, a little more investment would pay dividends, in saved time alone.

Bérenger Saunière seems to have prepared his clues in ways that would make it easier for a man of the cloth, with access to Saunière's entire domain including his secret room with the bulls-eye window and entry to the church pulpit

Fig. 7. 1. Saunière's domain viewed from the north-west.

Fig. 7. 2. The Church of St Madeleine is a mass of detail.

and to the *échauguette*. Knowledge of Latin, the language of
the Roman Catholic Church, goes with the job. It would not
have been long before an understanding of the Punic would
fall like a mantle upon the shoulders of Saunière's successor
as guardian.

Like the enigmatic phrases and words of Boudet's Punic
language, the painting and illustrations associated with
Rennes demonstrate that a portion of construction lines in
the paintings and other features are deliberately omitted,
else the whole thing might appear as plain as a shepherd's
staff.

Saunière's efforts at concealment were met with partial
success only. He could not and would not remove the final
marker to the hoard, as his efforts would certainly be
noticed by the villagers who would always be watching
every move once the whisper of gold and treasure had swept
through the parlours of Rennes-le-Château.

The *échauguette* or *tour de coin* and the other features of
Saunière's domain all served their purpose, and figure in the
geometry. The plan of his domain yielded up its secrets with
some reluctance when submitted to the ever-powerful key.

Of particular interest is the stone stairway with the flight
of steps sweeping up to the centre of the belvedere in an
impressive double arc, just begging to be matched to the
key. This unusual layout, covering the belvedere area,
includes the orangery and the Tour Magdala with its *tour de
coin*. The curved staircase and septum, central to the
belvedere, falls into place in the design in a specific manner
forming a part of two widening arcs. The twin spiral stair-

cases cried out to be the centres for our blue apples. When the centre is placed on the *échauguette* such that the spiral aligns with the round stair-well and the straight sides of the belvedere coincide with the relevant square on the key, then it appears that one of the nodes also aligns with the site of the hoard on the hillside. As alignments viewed on an aerial photograph is subject to the distortion that is a feature of this media, this suggestion cannot be relied upon without a proper survey to verify Sauniere's intent. This caveat applies, especially where the relevant portion of the photo is distant from its centre and the altitude range in the area is about a hundred metres, as in this case.

When incorporating these two spiral stairs, each centre located at an extremity of the belvedere, the pivot of each of key figures lies on those stair-wells. In this position the two opposing arcs sweep round to coincide with the curve of the banister rails bordering the grand staircase, which forms the central feature of the belvedere. Viewed from the garden, the inner curves of the stair spiral inward and the intricate pattern incorporates the curves of the inner handrails.

The precise alignment of the key upon the layout of the church and gardens can best be established after defining which of the existing site plans most accurately represents the ground. However, the layout of the church and of the adjacent portion of the village appear to conform to the key and one may wonder to what extent the village layout does predate Bérenger Saunière's modifications. The tapering angle of the southern side of the Church could be indicative of this. We may feel amazement at the attention to detail that Saunière displayed. Surely, such a mighty project would not have been undertaken without his having some grand objective in view.

The parish priest within him led Saunière to perpetuate the key to the mystery within the fabric of his little church, which he refurbished and redecorated to include those vital clues to both the location of the main hoard and to the cipher key. Yet, he achieved this in a deeply religious setting to bring his flock to Christ while carrying Rennes-le-Château from his world through to our present day.

His Church has a provocative style of adornment linking the promise of both a spiritual and a fiscal reward within its walls. The unusual architecture provided the backdrop for the Priest to lead his flock in their Christian worship. At the same time he maintained his dual rôle of pastor and leader in the community. This he achieved without disruption of the civic order that was rightly the function of the Maire.

The peculiar architectural style of the Church leaves a feeling of spiritual disquiet on approaching the arched entrance bearing the superscription 'TERRIBILIS EST LOCUS ISTE', 'Terrible is this place'. Above this is what appears at a casual glance to be our first skull in the guise of an angel or saintly maiden. Everyone entering the church is immediately challenged by the staring eyes of the forbidding statue of Asmodeus, who bears the stoup of holy water upon his head. He is the mythical guardian of Solomon's personal treasure which, one might imagine, includes the treasure of Solomon's Temple.

The stoup, which Asmodeus supports, bears the initials

'BS' on a red plaque. Yet, all is not lost, for, on raising our eyes, we see that four winged angels stand over him having the power to subdue him by the sign of the cross, with the admonition, *Par ce signe tu le vaincras*. The Templar motto *In hoc signo vinces* springs to mind leaving one in some doubt as to what sign is intended.

As the Priest of Rennes enters his chapel, which first appears to be a place of terror, he would pause before the stoup brimming with holy water, while reflecting on the image of the holy angels mirrored in its surface. As he dips his fingers into the stoup the water would spill over, like the tears of Magdalene, falling upon the back of Asmodeus' hand as the Priest crosses himself reverently, replicating the position of the hand of each angel to complete the geometry.

The initial trepidation on entering the little church, based on total incomprehension, is soon replaced. A feeling of tranquillity prevails, leaving the overall impression that the architect was a man of peace. For, as we now possess the key, this may be imposed throughout, the church, even upon the cowering figure of Asmodeus. The square shape of his clenched fist leads one to ask what is was that he grasped. Was it perhaps a staff? The centre of the key could traverse down his contorted limbs to the extremity of his foot, while tracing out strange patterns in its journey. Should one indulge in such fascinating dalliance many days would pass in a flash and then only the surface would have been scratched. We are talking of the dedication of many days to elucidate the spectacular contribution of the Priest of Rennes.

Bérenger Saunière left us many clues and in his personal

journal, we may find a picture of an angel holding Asmodeus in check by means of a chain around his neck. This is the repeated theme of Asmodeus supporting the stoup of holy water in the little church at Rennes-le-Château. Bérenger considered this important. As Saunière washed his hands before celebrating Mass he would catch a glimpse of his reflection in the mirror, which bore the inscription, 'Before Mass' and 'After Mass'; not just a reminder to wash his hands, but that all things have their opposites and mirror images do have their place in the ways of Rennes. He also left an interesting square cryptogram; a system of squares, circles, and triangles. In his journal, he wrote the cryptic text, which we have already briefly examined.

The square block bearing the twin triangles is taken from a book written in the same era as Nicolas Poussin and brought to my attention by Sandra Hamblett, the prime force in creating the archaeological Journal *The Rennes Alchemist*. Being an erudite student of archaeology, she has researched the origin of this figure as it appears in separate editions of the same book suggesting the possible refinement of the geometry. The two figures have been modified between 1621 and 1625, the date of the second edition.

The square plaque with the double triangle bearing a head in each corner occurred fairly frequently in mediaeval religious artifacts, an excellent example was exhibited in the British Library recently. Each of the triangles is formed by two adjacent keys. The second pair of keys is inverted, as demonstrated in de Sède's explanation of the BERGERE PAS DE TENTATION cipher in Henry Lincoln's book *The*

Holy Place.

The later version appears to be the same as the one that Saunière uses in his notebook. The various circles employ the sequence of curves generated in the key. Superimposing all four keys makes for rather a complex pattern but may be

Fig. 7. 3. Saunière's bookplate design central to Fig. 7.2.

reviewed in Fig. 7.3. The superimposed geometry indicates the four different alignments of the key, dexter and sinister upright and vertically inverted. One interesting aspect is the manner in which our Priest has incorporated this design as the centre of centres of his Church in a beautiful circular stained glass window with the complex structure beneath it illustrated in Fig. 7.2. in this culmination of the pattern of the cipher.

The dominant figure in the Church is the good St Anthony the Hermit standing upright holding his staff at the regulation angle when viewed from the side. Perhaps we should look briefly at him bowed in prayer as in Fig. 6.1. but now rotated about the eye of the scrawny bird perched on the left side of the picture. Thus the crucifixion and the skull become aligned and the tempting glass is tilted and spilled. The second move in the familiar sequence brings the hermit to his knees as he draws solace and penitence from the cracked wooden bowl from which he is about to sup. Yet like all these icons, they contain so much more.

As the actual technique was dependant on the skills of the architect and painter, the secret of the key was passed on through artists such as David Teniers and his son, and even through Poussin. There are recurring features that resemble vignettes in the landscape of Rennes in the work of David Teniers; for example, the weird flying creature that appears in *Tentation de Saint Antoine par l'ivresse* by David Teniers the younger.

Close to the entrance there stands a figure of two men, one of whom holds a cross, the angle of which is not 26.565

Fig. 7. 4. St Anthony turns from temptation as he resists the wine.

degrees. This in itself is sufficient to rivet ones attention in this hall of mysteries. Next to him his twin crouches in a similar pose to that of Asmodeus. Using the key, Fig.7.5 helps to clarify some of the precise geometry of this pair of half-naked figures. The length of the upright bar is exactly.four factors of Tau longer than the length of the crossbar.

Modern surgery has a penchant for separating siamese twins yet in Bérenger Saunière's time the reverse seems to be the norm. When the twins are conjoined at the head, which, of course requires the rotation of 26.565 degrees, some more interesting geometry ensues, as shown in Fig. 7.6. It is important that we remember that we have so far been using one set of curves and squares in the geometry.

There is so much hidden within this scene. The key align comfortably onto the kneeling figure but also fits in the same way over his bare knee whilst merging two opposing rectangles on the staff in the usual way. Thus it can be demonstrated that the head can be fitted over either knee or even upon the curved rock at the foot of the cross. As we leave Saunière's two faithful friends, heads bowed on the way to Genesareth, do we glimpse an 'H' on its side aligned with their staff? There is much to tease from this scene but what of the other half of the apple, or indeed, what of its other three quarters?

The fourteen stations of the cross must lead to Christ in the pathway to his crucifixion, yet for the Church of St Madeleine the configuration must also adhere strictly to the pathway to the key. In the second and third stations flanking

St Anthony the Hermit the basic layout can be seen. The half square must fit the width of the image with the two roses centred on the arc node and the tau cross. The wooden cross must match the lines of the key. Now the arc must curve upwards to the large rose intersecting at the next node.

Thus we have a picture set against the half square of the key. As the matching rectangle slides diagonally across the picture aligned with the key, the central arc slides across the picture and the various elements align with the key. In order to best see this effect, the photography needs to be taken from immediately opposite the picture to avoid distorting the image. To study this application of the key in all fourteen stations of the cross a complete set of true photographs would be required. To elucidate the intent of our Priest it would take the ego of that Belgian detective Hercule Poirot capped with the determination of a gendarme.

Poussin and David Teniers the younger had held the key. Now Bérenger Saunière held the key. Was this the key that secured the treasure chest of Rennes alone? Could it be a key that has already opened the treasure chests of Europe wherever the Knight Templars has concealed their hoards? Bérenger Saunière was not given to idleness. In his early years most of his efforts were centred on his studies and upon survival. To put meat on his table he hunted whatever game he could find, while he strove to lead his flock and obtain funds to renovate his dilapidated little church.

However, Bérenger had acquired the skill to use his new-found knowledge and had discovered the location of the main hoard of the Visigoth treasure of ancient Rhedae.

Fig. 7. 5. The vertical is 4 Tau increments of the cross bar.

Fig. 7. 6. Four eyes aligned generates the usual rotation.

Truly, this was a dangerous secret. How many lives had been forfeited in acquiring and retaining this prize? Bérenger had once remarked, in his own Languedoc tongue that he would keep control of it. How true! What else could he do?

Because the secret location was so close to the village, he could not excavate without explanations to the city fathers and not least to the Vatican. To reveal it would be to lose all. His future would be to become, once more an impoverished parish Priest, with dismal prospects despite having enjoyed such an exotic past. He must have realised that he would remain the incumbent; the custodian of the Visigoth hoard. This same destiny had rested upon a succession of people, some worthy and some dubious, as the centuries rolled by since the ancient sacking of Rome by the Visigoths.

In the past, the requirement for secrecy and security led those responsible to attribute a religious significance to the signs and seals. In this regard, oaths and secret knowledge were equally as important as self-interest. The aesthetic value of knowing something to which only a few of the elite were privy, is a great boost to one's ego and affords a certain status to the cognoscenti. To have all the outside evidences on display, of which the masses can make neither head nor tail, carries a certain aura all of its own. However, it could become a bit of a bore to one who is the only initiate.

To what extent did Bérenger Saunière confide in his soul mate Marie Denarnaud? Certainly, she gleaned some of the corn of knowledge but it is likely that many of the more tasty morsels were gathered in secret and only certain scraps of information fell from the feast of knowledge that the

Priest enjoyed during his various clandestine trips to Lyon and other European destinations. The financial aspect of funds transferred to the account of Marie is a matter of record. However, the risks of others sharing the secrets were ever present. Risks for the security of the secrets and the risks of her early demise in suspicious circumstances could not be ruled out. Certainly, the good Priest would not expose his most prized possession — not only a capable housekeeper but also his confidante — to the dangers from those who would steal crumbs of forbidden knowledge from the rich man's table. Surely, in his declining years, his would have been a lonely priesthood, a *solis sacerdotibus,* without his faithful housekeeper, Marie. Saunière must have felt this acutely after his two associates, Gélis and Boudet, had been brutally murdered.

How conscientious must have been this busy itinerant Priest, affording his valuable time to visit the sites! Travel could not have been easy in those years at the close of the nineteenth century. In the preparation for his clandestine visits, the time and effort that he might spend poring over maps, historical documents and works of art would prove worth their weight in gold. Maybe some of the more remote sites could be explored without the interest of the locals being aroused. There the wealth that had lain dormant for centuries might be retrieved and put to good use at Rennes. A devoted man who was prepared to extend his labours into the small hours of the morning, could achieve much in rescuing long lost funds from the hidden vaults of obscurity — some might say pillaging — rescuing by the

Fig. 7. 7. Dexter and sinister squares combine.

caring hand of a devoted Priest is surely a more fitting expression!

Gold has long been an acceptable form of currency and banks would be willing to purchase it with few formalities. Antique jewellry could have required negotiations that were more delicate. Researchers have reported that funds were transferred to the local bank account but ended up to the credit of Bérenger's faithful housekeeper and confidante (in certain areas), Marie Denarnaud.

In view of the complexity of the subject it seems likely that Saunière was handed information regarding the key by other Priests in a meeting to which they invited him. This he mentioned in his diary, as reported by Gérard de Sède. For Saunière to acquire a basic understanding of all of the complex functions of the cipher in a short time without assistance seems unlikely.

As the skill of the chase became more developed, Bérenger was able to reap the rewards of his efforts. Perhaps he was obliged to treat with wealthy landowners and to make covert agreements to share the spoils, receiving due recompense for the use of his special exploration skills. He would be able to entertain the heads of Europe in noble style. They would be eager to seek out this Man of God and man of hidden talents, and those not just of silver. Tales of Templar treasure from the genealogical records and archives of the great families of Europe would be retrieved from dusty lockers to take on a new significance. The whispering winds of the secret societies of France, including the Knights Templar, would carry the news from village to château. The

Vatican, bowed in prayer, had its ear ever close to the ground and it was not long before the high living of the Priest of Rennes excited Papal interest.

One spade laid at the entrance to the hoard would have brought an army of diggers from the village. It would bring an even larger army of prelates armed not only with tools for excavation but with tools to probe inquisitorial depths, perhaps as in days gone by, when the pungent aroma of toasted Templar rose from the musty dungeons of Carcassonne. What would it profit the Priest of Rennes? The source of future wealth would be forever dry, unlike the legendary springs of the Razès, which have provided their bounty winter and summer. He would be called to account for all his past largesse and forced to move from his beloved village. What would become of Marie, his Madonna and of the villagers and of the treasure?

Only for a fleeting moment would that disastrous course of action have flashed through his mind. He must have instantly dismissed the idea of an unguarded excavation in full view of the village.

His rôle was clear. No expense need be spared. The Templars of old would cry out from the dust and from the embers of the inquisitorial fires if he had contemplated less. Had they not provided the wherewithal for his venture? Were not their coffers laid open to pay for it all and more besides? The wealth of the Templars was founded upon donations given by the faithful in the hope of salvation. At the Carcassonne Episcopal Office Saunière stated in his response to Mgr. Beauséjour's enquiry as to the origin of at least some of the funds that had passed through his hands:

"Alas Monseigneur you ask of me the only thing that I am not able to reveal. Deep sinners to whom, with the aid of God, I have shown the way of penitence have given these considerable amounts."

Perhaps it was an oversight that he omitted to state how many centuries ago the donations had been made.

However, who could gainsay his denial of everything? Who could prove his complicity? Who could deny his good fortune, having such a well-heeled housekeeper — with such a well-turned ankle to boot? No actual funds had passed to the account of the impoverished Priest; however, his housekeeper had mysteriously come into a series of small fortunes.

Surely there would be a finite end to the sites to pillage or to the hidden resources to rescue. With the outbreak of the 1914 – 1918 War, the restrictions on European travel would seriously limit his activities, especially if by then the known locations had been exhausted. In addition, transfer of funds across war-torn boundaries would present further hazards and difficulties. It was a time of dearth, particularly as later the franc was changed and the currency devalued.

However, the desire for further building works generated financial pressures that drove Saunière to seek new sources for his enterprise. Of course, with the end to hostilities, normal traffic might have been resumed, but time was pressing. The Grim Reaper was lurking in the shadows, whispering, "I am there, and I am Death." Thus in January 1917, while the war raged in Northern France, claiming the

Fig. 7. 8. Two nodes and Tau centre on the rosettes.

lives of so many, his Maker called François Bérenger Saunière to account. Yet, before this, he had secured further funds; enough to enable him to plan extensive building works that are reputed to include the construction of a new tower. Perhaps he wished to restore the old fortifications that had been featured in the Poussin painting *Les Bergers d'Arcadie*. The Tour Magdala was just a little short to provide a clear line of sight correctly angled to the treasure and the other distant features even if one stood on the highest point of the *échauguette* as Saunière had done.

In our attempt to define the various aspects still awaiting resolution, we need to become more familiar with the domain of the Priest of Rennes-le-Château, François Bérenger Saunière, the man of mystery. Perhaps we should eavesdrop on his conversation as he sits in his library one autumn evening, near the close of his eventful life.

"*Les pipes d'Algerie sont les mieux*"

The words came through teeth firmly clenched on the stem of a rosewood pipe. The Priest smiled as he opened his tobacco pouch. He proffered it to the man sitting opposite, who charged his pipe after affectionately removing the meerschaum from its silver case.

"It has been a long journey, especially the last pull up from Couiza."

"Ah! Now you have been able to travel the new road. You are lucky, Monsieur, that you did not make the journey some years ago."

Your road might be well metalled but it is also very steep.

The horses made heavy work of it and my carriage is always heavy laden."

The Priest crossed to the hearth where the log fire had been freshly kindled. The thin wooden spills he held burst into flame and he straightened up, passed one across to his guest and then drew the flame into the bowl of his own briar pipe with the curved rosewood in his powerful hand. When both men had their pipes drawing well, Bérenger Saunière settled into his high backed chair.

"It is not easy travelling these days with the whole of Europe torn with war for these past years. Frontiers have been a problem and I travel less frequently now. That is why it will be important to plan my visit to your château very carefully."

"We must be discrete but the financial arrangements may be difficult. How can we arrange to dispose of this sort of – ah, materials without arousing suspicion?"

We cannot tell how much will be in gold coin and whether there will be artefacts and jewels, but the quantity will be enormous. However, I have a discrete jeweller. He will raise an eyebrow from time to time but it is clearly in his best interests to keep silent. As for myself," here his rugged face lit up in a cheerful grin:

"I have been known to keep a secret or two."

As the smoke curled up to the ceiling, the two men were busy with their own thoughts.

"What about the financial arrangements? In your letter you mentioned that you have established a bank account with a reliable banker."

"Yes, I suggest we should set up two new accounts for this little exercise. One will be in the name of my confidante, Marie Denarnaud and one under the name of Hapsburg, if that is acceptable. We cannot know what we will discover in the vault when it is located. Perhaps just a few skeletons lying there since that fateful time of the Templar purge on Friday 13th October 1307. But more likely sufficient in gold coins to re-establish the Hapsburg Empire once this Kaiser Wilhelm folly has been concluded and Russian politics have run their course."

"Yes, I am afraid this war has cost us all dear, and not only in lives. Our fortunes have been strained to breaking point, and for what purpose? How could those assassinations in Sarajevo of our Archduke Franz Ferdinand and Sophie have brought about such mass destruction? Surely, Europe has gone mad in these modern times. And what lies in the vaults of Rennes?" The guttural accent held a note of intensity and his knuckles cracked as he gripped the arms of the chair, drawing his body forward towards the Priest.

"There are things hidden here of which I cannot speak yet which I must continue to guard. It has been handed to me. I must keep it safe and well will I hold it. The vaults of Rennes have held their secret from generation to generation and it is not for me to unseal them at this time. There is much still to be done to ensure their security over the years that lie ahead. Even if I had wished to release this hoard I could not do it without putting at risk future enterprises, including your own little exercise."

"You must be well aware of the reason that I need to have access to this huge amount of gold. The politics of our empire are so dominated by the Kaiser that the only way that we can retain our independence is to restore our dwindling resources. It is only by strength that we can keep ourselves from being drawn into further hopeless and costly wars. Because of our geographical situation, we are overshadowed by Russia and dominated by Germany and will remain so until this crazy war ceases. I admit that we may not be entirely blameless and each nation has been drawn into the various phases of this conflict by dreams of expansion and conquests with prospect of a quick and painless victory. But as each phase of the conflict spills over into more bloodshed the leaders of nations have failed to understand that men have always been prepared to sacrifice all for their home-land, not the least being the Russians. Every day the news is fearful and it is so costly in human lives. Do not even think of the cost in gold."

"But tell me as a man of the cloth." He lent forward clutching his meerschaum and peered into the Priest eyes. "What will you do with all this extra money? I believe you have a few debts to settle. I gather it has been a while since your last little foray. But after that, on what can you spend all this fortune?"

"The vaults of Rennes are my priority. You have seen the church. I have completed that. I have built the villa Bethania, the tour Magdala, my belvedere and my orangery. Here may be discovered the great secret which guards the vaults of Rennes. However, in time, the walls may crumble and the glass panes of the orangery will break or be stolen. Decay is all around us. I am planning to undertake a major refurbishment. My domain will be restored to resemble the old walled town with its great new tower. This will never crumble and so the vaults with their priceless hoard will be preserved for posterity. There will be sufficient remaining to keep my wine cellar and table supplied for at least another century. We will live out our remaining years in a village assured of prosperity. Perhaps I will make just a few more forays once this war is over. This would be just to keep my hand in, you understand. I am not as young as I used to be and all this climbing hills is taking its toll. Gold can be a heavy burden to carry."

"I am sure you will bear it with fortitude. I look to the future, as must we all. The Hapsburg name and the Austro-Hungarian Empire is the future for our line. Who will be the one to carry the secret after you have gone?"

"There will be others in the future. Marie is shielded from certain aspects of this affair. I would not place her life in danger. One who stands in the pulpit of my little Church will see the way forward, but another may succeed. That is, if he can read the signs. One who will watch over this little flock as I have done will stand in the best position to learn the ways of Rennes. I can only be the forerunner but whom it will be that will follow, I cannot say. Neither can I foretell when the time is right. Nevertheless, my concern is to show him the way. The onus for this rests roundly upon my square shoulders. When the time is right there will be someone."

Saunière rose and stood gazing into the fire.

"Perhaps I have done my work too well and the centuries may roll past. The new tower is important. I have said

enough. Let us take a stroll on the belvedere before we turn
in. We can admire the stars that shine so brightly in the sky
here where they are not dulled by the glare of the city gas-
lamps. The night sky here is the thing I miss most of all
when I visit the cities of Europe."

The visitor rose from his chair. After knocking out his
meerschaum in the hearth, he replaced it in its silver case.
The two men went out through the door of the Magdala
tower into the clear starlit night. The heady oleander scent
replaced the lingering smell of tobacco as they savoured the
moment. The bright full moon illuminated every feature of
the belvedere and reflected from the sloping spire on the
orangery.

Bérenger Saunière lingered on the belvedere after his
companion had retired to the room that had been prepared
for him in the Villa Bethania. He paused at the head of the
wide sweep of the stairway, positioned so carefully, before
descending the steps. He was glad of the support that the
curved banister rails provided and gave a wry smile as he
recalled those early days laying out the 'steps of temptation'
as he called them.

His thoughts went back over the years since first he had
shouldered the task of recording for posterity the location of
his treasure. He had hoped that one day he would be able to
see this magnificent hoard. He had pillaged several of the
ancient sites including Templar deposits, hidden since the
great purge of 1307. The Visigothic ones fascinated him the
most. However, he had always regarded the proceeds as a
means to benefit those in need. It had always been a matter

of discernment to differentiate between those with wants and those with genuine needs.

He had laid out his domain with meticulous care to ensure that a path would always be there enabling someone to locate and eventually reveal the main hoards. Soon he would be able to complete the task by rebuilding the new tower as it was in Poussin's time. He would restore the wall around the north and west side of the village. With the tower seventy metres high, he would ensure that the angle of slope down to the hoard would be the correct twenty-six and a half degrees so that the sun would again cast a shadow to that point at noon on the 17th January and so match the cipher. He made a mental note to check the existing angle next January to verify his calculations.

"Ah! How I have wrestled with all of the problems," he exclaimed aloud as he recalled those nights when he had struggled to find some sense in the puzzle. Its complexity yet simplicity ensured that it would remain hidden until the time was right. Would the glazed orangery, surmounted by its marker spike, stand the test of time? However, once the new tower was built the orangery would have no further function. The building cost was nothing. It was simply a means of distributing money that would otherwise be lost.

Many would be employed with generous wages. There was still a small matter of a bill for his library to meet. It had been a minor irritation. He had enjoyed the challenge and was looking forward to starting work again, yet he was beginning to feel his age. He sighed as he felt the chill of night strike through his soutane remembering all those who had been privy to the secret. Now all had passed into the eternities. Violent death was no stranger to Rennes.

He shivered involuntarily and turned his footsteps toward the warmth and comfort of the Villa Bethania. Sleep now for tomorrow there remained so much to accomplish.

CHAPTER EIGHT

GOLGOTHA REVISITED

At last the time had come to renew my acquaintance with the Razès and its secrets. It had been many years since I had been to the village of Rennes-le-Château but I imagined that nothing much could have changed. During those intervening years numerous books have been written about the mystery that clung to the ivy-covered walls and rugged slopes of that hilltop village. This has served well its purpose in sustaining the fascination that the it has held for the world outside. Thus, the vital heart of the village continues to beat in harmony with the regular footsteps of the faithful as every visitor fashions his or her own theories and dreams while surrounded by the images and fantasies in the domain that Bérenger Saunière created for us. Neither has the Curé of Rennes-le-Château toiled in vain to provide a future for his flock.

Ryanair to Rennes started with a visit to their website. The clinching factors were the direct flights to Carcassonne and the low cost fare despite the airport taxes at Stanstead in both directions. Armed with my new Pentax MZ-10 camera fitted with the SMC Pentax-FA zoom lens, I set out on Thursday the 15th March 2000 determined to build up a collection of colour photographs for future use and to tie up some of the many loose ends that my book must resolve.

Carcassonne was the ideal airport for Rennes and the forty-minute rail connection from London's Liverpool Street station to Stanstead was ideal for me, as was the fifty percent rail fare for Ryanair passengers. When I arrived at Couiza there was no room at the inn because the château was not open to visitors at that time of the year so I had to make the climb to the village of Rennes-le-Château with the hope of finding a bed.

However, the village had already settled down for the night by the time I had reached the outskirts of the sleeping village. With no prospect of finding a bed for the night, I took the once-familiar path that ran below the castle and branched off down the hill. The night was pitch black and I was grateful for the image of the landscape in my mind. I remembered that a drystone wall flanked the steep path for about a hundred metres, after which there was a secluded grassy patch to the left where I might settle for the night. I scrambled up a bank and found the location. There seemed to be a lot of loose branches covering some very hard ground but it would have to do. So I settled down there under a black, cloudy sky and thought of my duvet cover and comfortable bed at home, which was warm and oddly devoid of a lining of sharp sticks.

The lowering clouds scurried across the night sky above the wind swept hillside overshadowed by the watchful eye of the château of Rennes lit by fleeting patches of moonlight. The first cold grey light of dawn threw the castle outline into stark relief as I savoured the total discomfort of the tangle of twisted and broken sticks that lay beneath my thin plastic sleeping bag with only my silver survival sheet pulled round me to alleviate the chill of that mid-March night.

The flight to Carcassonne the previous day had wrenched me through the membrane in my life that separated me from the daily cut and thrust of engineering projects on the one hand and the make-believe, or perhaps more real life on those rugged slopes of ancient Rhedae.

As the morning light strengthened, I could see that the landscape had been attacked by some mechanical bush-clearer that had macerated what had once been the encroaching scrubland. What remained was a layer of jagged branches with which I had become all too familiar during a long night. This had changed the landscape and even the Poussin seat where I had previously spent a comfortable night had been bulldozed to clear the thick scrub. Yet, the thorn bushes remained as fierce as ever. Some months later, my legs still bore the thousands of red weals where my thick denim jeans were no match for their talons. The spines had covered my legs with hundreds of red marks as the fine thorns penetrated my skin. One could easily lose an eye to their clutches. But I counted myself lucky that I did not lie down to sleep on one of the many wood ants nests that the dawn light revealed dotted about the hillside where I had slept, or at least passed the night dozing fitfully.

Soon after dawn, I heard the engine of the macerator roar into life. I kept well clear as it hurled branches into the air, cutting a swathe of cleared land through the bushes. Now that I had at last revisited the site after about a quarter of a century, I could see just how much the scenery had changed.

On the wind swept hillside overshadowed by the ever-watchful eye of Rennes-le-Château there had been many changes, yet over-all, it had stayed the same as it had been for centuries. Some of the rocks had crumbled and slipped due to the ravages of time and some of the land had been completely overgrown with prickly scrub and small trees. I had come unprepared to deal with the heavy undergrowth.

On the nearby hillside, the macerator was growling away as it tore into the bushes and trees, hurling timber fifteen metres from its hungry maw. The village had set up a ground-clearing project, which was too close for comfort. I had timed my visit to coincide with the operation, to see the extent of the activity. However, I had no saw to clear the trees and scrub in the specific area that interested me. Even a thick pair of gardening gloves would have provided some protection from the thorns. Despite the undergrowth, I could see that the particular location had not been disturbed yet my efforts to reach the entrance stones were thwarted. On my next visit, I would come armed with a saw. I always carried a compass but I needed to buy a hand-held GPS, Global Positioning System, to define the precise location of the various features in the landscape that were related to the clues prepared through so many generations.

As the morning light strengthened, I visited the parts of the landscape I once knew. There had been a great increase in the scrubland and smashed sticks lay everywhere except in those areas not yet reached by the machinery or where the terrain was too rugged. In the untouched areas, thick scrub threatened to engulf the fields. I wondered how close the macerator would be able to come to my drystone wall. I found that the Poussin Seat was completely churned up and its character changed. The vineyard had now become a mass of scrub, thorns and broom. It was almost unrecognisable after a quarter of a century and the bushes pressed so hard against the wall that I would have needed a machete or saw to squeeze between them. I found that the area where the cavern was situated remained untouched, though it was now overgrown by yellow broom scrub. I had expected it to look the same as previously, but the passage of time has transformed the area. After a brief stay I climbed back up the hill to the village to visit the museum and the Church of St Madeleine.

The stark line of trees, stripped of their summer foliage, could not mask the ivy-covered lines of the decaying castle buildings. The outline closely matched the dark structure that Poussin had made a central feature on the skyline of *Les Bergers d'Arcadie*. The difference was marked by the absence of the fortified tower. The walls had been breached during the fourteenth century and the stones may have been taken for inclusion in more recent buildings since the seventeenth century. I thought that one day I could portray that rugged skyline on the cover of the book I intended to write. That first book was to be the translation of de Sède's original story. Now that it has been published, you may judge for yourselves from its cover and from the painting, whether the image is in fact the ancient fortifications of Rennes. Previously, close examination of the painting had left me reasonably certain that the skyline central to the painting featured the castle with an identical outline to the present day but with a tower completing the seventeenth century skyline of Rennes-le-Château as seen by Poussin. From the illustration in Fig.6.9. it is clear that Nicolas Poussin featured this in the geometry of his painting.

The outline was too regular to be a rock formation and there appeared, to my eagle eye, to be a hint of castellated defences. Careful study under a magnifying glass seemed to confirm this. Alternatively, it was perhaps a figment of my vivid imagination. A detailed examination of the painting three hundred and fifty years earlier may have provided a more definite answer. However, these on-site observations did confirm what I had seen earlier on my transparencies.

The ramparts of the tower rose slightly higher than the château roof. They would have cast a long shadow at noon on the 17th January from south to north across that rough terrain stretched below the ancient walls of the fortified town. The steep incline beneath the battlements combined with such rugged country falling away to the Sals River below would deter any but a determined assault. The commander of such a force would need to have a specific aim in view to justify mounting an attack, at least from that quarter.

Yet, there had been a successful assault. De Sède records that under the rule of the Visigoths what was then known as the ancient town of Rhedae had two fortresses and four towers. On the main route to Spain, this important town boasted thirty thousand inhabitants. In 1361, Trastamare and his Aragonese mercenaries laid siege to Rennes-le-Château and stormed through a breach in the walls caused by the explosion of the powder magazine. He records that the attackers destroyed the ancient church of St John the Baptist, but to destroy the walls and fortifications would have been a pointless exercise if they had already gained access to this valuable strategic prize. (Page 83, *The Accursed Treasure …*). Ancient walls are more often destroyed by the peaceful acquisition of the building materials than by the labour of armies who are more interested in pillaging than in feats of unproductive engineering.

By the mid-seventeenth century it is likely that a good proportion of the walls would still remain standing and could have been included in Poussin's *Les Bergers d'Arcadie* should he have strolled past armed with his sketch pad or easel. From a practical point of view, the actual execution of his masterpiece would certainly not lend itself to any casual daubing on a wind swept hillside. He would have made his careful sketches, but this Master, closeted in his well-equipped workshop, would need all the facilities he could muster. Even in the design phase of so important a masterpiece as *Les Bergers d'Arcadie*, Nicolas Poussin would have needed every facility that he had available in his studio.

* * *

The recollection of my last encounter with the site on the hillside below the château when I faced my Golgotha, rose fresh in my memory. I recalled every detail of the dismal failure of the dig with the BBC. At that time, as I sat on the hillside under the noonday sun staring at the drystone wall, I was surprised to see that the rocks uncovered by my efforts were similar in outline to the shepherds in *Les Bergers d'Arcadie*. But what startled me at that time was that one of the rocks was in the shape of a skull with the two empty eye sockets staring at me. The recesses that formed the eyes were accentuated by the deep shadows cast by the sun at its zenith. It was indeed the Place of the Skull.

It struck me forcibly, all those years ago, that without the proper equipment if I were to proceed with the dig perhaps I would destroy forever this priceless piece of archaeological evidence that formed the proof that the location was indeed the correct place preserved over the centuries.

Golgotha was the place where the three crosses were erected and where Christ was crucified. I recalled seeing a photograph of that fateful site of the crucifixion and that too did indeed have a large rock in the shape of a skull with two shadowy dark recesses, just like empty eye sockets. More important, Poussin had depicted skulls in his painting of the scene and this I could not deny.

My lack of understanding of the cipher and the realisation that I had only scratched the surface of the mystery jarred me into action. I knew that I had insufficient resources to do justice to the dig and that it was foolish to continue. By the time Roy Davies arrived on the scene, I had decided that my best course of action was to abandon the excavation, at that time, hoping that the bushes would grow back over the rocks hiding the wall. I knew I would be the butt of endless humour and no one would bother to waste time wading through the brambles to see what a mess I had made. The least I could do was to replace the broken branches where they had come from as I passed by the spot on my way down to Couiza the following morning, knowing that one day I would return, equipped with knowledge, not just a long-handled mattock. The treasure was there and there it could remain until I knew sufficient to fully understand at least some of the mystery surrounding the site. However, what was sorely lacking was Bérenger Saunière's mighty finger pointing clearly to the treasure stating,

"Here be treasure," or at least, "X marks the spot."

Perhaps, in a couple of years I would be ready. That was back in 1974.

***

Now, as I sat on the drystone wall, what was still needed from my present visit was some firm proof at the hand of Bérenger Saunière confirming with exactness the precise location he himself had guarded so faithfully, if indeed such a precise marker existed outside of my fertile imagination. I had decided to return to the drystone wall and the Poussin Seat to search for the clue that had eluded me. Despite the belief that each visit I made could draw unwanted attention to me, I had taken the familiar path via the Rue de Pompe and picked my way through the thorn bushes. The sky had cleared and the sun was as hot as ever. I was certainly glad when I finally sat down on the wall. I wanted irrefutable proof from the lips of Bérenger Saunière or at least from his architecture that the place where I was sitting was his Golgotha, his Place of the Skull and not just the spot that all other evidences had cried out from the earth.

Suddenly it struck me in the eyes! It was Bérenger Saunière's flash of inspiration from the grave! Now, as I sat on the drystone wall, a brilliant shaft of light struck my eyes. It was the reflection of the sun shining on the few remaining panes of glass left in the conical spire on the orangery. Visible now that the trees had shed their leaves, the orangery spire stood out sharply against the silhouette of his Tour Magdala. Next to it, slightly to the west, I could just make out the top of the square orangery roof, though the sun was not reflected from it at that time. Like two eyes, glancing sideways down the hillside, the glistening all-seeing beacon had been specially designed to shine across the rugged landscape. No matter what the time of day the sun would still reflect from the spire.

I rose to my feet and took a compass bearing by taking a sighting on the *échauguette* that surmounted the tower. The compass card swung round to 180 degrees exactly and stayed on the 'S', showing that the line from where I stood, through the centre of the orangery to the top of the *échau-guette* was exactly north to south in a dead straight line.

However, not just the tower, but also the alignment pin-pointed the very top of his *échauguette* where he alone could stand to gaze out across his landscape. From that vantage point, he would see, rising above the orangery roof the spot that he knew so well and had spent so much time and effort with unlimited resouces to preserve. The reflected shaft of sunlight shone exactly onto where I sat in deep thought awaiting that blaze of inspiration from the long-departed Priest. I pulled out my compass again to check that I had not made some error in my eagerness for success. My oil-filled Suunto compass was selected from the range of compasses on the market. The card was damped and I had placed a red line at the sighting end of the body to eliminate any parallax error in taking readings.

I knew that the compass bearing on the orangery roof would be accurate and precise to within a degree. Immediately behind the glass roof the *échauguette* on the tower stood out in direct alignment. The compass point swung round to due south. The local magnetic variation shown on the map when calculated for the year 2000 was practically zero, being only one degree west. The compass needle stayed steady on the south bearing. I moved a few feet to the side and checked the bearing once more. This compass bearing was the confirmation that I sought.

I could not accurately check the angle of declination at the time. I hoped that it would match the 26.565 degree angle that I had expected to find but it did not seem to be sufficiently steep. My clinometer used to measure the vertical angle of dipping rock strata would have given me a precise reading but it was not something that I had considered bringing. Every piece of gear you carry becomes heavier as the sun gets hotter. After checking the compass bearings from a slightly different position in case of a local magnetic

Fig. 8. 1 The orangery now in a sorry state.

Fig. 8. 2. Lavender grows where none intended.

anomaly, I decided to return to the village. Everything must be checked from the Tour Magdala looking down towards the dry-stone wall. I climbed eagerly up the steep path to the village, anxious to check my findings from the top of the Tour Magdala. Despite the warmth of the day, I made good speed back to the tower. After having bought my ticket, I entered the tower and clambered up the spiral staircase to the castellated roof. Looking up, I could see that Saunière had mounted two stout iron brackets into the wall. These were to secure his ladder, which was no longer there. Saunière's ladder that he used to scale the *échauguette* was nowhere to be seen, at least for the visitors. The best I could do was to take a compass bearing on the spike on the top of the orangery roof.

From where I stood on the square roof of the Tour Magdala, the compass reading was exactly 360 degrees, due north. I was surprised to see that there was a prominent spike placed centrally on top of the orangery roof to provide an exact alignment for my compass reading. Contrary to my impression that the belvedere ran parallel to the points of the compass, the north south alignment was set diagonal to the belvedere, as was now evident. The landscape behind the orangery spire was mostly obscured by the trees but I knew exactly what lay behind the trees, having just walked up from that spot. I took some photographs, in order to provide useful confirmation of the alignment. Photographs taken of the orangery revealed the intricate pattern that Saunière had used when he designed the spike on the top of the conical spire that surmounted it, reminiscent of all the curves of the blue apples of Rennes.

For the return route to Couiza I decided to take the ancient route from Rennes-le-Château via the path leading westward past the Tour Magdala. There is a straight path leading down towards Couiza, which was probably used by the inhabitants of ancient Rhedae. Having enquired at the village, I received assurances that this path would still be viable. I set off in the hope that I would be able to approach the treasure location from that direction. The path led down at a gentle gradient but at the point where I wished to branch of to my right, when approaching Roc Fumade, I found that the route became more precipitous.

The path was almost obliterated in its lower reaches, as I found to my cost. Though it was well trodden for some of the way, it later disappeared into thick bush and was barely discernable in places. However, I decided to continue in the direction of Couiza and eventually arrived there two hours later after quite a tussle with the overgrown thickets. Saunière's new road was designed to come as close to the treasure as possible and provide reasonable access from the road by a gentle path now partially obscured by undergrowth but clearly visible on the aerial photos of 1967.

So there was a sound reason for the construction of the roadway he designed, despite the obvious difficulties he must have encountered in laying out the route without the road sliding off the steep cliff into the Sals River. Moreover, his road provides a clear pointer, which became obvious only when standing on the site and gazing towards the river, when the long straight section of road is directly aligned with the location of the cavern.

Fig. 8. 3. The complex spike surmounts the glazed cone.

Fig. 8. 4. The *tour de coin* on the Tour Magdala.

The architect of all this must have spent many hours in thoughtful planning of such a complex layout before embarking on a project of this scale. It would have been an impossible task, unachievable without vast resources to back up his genius. How fortunate we are that the Priest of Rennes and his Madonna were there to prepare the path. Now, there is a challenge for all of us who would follow in his footsteps, as shepherds in Arcadia.

CHAPTER NINE

SHEPHERDS IN ARCADIA

Directly I arrived back in England, I called in at my photography expert where I had purchased my Pentax to have my prints developed. The next day my prints were ready for collection and after receiving the photographer's critical appraisal I was able to review the results of my trip to Rennes-le-Château. I found myself once more peering into my trusted mirror stereoscope. The stereoscopic pair of photos came into focus as I carefully aligned them so that the two images coincided and sprang to life in my mind's eye, transporting me back to the village.

Far from the steep slopes of Rennes, the ideas and images from my recent visit had to be analysed and reviewed in a formal desk study. Such discipline was essential in order to tease out any wild speculation and fantasy from the strands of reason woven into the web of intrigue. Here and there facts shone like the dew, as the morning sunlight pierced the canopy of webs on that familiar hillside, bright with golden broom. Before my minds eye, lay the village of Rennes-le-Château and the Sals River in the deep cut of the river, with the ragged outline of Coustaussa standing guard upon its north bank and the finger of the shepherd's arm stretching up towards the village.

Stublein had taken the trouble to record the tombstone of Marie de Nègre d'Ables, Dame d'Hautpoul de Blanchefort, that had been so cunningly designed by Antoine Bigou so long ago. I had not been able to see the similar markings on the far hillside, even when viewed from the top of the Tour Magdala, but they were clearly visible on the aerial photos.

In his tombstone illustration, Eugène Stublein had placed his signature such that the 't' of the 'ESt' was crossed exactly in line with the arrowhead and the large dot on the tomb-stone. I wondered why. What was the exact location where Anton Bigou originally sited the grave before Saunière moved it? The graveyard is now in two sections at different levels separated by a wall and a row of steps. It does not seem likely that Marie de Blanchefort would have been entombed in the more distant graveyard, even if that area had existed in her day. While at Rennes, I had taken time to examine the various positions where it could have lain. There is a recent grave in the far corner by the wall, from which it would be easy to view the treasure site and perhaps, years ago, those letters on the far hillside. The letters are set out in massive lines of stonework, which could have been part of the ancient Rhedae. Now it is fruitless to speculate.

The question of orientation is also of interest. Was the central line of the tombstone aligned with the treasure site or in line with the markings on the far hillside or, less likely, just aligned with the other tombstones? To prepare such an elaborate conundrum as posed by these two gravestones would surely have been incomplete without some subtle use of alignment, possibly employing an angle vital to the cipher. A straight alignment of the treasure site and the stone letters seems a little too simplistic and there is a variance of at least two degrees. Alignment with the hillside and the access path to the site exists but I am not satisfied with anything less than an exact match. More work would be needed before any firm conclusion might be reached.

The Marie d'Ables tombstone should respond to the same rules as the Poussin paintings and deserves careful scrutiny. For example, if the duplicate image of the gravestone is rotated through the requisite 26.565 degrees such that the P - S logo is superimposed over the 'D+I, we find the ubiquitous skull and the key superimposed on the gravestone produces many interesting patterns, including the 'PAX'. It seems reasonable to superimpose the relevant square divided like an 'E' over the letter of equivalent size. Should the 'T' be similarly placed? If we examine the form of the letters, the 'E' takes the shape of three sides of a square with the middle bar terminating at the midpoint. The 'T' superimposed upon the 'ET' makes the top of the square and divides the square vertically. The 'IN' then repeats these vertical lines and draws the diagonal as required in the key.

The arc is the next figure to be represented in the sequence. As the Marie d'Ables tombstone is intertwined with the solution, superimposing the 'E' and the 'T' gives 'PAX' and produces a match with the spider but this is by no means conclusive. The tombstone is as enigmatic as the rest of the work of Antoine Bigou, who was the Curé to Marie d'Ables, but his work should follow a definite pattern of actions.

It is reasonable to expect the double-ended arrow that runs down the centre of the Marie d'Ables tombstone to define the length of one of the Tau measurements and the tombstone image should be scaled to match the key. 'PRAE-CUM', meaning 'before and with' or 'forerunner', clearly states that it is important for the first step. The 'P' of the 'P – S' logo is the only thing that matches, so this must be superimposed upon the 'P' of 'PRAE-CUM' so that the 'N' fits in the bottom corner with the 'LIXLIXL'. This generates the new arrow length, being the mid section, which is equal in length to the arrow and the width is equal to the next dimension of Tau in the key. The fourth Tau factor from the arrow dimension is equal to two images end to end with the E's matching and with another pair adjacent. This produces a large arrow with the centre of the helis central to the arrow. The spider is then superimposed upon the helis to match when the original arrow coincides with the edge of the Marie d'Ables gravestone. This figure is thus seen to equal the height of the large square and half of its width. Clearly the tombstone does conceal more than it reveals but perhaps one should pause for breath at this point.

Returning to the meaning of 'P – S', the initials in Latin

could well stand for *primo – secundo;* first and second or even
– sabbato, seventh. Now continuing this line of thought, the
Latin for thrice is *ter*. This idea knits in well with the ET IN
ARCADIA EGO theme, indicating a third application of the
key, TER. This occurs in Saunière's inscription cut on the
tympanum above the door to his St Madeleine Church, TER-
RIBILIS EST LOCUS ISTE. This starts and finishes with TE.
However, verified facts are preferred to wild speculation.

The tympanum above the door may be the first example
you will spot but you will soon become an expert in the
angles. On re-examining Fig.1.1. you may note the angle
and view it in a new light. Just another skull lurking in our
very first illustration! There is still much room for light and
knowledge on so many aspects of the ever growing mystery
surrounding this village. A complete knowledge of everything including the entire history of each person involved
will never be fully known. This is what provides such interest in this saga. There will always be a mystery surrounding
this little village, together with other treasures still concealed in a web of intrigue. Yet this book must home in on
the treasure site with a view to proper archaeological excavations as a prime objective.

Before Saunière's death, he had organised funds and
reputedly had prepared plans to build a much higher tower.
Perhaps he had wished to restore the village to the eminence
that it possessed before the ravages of successive marauders
and time had reduced it to the parlous state that greeted him
when he first was appointed its Curé. At that time, without
any concerted restoration work the church of St Madeleine

would have fallen into the same state of decay that had already overtaken the old Church of St Peter, with its bell tower that now contains only a wine press. A few remains of the former Church of St John the Baptist, pillaged in 1361 by the Aragonese mercenaries, are still visible in the village. The careful work of Saunière is already beginning to be set at naught. The orangery is dilapidated. His garden has been allowed to deteriorate and trees have sprung up where he would not have had them. The landscape has changed and though parts of it have always been known as *terrain vague*, rough country, it has far exceeded the original description in this respect.

In the church, the colour schemes have been modified and perhaps the layout is not as it was originally. Some door panels have been cut with fleur de lys designs by those untrained in the ways of Rennes. Not only does this disfigure the doors but also it further confuses the seeker after knowledge and may lead to a distortion of the image of the Curé who has contributed so much to the village. One might be led to believe that he was a subversive royalist seeking to restore the Merovingian dynasty to the throne of France. Yet, he was always a devout Roman Catholic at heart following strictly in the St Sulpice order of worship despite his enforced contretemps with the establishment.

At the time that Saunière started his ministry at Rennes-le-Château it must have appeared to Saunière to be a sorry little village. Nevertheless, he devoted his meagre funds and tireless energy to build his flock and their house of worship. When his efforts were crowned with the success they deserved, he threw his entire energy into furthering the welfare of the village. At the far end of the Rue de Pompe, the village pump still creaked and groaned to my hand but there is now a tap by a trough serviced by running water. For this, I gave grateful thanks to the Curé after my last visit to the thorns of Rennes in the midday heat. Saunière not only supplied piped water to the village and a road fit for his guests, but poured untold wealth into and through the out-stretched hands of the villagers and upon the surrounding countryside. There are tales of handouts to the poor and needy, such that they may have thought that they were truly in Sion with no poor amongst them. Monasteries and churches were in receipt of his endowments. He had a hard challenge to bring long dormant funds back into circulation and did not bury his one talent during his stewardship.

Back in England, the alignment on the map and the Tour Magdala required careful checking. I needed fully accurate compass bearings around Saunière's domain to confirm its layout relative to the north-south readings I had carefully checked, taking account of the magnetic variation at the date that the accurate readings were taken. The exact positions of all the aligned points needed to be established on the map to a high degree of accuracy. The various altitudes needed to be established to give me the angle of the line of sight from the horizontal. Why should this be important? Everything was important to Saunière so why not to myself?

The 17th January was a recurring date, appearing on some tombstones including that of Marie de Nègre de Blanchefort so carefully erased by Saunière, and by others at Rennes-les-

Bains. The significance of this date had not been recognised by the experts but probably related to the angle of the sun at midday or, lapsing into the vernacular Punic, LE CHEVAL DE DIEU A MIDI when the best pommes bleues may be picked. When the sun is at its zenith on the 17th January the angle of the sun to the horizontal should be crucial. This would be the angle of the shadow cast by the Sun, taken in a vertical plane, at that time. The direction of the shadow should be from south to north, 26.565 degrees from the horizontal, but who can measure to that degree of accuracy?

This crucial angle, unlike everything connected with Rennes and the cipher, must only have one answer. It can only be 26.565 degrees. The calculation for this is the 'Golden' value of arc-tan $0.5 = 26.565$ degrees, but the last 2 places of decimals aren't really significant, because Saunière or Poussin (or even Greenwich) wouldn't have been able to measure the angle of the Sun to 1/100 or 1/1000 of a degree, so it doesn't matter, apart from the requirement to draw an accurate key using CAD.

If a drawing is inaccurate when starting from a small square with an imprecise angle, then the error will multiply as the figure is enlarged. The key figure is drawn to three places of decimals on the angles and four places of decimals in the dimensions starting with a large figure, which is then progressively reduced.

Is it more precise to sight to the top rim of the sun, or to the lowest point? Measurement of the diameter of the sun made it approximately 0.6 degrees from top to bottom. It took less than one minute, with a metre rule and minimal mental arithmetic.

My Nautical Almanac confirmed the angle of the sun but I needed proper verification from the Royal Observatory at Greenwich. Armed with my GPS E-Trex I visited the Royal Observatory on the cold but sunny morning of the 17th January 2002 to ascertain the sun's angle at noon as seen at Rennes. The Observatory staff were most helpful, advising me to send an E-mail formally requesting the calculation.

While I was at the Observatory I tested my E-Trex on the meridian line there. Imagine my surprise when I discovered that the meridian now lies some distance away in the park as a result of more precise calculations. As this gave me some concern as to the accuracy of my instrument I was at pains to verify that this was indeed the case.

After checking once again the accuracy of my estimate the following E-mails were exchanged:

To Astroline 11 February 2002 16:40.

Subject: Zenith angle of the Sun.

I am trying to verify the angle of the Sun on 17th January at WGS84 location N 042 deg. 55 min. 41.4 sec. E 02 deg. 15 min. 44.2 sec. The zenith time would be useful as well. I believe the angle would be about 26.5 degrees but I would like it as accurate as possible. Does the angle vary much from year to year for example in 1917? I am hoping to include this in a book and wonder if you could answer this odd query. Thank you for your help on this knotty problem.

Regards,

Bill Kersey.

<u>Monday, February 18, 2002 5.52 PM.</u>

From Robert Massey. To Bill Kersey.

Re: Zenith angle of the Sun

Dear Mr Kersey

The software we have doesn't give latitudes and longitudes to the nearest second and only gives results after 1980. To give you an answer I will need to know a specific time of day —. The Sun's altitude changes constantly.

Yours sincerely

Dr. Robert Massey, Royal Observatory Greenwich.

<u>19 February 2002.00:21</u>

From Bill Kersey. To Robert Massey.

Many thanks for addressing this problem. The exact time is not certain but I am interested in the altitude of the Sun at its maximum altitude, which could be noon but might vary from this by virtue of not being on 0 meridian, also any daylight saving times that might possibly apply in the winter there.

I imagine the Sun's path would be fairly low in the sky and would only attain a maximum of 26 or 27 degrees at its highest point.

I am sure this may appear to be some dumb question but it is an important issue for the purpose of what will be an interesting book. The issue as to whether this has varied over the last hundred year is not so important, particularly as the data is not readily available without reference to old almanacs.

My calculations make it to be about 26.5 degrees but I am

certainly not an expert and would value your findings.Regards,

Bill Kersey.

Tuesday, February 19, 2002 9.55 AM.

From Robert Massey. To Bill Kersey.

Dear Mr Kersey

The calculated maximum apparent angle is 26.4 degrees at around 1201 UTE (equivalent to GOT).

Yours sincerely

Dr Robert Massey

19 February 2002 11:53.

From Bill Kersey. To Robert Massey.

Thank you very much for this most useful information.

Regards,

Bill Kersey.

The Royal Observatory verified the angle of the Sun on the 17th January at Rennes as 26.4 degrees approximately at its zenith, which is almost exactly at noon, Paris time. This degree of accuracy should be acceptable to most, though I cannot speak for Nicolas Poussin who is a perfectionist. Sir Isaac Newton may also declare an interest and not only because of the apple but perhaps because of his interesting memorial in Westminster Abbey.

At this point, it would appear to be vital to explain just why the 26.565 or 26.4 sun angle has assumed such an important position in defining the location of the hoard. Surely, it is crucial because of the following reasoning:

1. The aerial survey and ground exploration have defined the position of a possible hoard.

2. The site turns out to be due north of Saunière's tower.

3. So the mid-day sun, on any day of the year, casts a shadow of the tower in the direction of the site.

4. The shadow falls short of the site, because the tower is not high enough.

5. After Saunière has discovered, or been shown, the hoard, he is aware of Poussin's pictures, and learns how to use the hidden Golden angle in updating or removing the trail of clues.

6. He therefore builds the Tour Magdala and the orangery as an alignment marker. The various panes of glass, set at an angle each, in turn, reflect the Sun's rays from its glazed spire to alert us to its presence. The buildings of his domain together with the other edifices and gardens form a significant landmark. Many of the main graphic clues he incorporated in his domain and in the St Madeleine Church. The precise location of the hoard is indicated when the orangery spire aligns exactly with the *échauguette*.

7. Saunière would have liked the end of the shadow to fall on the site, and probably considered that the ancient fortifications satisfied this condition.

8. He realises that the shadow of the original tower would have conformed to the 26.565 degree angle requirement at mid-day on only two days of the year: 29th November and 17th January. He is determined

to build a higher tower, so that the tip of the shadow will fall on the site on 17th January He dies before he can succeed.

9. His new tower was going to be 70 metres high, according to Gérard de Sède. So the sixty million franc question is: How could he design a new tower to fulfil these requirements? Can it be shown that a tower of this height, erected in the place he had earmarked for it, would, at midday on 17th January, cast its shadow upon the site that has been defined?

A positive answer to this question would go a long way towards understanding the problem that Bérenger Saunière faced in those final years of his stewardship. An answer may also contribute towards a successful archaeological exercise. Analysis of this problem would be dependant on accurate GPS results. Global Positioning System equipment would give locations, and altitudes with a degree of accuracy that would be sufficient to resolve the problem, I hoped.

The one thing that Saunière would have experienced great difficulty in controlling was the golden orb in its path across the heavens and the angle of the Sun at noon. Thus, he would need to construct a new tower to form a colossal sundial.

Saunière had secured another tranche of funds to support his new and ambitious plans to ensure that the hoards of Rennes would not be lost without trace after his orangery fell into disrepair. Though effective as a marker, the spire and orangery were ephemeral in terms of the centuries-long endurance of the hoard held in his vaults; his by virtue of his custodial stewardship. The plans of his new enterprise were reputedly stolen in the 1930s, but it seems that he had planned to restore the village to its state in Nicolas Poussin's time; namely, around 1640, when this great artist painted *Les Bergers d'Arcadie*.

If the village were to be restored to its original state, would that not revalidate the key to this seemingly eternal treasure? Were not Nicolas Poussin and his works of art more famous and eternal than a Priest of the countryside? Let no expense be spared. The village must again be walled to the north and a great defensive tower constructed to overshadow the fateful spot in order to restore the scene in *Les Bergers d'Arcadie*. If the battlements of the tower were to cast the correct shadow such that the angle of the sun at noon on the 17th January would extend to mark the hoard it would certainly require a tower taller than the Magdala, which subtends an angle of approximately fourteen degrees. If the high point of the tower was near to the position of the orangery, which would then be redundant, then the height of the tower could be less than if it was situated where the *échauguette* on the Tour Magdala stands. The new tower would then be closer to the treasure site. This would mean that the specific angle for the shadow would be achieved without requiring excessive height for battlements of his proposed tower.

By the end of 1916, the funds were probably in place and certain checks on the new designs were required before plans could be launched. Bérenger Saunière rose early on that fateful morning of the 17th January 1917 and hurried through his normal duties. He must have set off early for a gentle constitutional down the steps near to the ancient pump and well, which supplied the water so crucial to the village since those mighty days of Rhedae, capital city of the Visigoths. Then, striking to the right along the path at the foot of the wall, he would soon reach the path that led steeply down to a certain raised area where a rocky wall flanked a level area amongst those rugged hills. He reflected that he would have dearly loved to drive an automobile down to the bend at the end of a long straight section, he had hoped to possess one, but a parked car would have attracted too much attention from his eagle-eyed parishioners. He struck off from the path down the slope and paused to take a sip from the spring, now flowing freely with the winter rains. He followed the track to the vineyard and along the path through the vineyard along the drystone wall turning his gaze towards the village above him. His hand trembled as he aligned the compass on the orangery spire. The *rose des vents* or card of the compass swung wildly at first, but as his hand steadied, the south mark on the *rose* and the 180 degree mark aligned exactly with the shining glass spire with the *tour de coin* standing sentinel behind it. With his compass and level in hand, he verified the bearing to the orangery and the Tour Magdala and using his level, he verified the vertical angle. This figure he could use to precisely determine the correct position the new tower.

However, he must make haste. He consulted his fob watch. It was already coming up to eleven in the morning. No longer a man in his youth with a fowling piece chasing the red-legged partridge, he struck out across the muddy patch where the spring rose and hurried up the path towards the village. A gentle stroll down to a parked car would have suited him better. He arrived breathless and sweating despite the winter chill. By the time he reached the door of the Magdala, a glance at his watch revealed that it was five minutes to noon. The door was locked and he fumbled for his key beneath his soutane. Hastening up the winding stairs, he reached the tower roof. Under cover of the dark the previous evening, thank goodness he had placed the ladder against the *échauguette*, thrusting the two prongs into the iron loops he had designed for that purpose.

Climbing the flight of stairs had left him breathless and as he grasped the ladder a great heaviness clawed at his legs. He climbed to the crenellated top and swung a leg over, hampered by his soutane. Turning, he checked his watch. All was well; two minutes to twelve. The sun was at his back and its rays reflected straight back into his eyes from the glass panes in his orangery. He could see the shadow cast by the tower stretching down due north, like a finger pointing to a spot where a rock in the shape of a skull lay hidden behind a clump of bushes strategically placed. The shadow traversed west to east but he could see that it was well short of that place of the skull, his Golgotha and passed well to the south. He rested the compass on the stonework to steady it as the *rose des vents* swung unerringly to the north mark showing 360 degrees aligned with the orangery spike atop the spire centred on the precise spot on the ground where he had stood earlier that morning.

The new tower he planned would need to be much taller, maybe fully seventy metres in total. He marked in his mind the spot on the landscape where the shadow finally reached at the sun's zenith as the hands of his watch joined at twelve noon. Elated, he realised that he had achieved all that he had set out to do that morning. He had met his deadline, just. As he started down the ladder, he felt a touch of vertigo. By the time that his feet met the firm stonework at the top of the tower, he felt a mist rising before his eyes. He moved through the heavy doorway at the head of the winding steps leading down to his library and steadied himself against the wall on the way down. That lead weight in his legs and the winding stairs increased his dizziness. Yes, he was no longer a young man and he thought that he must hasten the work to mark for ever the place of the skull. He slumped in his chair and clutched at his chest. The pain racked his body as he attempted to stand.

"Marie, I must find Marie."

He lurched to his feet and tottered to the door of the Magdala tower.

"Golgotha, Golgotha," he gasped. He had to complete his work. Words from his Easter sermon crowded his brain.

"*Eloi, Eloi, lama sabachthani*." He gave a muffled cry through his clenched teeth; his powerful fingers tore at the searing pain in his chest as he collapsed across the doorway.

Some time later, they found him and carried him to the villa Bethania. Marie was there and tended him with tearful eyes, bathing his brow with a linen cloth.

"My master," she murmured tenderly, "Oh my God, my

God, why hast Thou forsaken him?"

For several days, his fate hung in the balance as Marie
Denarnaud watched faithfully by his bedside day and night
except for a short interval while the Curé came from the
neighbouring parish to administer to him. Who knows what
Saunière talked of with Marie or with that Curé as he fought
for his life, knowing he had so much still to accomplish? The
money meant nothing to either of them and they both had
intense memories of their early days of grinding poverty to
be followed by those years of largesse as the benevolent
Priest strove to restore those hidden funds to circulation.
Neither wealth nor prayers could stay the Grim Reaper and
thus an era closed for a great man in a tiny village of mystery
that has never lost its special attraction, nor yet revealed its
great secret.

CHAPTER TEN

STEPS OF TEMPTATION

In 1790, the Academy of Science was charged with the task of measuring the distance from Dunkirk to Barcelona. This major survey took from 1792 to 1799. From the results, the French were able to deduce the length of the Earth's meridian – a great half-circle joining the earth's North and South Poles. The length of this curved line formed the basis for standardising the units of measure, not only for length but also for determining units of weight and volume — all related. One twenty-millionth of the meridian length from pole to pole was taken as the base measurement and named the Metre. The new Metric System was instituted by decree on the 2nd November 1801 and became obligatory in France from 1st January 1840. The

old rule of thumb, *le pouce, la toise, l'aune* and *la ligne* no
doubt lingered in the hearts of many but the precision of the
metre has even overtaken the English equivalent of the *pouce*
– the inch, due to the elegance of the unified metric system.
However, I must admit to my affection for the troy ounce,
particularly when used as the measurement of the gold yield
from my claims in Rhodesia. The *pouce* or inch, the foot, the
yard and the mile still have their traditional place in my own
concept of size or distance.

Perhaps the idea of a Templar Measure had been inherited
from the Temple Measure. Just what exactly would a
Templar have used as a measure? How long is a Templar
Measure? Precisely as long as a Templar would want it to be!
The arch formed by the interlocking key was reminiscent of
the Royal Arch degree in Masonry, which existed in the
ancient Masonic degrees and might have had its origins in
some way connected with the key. This degree probably
existed as long ago as the period when the Knights Templar
were in possession of the site of the Temple of Jerusalem
during the crusades.

***

Precision measurements on *Les Bergers d'Arcadie* had not
been established at this stage in the investigation, but the
reader will have gained a background to the ways of Rennes,
which form such an important part of the strange world of
Bérenger Saunière, the most diligent custodian of the secrets
and treasures of Rennes-le-Château. But this could never
have been his main source of income. However, it was his
main cause for vast expenditure. Our Priest was also the

keeper of a key that unlocked for him, through his newly acquired expertise, the Templar hoards of Europe. Much of the wealth he spent liberally in his priestly duties caring for his flock. However, his expenditure on the maintenance of the path to his special treasure cost him dear. It must be said that he loved his work in the environment he created. This key may disclose many treasure chests already pillaged. Some sites will remain forever undefiled.

The painstaking task of unravelling *Les Bergers d'Arcadie* did not all happen overnight and not in one day. The learning process was dependant on moving forward, following one hypothesis and sleeping on the findings. Working on the problems late into the night was not practical. Firstly, other commitments required my full attention during the day and sleep deprivation was counter productive. Secondly, the mind is active during sleep. The brain often reorganises and files the thoughts and actions accumulated during the course of the day. The brain appears to relate recently acquired data to existing information already stored in the archives of the mind.

I had amassed a vast amount of relevant information and even more misinformation. Much had been written and this provided a background to the progress of the story in the modern world. But little, if any of the basic facts that Gérard de Sède expounded in *The Accursed Treasure of Rennes-le-Château*, had changed. Some of these facts that are needed to discern a way forward are summarised in the next few paragraphs.

Various paintings either give the key or use the cipher,

including Saunière's painting of the skull next to the maid in
the landscape, and his large wall painting depicting Christ
inviting all who are heavy laden to come to him. His stations
of the cross, probably based on other similar works, need
serious consideration, having been prepared and installed by
Saunière as a guide to the earnest seeker. Other useful
paintings include the Chatsworth *Arcadian Shepherds* and *Les
Bergers d'Arcadie*. Teniers paintings of St Anthony contain
skulls and crosses. There is also the *Et In Arcadia Ego* by El
Guerchino to consider. We would be well advised to limit
ourselves, to avoid over-saturation of the brain. We should
not overlook those things that are conspicuously absent from
Saunière's domain. These items include the painting of *Les
Bergers d'Arcadie* and the two tombstones of Marie de Nègre
that our Priest disposed of so effectively.

We have the *helis pomata*, but we need to continue work
on the paintings as the problem is only partially solved. If
we work on *Les Bergers d'Arcadie*, which contains the key we
may be able to define the range of dimensions that Poussin
used. There are various photographs of this painting, which
have been filmed over the years. One of the photographs I
have used was from Scala in Florence and was taken just
after the painting had been cleaned, so the colours were still
relatively bright, considering the age of the painting. This
photograph transparency was made at least thirty five years
ago so does not show the ravages of time and care that the
painting has since undergone. My first transparency was
supplied for research purposes only, but this has been
replaced by a transparency for which copyright has been
secured from Scala.

When asked how he achieved his masterpieces Poussin replied,

"I leave nothing to chance." He is the man with whom we must work. The famous Fouquet letter (Lépinois, *Lettres de Louis Fouquet, pp 269*) indicates the possibility of some great secret. Let us examine the translation from Sir Anthony Blunt's record. (De Lépinois, Ernest De Buchère and De Montaiglon, Antoine. *"Nicolas Poussin. Lettres de Louis Fouquet à son frère Nicolas Fouquet,"* AAF, 1862, pp. 267ff.

M. Poussin…and I have been engaged in certain things, of which I shall shortly be able to discuss with you at length, which will give you, through the means of M. Poussin, some advantages … which kings would go to great lengths to extract from him, and which, according to him, no-one in the world would ever retrieve in the centuries to come; and what is more, is such that without a great deal of expense would even be able to produce a profit. Moreover, this comprises of things that are so difficult to discover, and cannot be equalled or of better value than anything on the earth at this time.

This letter was sent on the 17th April 1656 by Abbé Louis Fouquet, residing in Rome, to his elder brother, Nicolas Fouquet, who was Superintendent of Finances at the Court of Louis XIV in Paris. Nicolas Fouquet was arrested in 1661 and held incommunicado, by order of the King, right until his death. It is likely that the subject of the letter relates to our little enquiry.

The implications of this letter may produce a mixture of hope and despair. The letter engenders hope that in our grasp is a painting that holds the encryption of a priceless key to undreamed of advantages. This is countered by despair at our inability to unravel the cipher that is destined to remain forever beyond our powers to solve. His famous paintings were the medium that Poussin used to express himself in a manner so shrouded in secrecy that his innermost thoughts are impenetrable, almost. How best to probe his mind? He went to great lengths to ensure that someone would appreciate his genius and humour one day. He was a patient man and seemed prepared to wait for the centuries to flow by before receiving his accolade.

The inscription associated with the Arcadian theme has always been a source of conjecture. Though it appeared in the earlier El Guerchino *Et in Arcadia Ego* painting, it has been associated with the mystery and appears on the Marie de Nègre tombstones. Here it is partly shown in Greek characters, the form of which have been employed to good purpose, although there is an obvious connection with the location of Arcadia in Greece.

Where Rennes is concerned we must expect multiple connections and meanings. 'Even in Arcadia am I (death)' is the generally accepted interpretation. The skull, used to depict death, is clearly emphasised here. To achieve a mere *double entendre* from this is surely admitting defeat.

Much of the first chapter of this book has relevance in this story and is there to implant in the reader the seeds of thought. The compass card swung as the *Richmond Castle* took up its course from Las Palmas. The word card is derived from the Latin hinge while ego clearly refers to the head. Consider the Punic form ET IN ARC CARDIA EGO. ET in an arc hinges the head. We use the arc, not the full circle, in the construction. Now consider that 'et' implies a repetitive action and 'T' refers to Tau (the golden ratio) we have a possible instruction. The 'ET' may be the shortest word of little significance but this may not be the case. One could dwell long and hard on those two simple letters,'et'. The letters of the alphabet may relate to certain parts of the key. For example, the 'T' may represent the conjunction in the Tau cross. No speculation on this can be verified if we fail to enquire of a Past Master. Which painting is the best one to use to gain insight? Perhaps it is best to refer to as many as possible.

The Sun's chariot of fire drawn by the relentless *cheval de Dieu* in its journey across the sky in its *arca dia* has assumed greater significance, especially when linked to the central *ego*. The horse's arched mane of our knight chess piece reminds us of not only the knight's move of the key, with its step forward followed by the diagonal move, but also of the arc in the key as it traces out the move. The figure of Asmodeus, the *daemon de guardien* crouching at the entrance to St Madeleine will surely yield up its secret if we submit to the discipline of tracing out the course of the sinister and dexter along its contorted limbs.

The definitive solution is more readily found in Poussin's more recent *Les Bergers d'Arcadie* containing the shepherd, clothed in red and holding his staff. The staff clearly has been given a specific length, whereas the other two staffs appear to have no clearly defined length and the others do have distinct bends. It is necessary to resolve all of the main dimensions that the artist had used in linking the progressive sequence through the golden section, or Tau. It appears, from x-ray information, that Nicolas painted these staffs early in the composition. The golden section construction is based on rectangles and squares. Poussin used squares but how big did he make them? We need to consider what he decided to use as his basic unit of measurement.

LES BERGERS D'ARCADIE

Original Sequence	Dimension in Inches	Revised Powers of Tau	
15	46.978713763747	10	Picture Width.
14	29.034441853748	9	
13	17.944271909999	8	Staff (Inches).
12	11.090169943749	7	
11	6.854101966250	6	
10	4.236067977500	5	
9	2.618033988750	4	
8	1.618033988750	3	
7 Staff	1.000000000000	2	Thumb.
6	0.618033988750	1	
5	0.381966011250	0	*Pouce*/Inch.
4	0.236067977500	-1	
3	0.145898033750	-2	
2	0.090169943749	-3	
1	0.055728090001	-4	Rather Small.

If we play around with the values of Tau, we can produce

a table giving the staff a notional length as one, our base unit of measure in the initial hypothesis. The various copies of the painting that I had acquired were all of different sizes. Only at the early stages could the actual size of the painting be ignored while concentrating on the crucial factor, the ratios within the illustration. So I settled for the largest and most clear copy. A sequence of fifteen values for powers of Tau, increasing and decreasing from one are shown in the table. The use of twelve places of decimals is irrelevant and beyond working limits but may be of interest to some. Each value for Tau is the sum of the two preceding values.

In the left hand column item 7 of the sequence, the staff length, has a Tau value of 1. The sequence of values is taken as from 1 to 15. The relationship between the length of the staff and the picture width is 1 to 2.618. However, item 15 of the sequence has a Tau value is 46.9787, which is very close to the width of the whole painting when measured in inches. The centimetre equivalent is approximately 120 cm. Professor Cornford gives the overall painting width as 120 centimetres, or 47.244 inches. We must permit Poussin the possibility of some difference between his measurement in 1640 and that of today. There is some uncertainty in the actual width of the painting if we consider the dimension of the frame, the original dimension, the dimension three and a half centuries later and the actual original width of the area of display, as delineated by Poussin at the time of painting. In centimetres, this is given as between 119 cm. and 121 cm. dependent on which catalogue is used.

Because of the constant relationship, which exists in the

Tau scale, using the right hand column we now allocate the overall width of 46.978 inches to this power of Tau, (item 10 in the Tau Sequence in Inches column). The actual length of the staff in inches is thus now equal to item 8. The result is that the Tau value of the distance between the thumb and forefinger of our staff holder appears to be 1 unit.

Thus, these values have been related to the width of the painting expressed in inches, as in the top line of the table, acknowledging the difference amounting to about a quarter of an inch in the estimations of the width of the painting. This now gives the distance between the forefinger and the thumb a value of one inch. This is also the full length of the thumb, comprising the two phalanges and the metacarpal.

Poussin has painted the thumb with a straight line that extends along the upper limit of the thumb (see Fig.10.1). The quarter of an inch difference in the overall width of the painting equates to Poussin's inch being 1.0056 of our inches. This is not bad for our struggling artist. Perhaps we should not be two harsh on Poussin and attribute this minute difference to the coefficient of linear expansion of his ruler on a hot day in Rome or the width of a hair of his paintbrush, making his measurement out by 1/200 of an inch. The angle of the two thumb and forefinger lines conform exactly to the key line of the Red Shepherd's staff. The angular relationship between the staff and the other bones of the hands is present throughout the painting.

While on this subject of dimensions, it is of interest to note that the height of the painting is twice the length of the Red Shepherd's staff. The Louvre kindly let me read the file on Les Bergers d'Arcadie but the information concerning the uncleaned portion along the top of the painting, that lies concealed behind the frame, was not mentioned. It was not until Andrews and Schellenberger's book *The Tomb of God* was published in 1996 that this additional flap of canvas was common knowledge as illustrated in Plate 9 of their book. It is not clear why the frame is smaller than the painting but if the whole painting were visible, that would tend to high-light the importance of this staff in relation to the overall dimensions of the painting. Thus, we have a simple link between the staff and overall dimensions, namely the height is twice the staff length and the width is two steps up on the Tau scale.

We seem to be making progress with the painting and can disregard most of those twelve decimal places as the point has been made. You may also share some of my admiration for Nicolas Poussin. There is more to follow. Align the line that matches the width of the painting along the tops of the staffs through the eye of the Shepherdess.

Which of the five lines should we use? To clarify this, we must first define whether the key is reversed. When the key is oriented with the centre of the arc placed in the left-hand rectangle we shall call this 'sinister'. The mirror image places the centre in the right-hand rectangle and is called the 'dexter'. The orientation can be labelled according to the location of the axis of the arc of the square in question. When at the top we will define it as 'T' because the square resembles a 'T'. When the axis is to the left we can refer to it as 'E' because the square looks like that letter. The corners of the squares will need letters to define them. In sinister,

Fig. 10. 1. The relationship of painting width to staff top.

Fig. 10. 2. Almost a match.

Fig. 10. 3. The thumb and forefinger with key.

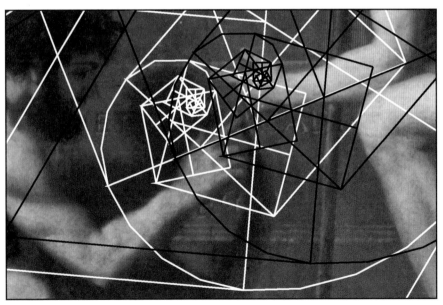

Fig. 10. 4. Sliding motion of the key.

starting with the arc corner moving clockwise use ABCD for
the corners and in dexter those same letters would be used,
being counter-clockwise. This seems a great system to avoid
where possible and is not as defined in the key!

To put this jargon into practice, place the sinister T, Tau
seq. 10 across the top of the two staffs and the Shepherdess's
eye to match the full width of the painting. The T, Tau seq. 4
is then aligned with the Blue Shepherd's staff. Now place
the sinister T Tau seq. 8 on the Red Shepherd's staff using BC
and the dexter T, Tau seq. 8 on the White Shepherd's staff
using the mid-line. Now both the Tau seq. 5 squares are
aligned and we do have the arcs to form an apple centred on
the White Shepherd's face, as in Fig. 10.6.

The shepherdess, seeing all this, casts an approving glance
on the scene. However, no smile touches the corner of her
mouth. Who knows what secrets she shares with the Mona
Lisa when night falls in the sleeping Louvre Museum?

Nicolas Poussin, being a Frenchman would use the word
pouce for that vital measurement we call an inch. Having
generated our key figure, we can now superimpose it over
the hand such that square side 3 Tau is placed twixt thumb
and forefinger with the side of the square lying along the
thumb. As we trust the painter implicitly, we would expect
the angle between the sides of the two adjacent squares to be
a right angle plus 26.565 degrees, which of course it is. We
have an expectation that the length of the sides will have
decreased proportionally, that is 0.1618 being the 2 value of
Tau (as shown in the table). Wrong! It is of course 1 unit or
1 *pouce*. How could a thumb be less? Here lies a message

from Nicolas. Of course we can see that, in the painting, the figures are not life-sized but drawn to scale. Thus, the length of the first phalanx of the Red Shepherd's thumb cannot be the standard length of one inch, or *pouce*, as in the basic unit of measure. As near as can be measured, it appears to be 0.382 inches or two steps down the scale. But on careful examination the Red Shepherd's fingertip is not on the square but on the arc node!

What does Poussin expect us to deduce from this little exercise? We can place the 1 Tau square in either position, either rotated or reversed. We can also superimpose the painting to replicate the possibilities with the key. We are suffering from a surfeit of possibilities again.

This leads us to now examine *Les Bergers d'Arcadie* painting in a different light. We are searching for the key, apparently held by Poussin and Teniers, mentioned in the parchment cipher. Here we might assume that the original parchments were not fakes. We may have the copies that Saunière made or copies of two of those copies. Let us assume that the result of unravelling the anagrams and coding is correct, wherever it came from. That Poussin and Teniers guard the key. We know that the *pommes bleues* exist, being the basis of the construction of the key as defined by Poussin. On this assumption, let us proceed to success or failure. We have become familiar with the *helis pomata* that fits the paintings and the geometric pattern, which will either stand or fall. We must put it to work.

To construct this *helis pomata* we make it in two halves and then combine the left and right portions, the one being a mirror image of the other. The obvious choice what to use as a basis for measurement must be the the Red Shepherd's staff. We need to construct a square with sides of that dimension, though other squares will be smaller or larger. All squares will be in golden section relationship to this staff length. This becomes easier to understand as we become more familiar with the key and its mirror image. By now, I am able to generate CAD drawings to several places of decimals with precise angles. This replaced the painstaking pencil and compass work, not forgetting the eraser. Now, by using CAD, several copies of the key, identical in every detail, could be produced.

By using the computer, the challenge of varying the scale is easy to resolve. Several transparencies are needed and these must fit the length of the staff or the unit length for the particular image under investigation. When first building a figure it was practical to start with a square side equal to the staff length. Theoretically, it is easier to start using a small size and construct the figure in ascending sizes, finally reducing it to the required size on printing. In practice, it is easier to commence with a large calculated size and draw a succession of lines decreasing in size by Tau, at the correct angle calculated to three decimal places. Later construct the figure on this basic pattern. After checking it, produce two transparencies to the exact scale required. At this stage, to work with more than two is confusing. Later, one achieves a greater capacity for confusion.

Taking one key figure, place it over the painting and move it around so that the Red Shepherd's staff exactly matches a straight line on the key. It is possible to match the staffs of both the Red and Blue Shepherd's staffs at the same time. If this is not achieved, then turn over the transparency and try once more. This exercise will make you reasonably familiar with the picture and the transparency.

It is only by actual practice that familiarity with so many of the complex relationships is achieved. A relationship exists between their relative position and their angles. The angular and length relationships are complex and can become time consuming. A more complete explanation is given in Appendix C. This collection of numbers representing both distances and angle defies normal, rational thought processes and is an excellent barrier to the elucidation of the mystery, but is nevertheless crucial.

Another angle that catches the eye is the angle formed by the arc. This is therefore a right angle less the 26.565 degrees, being 63.435 degrees approximately. At Rennes these two angles predominate everywhere you look. They appear above the entrance to the little Church of St Madeleine and in everything therein. This includes the paintings, the crosses on the Teniers paintings and everywhere you cast your eyes. Life for you has changed at a stroke and will never be quite the same. It becomes more complicated when you consider that there is a mirror image to this in the other half of the *helis pomata*.

When we hold the two portions of the key, we have reached a plateau. It is interesting to try various positions with a one half of the key when the relationship between the two long staffs can be recognised. Curves matched to the

position of a hand, eye or ear may be related to the key. The
key constantly changes its relationships as it components
move around the picture. Still there is no definition as to the
relative positions of the two halves of the key despite all the
achievements so far!

***

Another facet of the Nicolas Poussin enigma and Les
Bergers d'Arcadie becomes apparent as we move the two
transparencies across each other, like a good chef kneading
dough. We will note that the highlighted areas frequently
reveal the admonition to RCAD, which, on examination,
looks like READ. For those who have read Henry Boudet's
definitive work on the subject, *The True Celtic Language and
the Cromlech of Rennes-les Bains,* he acknowledges that the
English tongue is important. Referring to page 107 of *The
Accursed Treasure...* we quote:

As an example, take the word '*Cayrolo*' (a place-name often
found in Languedoc). This comes from '*caire*', which
denotes a squared stone, in Latin '*quadrum.*' Nevertheless,
Boudet pretends, against all the evidence that '*Cayrolo*'
comes from three English words, namely 'key,' 'ear' and
'hole.' This enormity is only inserted in order to draw
attention to the key passage.

Perhaps we underestimate M. Boudet and his desire to
emphasise the importance of English.

The ways of Rennes are noted for their inter-lingual
puns. Those who are offended by his method of alerting the
reader to a link between the ear and a key with the covert
reference to a square may prefer to read on with their eyes

closed. M. Boudet's thesis is based on the genocide of all languages and the wanton destruction of etymology in any shape or form in the pursuit of his Punic linguistic master race. The advantage of this is that no other language can derive so many meanings from any irrational collection of sounds. The student will emerge from his studies, his hair turned white and muttering in a certain jargon.

If we take a closer look at the cipher solution to the parchment as communicated by De Sède and reported in the Appendix of *The Holy Place* by Henry Lincoln we must be astounded at the complexity of the method of unravelling the coding. Surely, the wording of the final text must be vital and no less complex to unravel. We have resolved, in part, the *pommes bleues* portion of this text. So, let us now consider the first portion.

BERGERE PAS DE TENTATATION QUE POUSSIN TENIERS GARDENT LA CLEF

We can accept that Bergers alludes to *Les Bergers d'Arcadie* but implies a reference to the shepherding of the searcher. In the interests of style, one has a tendency to insert ET between POUSSIN and TENIERS; one should never under estimate the importance of ET. We have discussed the importance of *pouce* in the geometry. *Pas de tentation* gives an allusion to Teniers with reference to the many paintings of St Anthony the hermit's resistance to temptation. The *pas de tentation* might mean that we should look at the painting in part only, excluding the tempting shepherdess or including the shepherdess only. It could also mean 'in the steps of temptation'. These are the accepted interpretations. The '*pouce*' is crucial in the geometry. A pun on '*pouce*' might be expected in the cipher. Without temptation '*que Poussin*'. 'Poussin without sin', or '*p**ouce*'. The 'in' might possibly be an abbreviation for inch. I feel another pun coming on. Do they have no respect for a name? 'Ten ears' or the shape of an ear in the ten figures that increment from the very small to the very large and make up the key, consisting of a square and an arc. It is uncertain whether a linguist would approve of these aberrations. However, if push came to shove, a Times crossword expert may not be averse to stooping to such depths.

* * *

Much has been achieved, but we have not given sufficient attention to our Master of instruction. How did Nicolas Poussin intend that the key should be created from *Les Bergers d'Arcadie*? We have achieved the rotation of the forefingers as they trace out the scythe shadow and the rotation of the head on the knee. These steps are certainly not entirely self-explanatory, so we need to identify where the key arcs and squares fall upon the painting as the moves progress. We must follow where we are lead and learn the lessons.

The Red Shepherd's index finger is moved down the painting as it follows the left side of the shadow. The Blue Shepherd's index finger, following the right side of the shadow forces the clockwise rotation of the overlay by 26.565 degrees when the overlay red shepherd's head aligns with his own knee. The Blue Shepherd is now wearing the white hat. As we know this angle it is possible to find the centre of rotation, knowing that it will fall on a line at right

Fig. 10. 5. The complex merge in *Les Bergers.d'Arcadie*.

Fig. 10. 6. The staffs match the key with sliding squares.

angles to the start and end index fingers as illustrated in Fig.
6.10. One definitive length, so far, is the distance moved by
the Red Shepherd's index finger, but the distance between
any two points on the superimposed images could equally
apply. For the sake of clarity, we shall name the lower copy
Primo (first) and the overlay we shall call *Secundo* (second).
As there are two main movements required to this point,
one could argue that the 'P – S' should be reserved for these
first two moves, but this arbitrary choice can stand at this
stage.

As the Red Shepherd's head spins counter-clockwise
(*Secundo* or S) upon his own knee, (*Primo* or P) he receives a
severe crick in his neck. As the forehead and the knee slide,
the actual centres of rotation are determined by intersecting
radii for the kneecap and similarly for the top of the face.
These two points are established and the centre of rotation
on the knee is confirmed when the 'E' and the 'R' are superimposed then the second 'R' with index finger is on the
knee. The third point that is fixed is the red shepherd's
index finger in his sandal loop. This is the only marked point
in what is now a straight line joining these three points. The
midpoint turns out to be the knee rotation point. To put you
in the picture, these three points are equidistant.

The horse of God moving across the heavens presents an
allegory for the arc traced by the Sun, and the critical angle
at midday on the 17th January springs to mind. We have now
achieved in this '*daemon of a guardien*' two halves of the key
represented by two mirror image Tau spirals. We have now
established that they can be centred on the two hands that
are central in the *Les Bergers d'Arcadie* painting. We also know

that the index fingers of these two hands were used to trace the outline of the shadow and to define specific points such as the white shoe fastening.

If we introduce the key to these two hands and then trace out, what does that produce? Before moving down that route, it is important to carefully study the painting. With both keys in position, the two staffs do not align with the boxes or squares. However, they would do if they were jointly slid upwards and to the right. Poussin is trying to tell us something because for the first time both squares would then match the tops of the staffs exactly when both of the staffs coincide with the boxes, as in Fig. 10.6. The sliding movement must surely be part of the system. Er we leave this, if the copy of the painting is slid to the left until the staff pokes the shepherdess in the eye her foot has advanced one pace and the 'E' coincides with the 'R'. The rotation point of the knee now bears the other 'R'. A faint 'PES' could be read diagonally across the back of the Blue Shepherd which, if followed up brings the 'R' to the end of the thumb. This enables the arc 'EG' to be drawn centred on the thumb tip. This does not seem a valid entry into the geometry and is not definitive despite being a step by the shepherdess.

We must check the direction and distance of movement of the boxes. This we see is achieved by sliding one box across itself so that the base of the box coincides with the original position of its top. Thus everything now matches except that the the P and S boxes do not exactly line up. The details must be absorbed and we can see that the distance moved is exactly equal to the width of a particular rectangle.

Returning to the position of the key on the Red

Shepherd's hand with the index fingertip at the arc node, the arm shadow replicates the arc. Slide the key along the line down from the arc node until the shadow curve matches the arc. The index fingertip now points to the Tau point and the two rectangular cells coincide. Note the various positions of the 'E's at each stage. Each step can be repeated for each curve of the shadow. The sequence being the outer curve of the shadow, the inner curve, the shadow of the head, the head and finally the beard. This brings the Blue Shepherd's staff in conjunction with the side of a square.

But how did we come to place the key on the hand in the first place? Though the little piece of white cloth above the tomb is an important golden mean centre. But exactly in the centre of the painting, as it appears in its frame without the extra uncleaned portion, there is a square with a large 'T', as indicated by the pointing finger. Surely, we must place the matching square over this. It fits! So do other significant points including an arc node resting on the partly obscured 'E' of 'EGO'. Not that one just yet; it has to be sinister and upside down! That is better, now the side of the square is parallel to the staff. Slide the key down from the arc node until a line matches the staff and the thumb line is in the right position. This is how the key is placed correctly to start.

For those who would skip to the end of the book for an easy answer to everything, avoiding the diligence you, the Reader have exercised, they will be unsuccessful. The method of manipulating the paintings is based on these last movements. But a reverse transparency is required to match the central square, slid sideways such that the hand of the White Shepherd is across the Red Shepherd's eye. With a Key for each transparency, the two reversed images can move in conjunction. Safe in this knowledge, the Reader will be able to enjoy the rest of the book without suffering the continued mental turmoil, as he reads between the lines. While the Author's continues his quest, wrestling with the key, the Reader will smile inwardly as the Author's struggles through darkness to discover these hard-won principles.

But what about the White Shepherd's staff? What is the angular relationship with the staff of the Red Shepherd? It is an understatement to say that it is difficult to determine Poussin's logic. There appears to be a seven to one Tau angle relationship between the two staffs, but how does this fit in? Abiding by the rules, one must place the dexter key with the centre line equal to the length of the Red Shepherd's staff upon that of the White Shepherd. This centre of the key matches his features to a T. Placing the sinister key to make a little skull with the dexter we find that the side of the square matches the Red Shepherd's staff exactly. We would expect nothing less from Nicolas, the Master. In completing this little exercise it can be seen that there are now two matching boxes that include the skull figure, the dexter and sinister could be slid across each other, should one so desire.

Both of the squares mid-points are set at the base of the White Shepherd's staff inviting a rotation centred there so that both squares coincide resulting in the White Shepherd's key centres on some matching foliage.

Regarding the relationship between the key and the left

hand, one must knead the dough once more to learn. It will
be noted that a match is achieved by using the arc to match
the hand. Again, a match is obtained by sliding the square.
Again, *lecis quod fecit,* learn what it does.

We seem to be establishing a relationship between the
two parts of the key, as used in certain relevant pictures.
One image may be slid across another, and we shall see how
this principle applies to the Marie de Nègre's tombstones.
The LIXLIXL at the bottom right of the stone is a repetition
of the letters LIX. With the first three letters are placed
over the next three, it produces a shift to the right, which is
repeated producing various effects. When generating the
mirror image by reversing one half of the key, turning the
key over from right to left, we must realise that a different
effect is obtained by turning the key over from the top to the
bottom, which would create an S effect with the curves.
This type of curve (an ogee) can be observed in *The Arcadian
Shepherds* at the right hand side of the tomb.

David Teniers the younger painted fine works depicting St
Anthony the Hermit bearing his Tau cross on his sleeve or
cowl. To demonstrate the sliding effect using the St Anthony
and St Paul painting with which many are familiar, we may
learn an important principle. The skull is superimposed
upon the cross using the mirror image of the painting. This
concept may have brought the Templars into disrepute when
the inquisition accused the Knights Templar of using a skull
in their rituals. By innuendo, it could appear that they were
engaged in dubious practices not in keeping with Christian
standards. In the Teniers painting, we must remember ET

IN ARC CARDIA EGO. With the back of the skull to the right of the cross, with the regulation rotation to the left, of 26.565 degrees we place a fine plumed hat on St Paul, while at the same time St Anthony dons a small Jewish skullcap. This demonstrates that the elaborate frame holding the painting may well have been the original frame, probably designed by Teniers. The idea of capping was encountered when *Les Bergers d'Arcadie* was first rotated. Now why would St Paul require such a plume? To answer this question the key must be applied. The plume on his hat exactly matches the 26.565 degrees when the key is used.

***

To give validity to the geometric pattern of the key and its relationship to paintings it was important to establish that it could not be applied to just any painting or collection of random lines In this important test failure met my every attempt to apply the key to random paintings not associated with the key yet it did confirm the complicity of Leonardo da Vinci and the Pre-Raphaelites.

To review progress and to take stock of what has been learned so far would be interesting. Do we have a clear understanding of the cipher? We have a formal design that has been extracted from various paintings and designs and which may have universal application in all the paintings or layouts. Though it matches line for line yet it still gives no answer as to what is intended. True, we can readily locate points on the ground by using this key in various ways. We still lack a proper sequence of events. The pattern or key may fit in the lock and will turn yet no creaking of rusted hinges or 'Open Sesame' is heard as the front of the tomb swings open on silent hinges. But to quote Sir William St Clair:

"If thou canst comprehend these things thou knowest enough." It is enough to make a start anyway.

"Bravo, you are beginning to learn the ways of Rennes." Two eyes you are. Two eyes you be. I see you are two eyes for me. Yes, we are beginning. Here we could end. We know that there is a cache of something of extreme value in a vault just a few metres below ground. We know its exact location, as indicated by the alignment of the shadow cast by the noonday sun on that fateful January day. We know the shape and approximate dimensions of the vault. We know that various people over the centuries were at great pains to record its presence but felt that it was important to not reveal the location.

It must be about time that the whole mystery should be exposed to the midday sun. The heart of the *pommes bleues* rotting core lies open to the world that the people may judge it for what it is in all its varying flavours. If we think that everything will be revealed and the ghosts of the past laid to rest, we delude ourselves. Certainly, we shall know what is buried there. Until that moment, we can speculate and pontificate. Many will covet and lay claim to it long before the first pickaxe rings against the ancient stones. Will more die before it is retrieved or perhaps when it has been retrieved? A solemn thought on which we all may dwell.

CHAPTER ELEVEN

SAUNIÈRE'S TOWER

A GPS sensor was the only way that I could establish once and for all the exact position of important locations such as the entrance to the main hoard at Rennes. I purchased a Garmin E-Trex Global Positioning System instrument on my return from Rennes. This handheld device looked like the current mobile phone and picked up the signal from the numerous orbiting satellites enabling it to display the location of the instrument to within a few metres. At that time the system was rather inaccurate as the signals transmitted from the satellites were subject to the built-in errors designed to deny an unfriendly power the extremely accurate tracking facility that might possibly make it easier to place a guided missile with great precision

on a strategic target. Nevertheless, it would be useful to
have such an instrument to give a guide to the position of the
various critical locations on the ground. The accuracy of the
altitude reading was also subject to this imposed variation
making these results virtually worthless. But I could always
work with the map contours combined with the altitude
reading using my tracing stereometer applied to the aerial
photos of the area. However, in May 2001, the USA
Government removed the built-in error factor and from
then on the E-Trex could be accurate to within fifteen feet
or four metres and I hoped that the accuracy of altitude
readings would show some improvement.

I needed another visit to Rennes-le-Château particularly
to photograph the drystone wall and to take GPS readings.
I purchased a folding saw and made my preparations. Rail
travel became a real alternative to flying to Carcassonne. I
needed a couple of days in Paris, and the new high-speed rail
to Perpignan via the Channel Tunnel and Paris had just been
introduced with a burst of low fares. Accompanied by my
wife, we opted for the rail trip with a break in Paris during
the forward journey on the Monday and a night stopover on
the Thursday night on our return. As it turned out,
Narbonne would have been a more convenient destination.

We had to pay a courtesy visit to the publishers of *Le Trésor
Maudit de Rennes-le-Château* at the Avenue Marceau on the
Monday. This was at the crucial time when I needed the
completion of the contract for the translation rights. This
book was an essential part of the strategy in my programme.
Gérard de Sède had completed the first major study of the

mystery in which he clearly defined many aspect of the background without indulging in flights of fancy or wild hypotheses based on leaps of logic. De Sède's book has formed the basis of most, if not all subsequent writings on the subject and any reiteration of this would be superfluous. Far better, I thought to achieve publication of the English translation attributing the honour where it so justly lay, for de Sède had picked up the tale and written an excellent objective study of the geography and historical events that surrounded the people and the places involved.

Because De Sède made such a good job of his research, we can all benefit from his work and come to grips with the problems. It can take the student from pure bafflement to a reasonable comprehension of the ciphers and challenges that faced the Priest of Rennes. That first translation was really for my benefit and was started by my father back in 1973 based on the copy I had purchased from Hachettes.

On leaving the publisher's office, situated on the Avenue Marceau, close to the River Seine, we took a pleasant stroll by the river as far as the Place de Carse at the entrance to the Louvre. The Richlieu Gallery held the French paintings of the XVII century. My memories of my previous visit were of a rather guarded access to the art treasures. The *Mona Lisa* was then preserved in subdued lighting in a special area. Now she gazes down upon the crowds from behind a special type of glass that protects this masterpiece from the effects of the constant popping of flash bulbs. It came as a shock to see the halls of the Louvre filled with camera enthusiasts and artists busy copying the great works of art.

Turning to one of the Louvre staff, I enquired about the artist busy at their easels. He told me that it was always open season at the Louvre for photographers and artists with the proviso that any copy made must differ from the original at least in the overall dimension of the painting else it could be deemed to be a forgery. The French take their art very seriously.

I had left my camera with our other baggage at the Gare de Lyon. I was determined to return with my camera on our way back from Rennes, as I had arranged a night stopover in Paris to order some more aerial photography. I needed a special photo of that part of *Les Bergers d'Arcadie* painting, which showed the old château and village. This could be identified by its similarity to the existing château with the distinctive shape and features of the same scene today as shown on the cover of *The Accursed Treasure*...

I well remember the scene from the last uncomfortable night spent on the hillside below the castle as I awoke on that cold grey morning with the dark outline of the château looming above me. I needed some good shots of the whole painting to work upon. Also I needed some photos of the ivy covered wall for the front cover. Originally I had intended to take these scenes from my photograph transparency that I had obtained from Florence. That photograph of *Les Bergers d'Arcadie* was taken in its pristine form, just after it had been given its first careful restoration and before it suffered at the hands of the later restorer. However, I would prefer to take my own photographs now that was a possibility.

Also, a couple of my own photos of the full painting

would come in handy for the work I still needed to do on the Poussin painting to recreate the results I had obtained a score of years earlier. I needed to draw out every nuance of meaning that the great artist had put into the preparation of the painting as he sat on the Poussin seat.

On reflection, much of that work must have been in the form of sketches to be carefully set into the painting behind the locked doors of his studio. Each of the sketches would contribute to build his masterpiece. With his combination of precision and technique, he created his message to the world. He did however believe that his work would never be completely understood. Perhaps he was right about that too. But he left nothing to chance.

Fig. 11. 1. The tower in bygone days.

When we found Room 33 in the Richlieu gallery of the Louvre, the painting was hanging at eye level. Amazingly only a cord separated it from the public. The painting, which had occupied so much of my thoughts, was right there before my very eyes, so I was able to examine every detail.

I had not come prepared as I had left my magnifying loop in my baggage and, from the front of the painting, I was unable to find any trace of the holes in the canvas that were reputed to be visible from the back of the painting. Truly deceptive in its uncomplicated appearance, the apparent simplicity of the design surprised me though this painting was so precise in its dimensions and angles. Perhaps some of the fine detail had been cleaned off over the centuries and it had that dark tinge associated with old varnish. Certainly, we know about the cleaned area on the horizon to the right of the tomb that altered the painting's earlier appearance some time after the Scala photograph was taken. This renovation of master-pieces is not without its hazards. We decided that we would revisit the Louvre, armed with my camera, during our stopover in Paris on our return journey. We left the Richlieu gallery and took the Metro to the Gare de Lyon to catch the Eurostar to Perpignan.

We did not reach Perpignan until midnight and picked up our self-drive car the next morning. The magnificent scenery kept us in awe as we drove to Quillan through mountains cut by deep gorges where river and road jousted for pride of place. We stopped for lunch at Quillan before pressing on to Couiza where we branched off to join the steep winding road that led up to Rennes-le-Château. We drove through the village and parked where the magnificent view across the Aude and Sals Rivers stretched before us.

The hilltop empire of Bérenger Saunière was created in part to disburse untold quantities of money and in part to preserve even greater treasures. He had built the road to the village. The winding route he planned for this road was very different from the direct route from the castle at Rennes leading directly towards Couiza Montazels. Yet, the new road had the advantage of linking more villages. Part of the route led near to the area where the Rennes main treasure remained hidden. Access to this spot from the old road was not an easy matter. Yet, the new road gave no obvious clue to the hoard unless one was aware of the alignment of the portion of the road as it zigzagged up the steep hillside.

The little St Madeleine Church, with its many strange clues built into the striking architectural features, produced an awareness of its deeper significance, as did the monument bearing the inscription *Mission 1892* that Saunière built to commemorate his remarkable challenge. The villa Bethania, built to his own design remains enigmatic in its message and was used to cater for the needs of his distinguished house guests. Overlooking the fields at the northern end of the belvedere or walkway that curved along the ramparts, Saunière had positioned his glass-covered orangery with its conical spire.

At the other end of the walkway, at the extreme south west of the village, stood the square tower, the Tour Magdala, with its cylindrical staircase winding up to the flat roof which gave such a magnificent view for miles. A still finer panorama was spread before the crenellated top of the *échauguette*, which stood some four metres above the square tower roof. However, this magnificent aspect was denied to the masses, as there was no visible means of access. All these edifices were startling to the eye and shrieked of mystery and intrigue.

I looked across in the direction of the treasure and could
see that the tower was situated so far to the south west that
it was necessary to look diagonally across the walkway,
through the conservatory to locate the spot. Even then, it
was partly obscured by a tree that had sprung up over the
years at just the wrong location. Knowing what great pains
the Priest had gone to in order to construct his tower there,
and being aware of his emphasis on detail, there must have
been an important reason behind his choice of location. My
interest was centred on the alignment with the orangery
spire.

The wily Priest made it difficult to gain access to certain
parts of his domain, such as to the *échauguette* or to his small
quadrant-shaped room with the bulls-eye window accessed
by a concealed door or even to his pulpit.

Bérenger Saunière was said to have had a cannon hidden
in the tour Magdala. Rumours were widespread during the
Great War. Was this just a malicious lie spread by those souls
who revelled in those few times when our Priest was
strapped for cash? The rumour of Saunière's canon might
well have been based on a chance remark that he made.
Access to the very top of the *échauguette* or round tower was
denied to all except those privileged few Saunière allowed
to climb his ladder. Certainly, it was not to fire his imagined
cannon! Where would he have concealed it? Where but out
of sight, at the top of the round tower, ready to be run out
to menace the surrounding countryside? Saunière was a
man of peace. They may have observed our Priest taking

compass readings and angles from this vantage point. Obviously, he was pinpointing possible targets for a future hail of grape shot.

The imagined cannon was concealed from the gaze of the villagers but was not impervious to their snide gossiping. An archer could stand atop the high tower built to contain the circular staircase and provide a watch-tower. Its centre would lie exactly above one corner of the Tour Magdala at N 42° 55' 41.4" E 02° 15' 44.2" Alt.524m (level with the top of the stair). There the archer could peer through any one of the firing slots and direct his arrow in any direction, just like looking through a gun sight of a cannon. He could not fail to see the shining point above the glazed orangery like a beacon on the walls of Rennes-le-Château.

Fig. 11. 2. The silent vigil of the guardian rock.

Now if he were to descend the anti-clockwise winding staircase from Saunière's Magdala tower in the 'trick of the corner' or *tour de coin*, he could descend into the long gallery below the belvedere As he walked along he could gaze out through the four circular windows as the gallery curved round. At the far end of the gallery he would be faced with another spiral staircase, which led up to the very centre of the circular beacon, formed at the corner of his orangery. If he was to align his sights from the highest point on his tower and drew mightily on his bow, his arrow would fail to strike gold but would come to rest in the fields below the castle or strike the trees now grown over the years. Yet, his line of sight would extend to a deserted point below on the hillside, where it would be certain to strike gold. There would be a line of rocks forming a drystone wall. One stone, shaped like the head of a shepherd long dead, would gaze upwards through the mists of time with unseeing eyes towards the archer. This was the death's head stone set to watch over the treasure of Rennes-le-Château. It is there; a death's head! Any arrow falling there would strike true to the heart-shaped *pommes bleues*. For Sion is the pure in heart and it is Sion where the treasure lies.

Yet, no arrow could pierce the heart so deeply nor inflict a wound so painful or hard to bear as the wound to Marie Denarnaud's heart when she exclaimed in her anguish,

"It is finished." It was at the fateful time when the Priest and the architect passed from the world of Rennes. A heart replaced by the empty eye sockets of a skull. To Marie the gold of Rennes became but dross. No matter that the crenellated tower formed the back sight for the bowman's aim and the foresight formed by the orangery spire lined up exactly with the midi of the *pommes bleues*. Here lay the ancient site carefully sculpted into the scenery of ancient Rhedae. It blended unnoticed into the background of land, cultivated in part, but interspersed with steep, rugged areas, which were only kept in check by the sheep and goats.

The treasure could lie hidden for another century for it could never restore the splendour that existed under the ever-watchful eye of François Bérenger Saunière. The dense layer of bushes would always cover the skull shaped rock unless some wild prospector would hack them to the ground. Now an English oak sapling is planted there and marks the spot for posterity at WGS84, N 42^0 55',56.9" E 02^0 15' 39.5" altitude 410 metres. The altitude reading is based on average sea level at Marseille and these true north figures are 3.5 seconds west of the 3615 IGN map grid north at Rennes-le-Château.

Time spent at Rennes-le-Château could not be used in reminiscing and there is always plenty to do. Much of my day was taken up with GPS readings as close as we could get to the points of particular interest. The drystone wall required several readings at both ends of the cavern site. The folding saw came in handy. With much effort, I managed to squeeze down between the wall and the bushes. I ended up with my feet in the air and was able to saw enough of the branches away to be able to take some photographs of the skull rock. On the way back to the village, I leapt into the long grass to locate one of the shepherds' square huts and took GPS readings for that, being N 42⁰ 55',52.9" E 02⁰ 15' 39.5" altitude 432 metres.   Opposite the rectangular entrance to the hut there was some arc-shaped stonework that replicated a node point with a hole in the centre. The other hut, which is rather more dilapidated, is situated next to the path and so it was easy to obtain that GPS reading of N 42⁰ 55',49.4" E 02⁰ 15' 49.7" altitude 452 metres.

Fig. 11. 3. A shepherd's hut built to stand the test of time.

Another point of immediate interest was of course the *échauguette* but it was not practical to take a reading exactly on top of it without a ladder so an additional four metres needed to be added to the GPS altitude reading. Also the GPS reading for the orangery spike was needed, but this had to be verified later as the metal framing obscured the signal from the satellites making it difficult to obtain an accurate reading. An additional amount of three metres was added to the altitude reading, which was taken at ground level, to estimate the height of the curiously shaped spike on the top of the orangery spire. However, GPS readings are not always reliable when overhead obstructions are present and accuracy dropped from four metres to thirty metres so that exercise might have been purely academic. As we drove down the hill to Couiza, we took several readings at the 372 metre spot height at the bend in the road marked on the map where a little stream flows. This is probably the flow from the *Lacrimae Magdala*. This location was at N 42⁰ 55',59.0" E 02⁰ 15' 51.0" altitude 372 metres. The accuracy shown on the ETrex was within four metres and the readings for altitude did prove to be in agreement with the map, thus increasing my confidence in the other altitude readings.

We spent a long time time in the Church and took some photos of Asmodeus and his friends including the life size model of the man bearing a cross that was set at an angle other than the regulation 26.565 degrees. The architecture including the fourteen stations of the cross absorbed our interest. Our visit to the church was followed by a meal at the Pommes Bleues restaurant but we did not eat any Helix Pomatia. They are far too convoluted for me.

The following day we visited Rennes-les-Bains. We called at the Church there but the building was locked. However, the churchyard was open and was most interesting but we were of course unable to see the Rennes *Lapin* painting, mentioned by de Sède, (*The Accursed Treasure...* page 111) which was a pity. We returned via Axat to Perpignan after a delightful drive through the breathtaking scenery.

It was not until 11th March 2002 that we returned to the Louvre to take some photographs of *Les Bergers d'Arcadie*.

The Louvre was open on this visit and on entering the Richlieu Gallery my eyes first fell upon Nicolas Poussin as he gazed out from his self-portrait with a look, which I thought to be a little condescending, wistful in his inner thoughts as he contemplated the proportions of his masterpieces.

"Why should I cast these grains of truth before the masses who would rake through the husks; but never in centuries to come will they savour the kernels of wisdom they contain? They will trample down the corn and never glean the fruits of my labour."

Perhaps he would be resentful of my intrusion with my camera into his private sanctuary, or would he welcome the appreciation, if only in part, of his genius?

A row of seats ran down the centre of the Richlieu gallery providing a luxury only experienced by those who have walked the long corridors of the Louvre or abandoned the sanctuary of the sunny kerbside tables of the Rive Gauche to tread the streets of Paris. From this comfortable vantage point, I was able to study the familiar lines of the *Les Bergers d'Arcadie*, which hung on the far wall. Although the picture has been cleaned at least once, the darkened varnish masked much of the brightness of the colouring that surely existed in the mid-seventeenth century. Now, it seemed difficult to pick out the fine detail. Perhaps this was why Nicolas

Poussin's gaze was somewhat askance from his self-portrait on the adjoining wall. The horizon on the far right of the painting had certainly changed over the last few decades revealing more sky than was previously visible. A deliberate attempt to disfigure the painting is not at all likely though it would not be the first Poussin masterpiece to be attacked and vandalised in recent years, possibly by a person who thought he knew more than he did. Time had taken its toll.

Yet, the ageless painting retained some information, which I had come to check. Part of the dark mass on the skyline in the very centre of the painting bore a strong resemblance to the photograph I had taken from the hillside to the north of the château where I had slept on that cold and windy night in March 2001. The difference being that the castle now had no dark mass to its right. The burning question was whether a detailed examination of the painting would show this to be a rugged outcrop of rock – it did bear a certain resemblance to Rocco Nègre, or a round tower, castellated, standing guard over the château and town of Rennes as seen by Poussin in the middle of the seventeenth century.

Gérard de Sède spoke of a tower that was in existence in the past when the town was besieged and the walls breached (see pages 82 and of *The Accursed Treasure* …). Fortifications may be breached but it takes several centuries of transporting stone for new building works to completely remove a structure as massive as a defensive tower.

In order to examine closely the dark mass above the tomb in *Les Bergers d'Arcadie*, I took several photographs of the area around the top of the tomb while in the Louvre. I compared these with my transparencies using a magnifying glass, the combined 3X optical zoom, and the 2.5X digital zoom at various exposures with my Olympus Camedia. I had bought the digital camera to provide the TIF images needed for the illustrations in the book. Careful examination of the photos confirmed that the painting appeared to represent a circular, castellated tower, elongated to join with the castle of Rennes-le-Château. The possible foundations appeared to run along the existing line of the perimeter path to the north west of the village. The is a line of rocks just to the north west of the belvedere that might have served as the original foundations. The ancient water pump is practically outside the existing wall and might have had some exterior fortification to protect the vital resource against attack.

The tower contained a dark patch similar to a window, though larger than one might expect to find in an ancient defensive structure. The impression was that Poussin had intended that portion of the painting to represent the skull hitherto so conspicuous by its absence, until the first turn of the key unlocked the tomb and its grizzly secrets.

Other paintings have proved far easier to interpret. It was reasonable to assume that Poussin meant to portray the village as he saw it from the treasure site on the hillside whilst depicting a possible skull for the diligent searcher. If the painting did indeed give a true picture of the village as seen from the treasure site, then that alone would have been sufficient reason for King Louis XIII to keep the painting locked in his private chambers for many years, as is claimed.

The GPS results were transferred to the aerial photos and related to the map. This enabled me to establish the exact locations of places of interest and gave sufficient information to review the feasibility of the new tower that Saunière was planning to build. Analysis of the GPS results revealed that the horizontal distance of 482 metres separates the hoard from the *échauguette*, which Saunière has positioned as far south as possible. Should Saunière have wished to make a more permanent pointer to the hoard, then he could well have determined to build the new tower like the former tower that had watched over the hillside for centuries.

If the passage of time and the challenges of life and death removed the few who held the knowledge, the key and its purpose, what then? What would become of the remaining apprentices? Life is precarious now; it was so in Saunière's day. Was he prepared to leave this life on that day in 1917? Had he made proper provision for the key? Yes, if he had left a puzzle that was not inscrutable! Yes, if he had passed the key to his soul mate, Marie. Yes, if he had exhausted all the funds in the coffers and caches. Nevertheless, Bérenger had just drawn up plans to construct a new and exciting building programme. What was the justification for this sudden expense, and why was it particularly important to our Priest, when he had so recently recovered from a period of financial calamity and was not in the best of health? He could have been motivated by an urge to clarify or alter the detail of the great enigma that Saunière had created by his earlier building exploits. It seems that he felt compelled to leave for posterity yet another pointer to the treasure he guarded and to the key that he held.

Using the 26.565 degree gradient would generate a height of half the horizontal distance, being 241 metres. The altitude of the hoard is 410 metres and the altitude of the level ground at the Tour Magdala is 507 metres. If the new tower were to be built in the most northerly position where the new wall around the village would stand, it would lie approximately on the 500 metre contour line (see appendix D). The distance between the hoard and the tower would then be 380 metres when measured horizontally. The Golden angle would require a vertical height of 190 metres. 90 metres of this would be provided by the steep hill, being 500 less 410 metres. The perimeter wall could be as much as thirty metres high if necessary. The existing wall is not far short of this in places. Saunière would then have to build a tower of 70 metres height at the most northerly point in order to fulfil his requirements. The building works would provide a good earner for the villagers, return to circulation a supply of finance and provide a permanent feature for the village. In addition, the valuable hoard would be identified eventually, assuming someone could interpret his message to posterity or until the Poussin painting could be fully understood, so permitting the architect to rest in peace.

CHAPTER TWELVE

ROSSLYN CHAPEL

Even a small diversion from our tale might provide a welcome break from the obsession with the key so perhaps a discussion about middle-eastern temples might be in order. Asmodeus, the mythical keeper of the treasure of Solomon's Temple, went through some difficult episodes as the Temple was desecrated and despoiled from time to time. Robbed of its treasures by various kings, it was later cleansed by Josiah and Hezekiah. Finally, Solomon's Temple was burned to the ground and destroyed by Nebuchadnezzar. All the valuables therein were carried into Babylon. However, the vessels were preserved and returned under Darius and Cyrus.

The layout of the Temple of Solomon was repeated in

later temples and one might assume that the Temple of Zerubbabel was of similar design and was sited where the former Temple had stood. The Persian kings provided the materials from Sidon for its construction.

This Temple of Zerubbabel underwent turbulent times, with pollution and pillage similar to that suffered by Solomon's Temple. Perhaps it would be unfair to blame this upon Asmodeus. However, this Temple survived Herod's actual assault but was partly destroyed by fire when Herod captured Jerusalem in 37 B.C. The Lord does not take kindly to the pollution of His Holy House and when Ptolemy Philopator entered the Holy of Holies in 217 B.C. he was carried from the temple courts more dead than alive after having been smitten. Even in the time of Moses, when the Tabernacle served as the mobile temple of the Israelites, the High Priest entered the Holy of Holies, only after much purification, just once a year on the Day of Atonement. Then, as in subsequent Jewish temples, the High Priest entered with a long cord tied round his waist so that, should he be smitten, he could be drawn out by means of the cord.

Contemporary to the era of the Temple of Zerubbabel, at the time of Alexander the Great, Tyre was besieged and a Temple was constructed, contrary to Mosaic law, on Mount Gerizim in Samaria. Manasseh was the Temple's first High Priest but those Jews who had violated the Mosaic Law used this Temple. This undoubtedly led to friction between the inhabitants of Samaria and the orthodox Jews. This enmity seems to have still prevailed whilst Jesus walked the Earth. Even in those days, the religious observances of Samaria were clearly regarded by the Jews to be counterfeit worship.

However, the Samaritans made minor adjustments to the text of their Pentateuch in Deuteronomy 27:4, where they substituted the location, 'Gerizim' for 'Ebal'. In Exodus 20, they made a small change to the text, thereby achieving divine authority for the site to their own satisfaction. It was recorded that Hadrian later erected a temple of Jupiter Capitolinus on the site. This location still has some religious significance for the Samaritans even to this day. Such is the tortuous nature of many men that they would presume to manipulate the mind of God to ensure that He is compliant to their every whim. However much they might delude themselves, certainly to their own gratification, they are unlikely to secure the approval of The Almighty; much less His compliance.

Herod, after eighteen weary years of ruling over the Jews, felt that to the best way to win their favour would be to rebuild the Temple of Jerusalem on the same site that the previous temples had occupied. He amassed the materials before the commencement of building operations. The foundations had to be built up from the valley in places, to establish an area with sides of approximately one hundred and eighty metres in length. The overall area formed approximately a square and was considerably larger than the area on which the previous temples had stood.

Once the building materials were assembled, the work was entrusted to the hallowed hands of the Priests. Construction of the Temple itself took less than two years, though completion of the cloisters and outer enclosures took a further eight years. Work on the site continued until about six years before the Temple was destroyed once again.

'Titus conquers Judea and lays Jerusalem waste, killing six hundred thousand people.' (Esubius, *Chronicle*, Vespasian 2, A.D.70).

Nevertheless, the Temple of Herod was in full service during the time that Christ was on the earth and various incidents that took place in the Temple are recorded in the Gospels. Surely, the Temple was important in the unfolding of events during the life and death of Christ, not the least being the moment when the Veil of the Temple was rent at the time that Christ died upon the cross at Calvary. Thus, the site of the Temple was again polluted and the Lord again withdrew His presence. The Temples were constructed to the honour of God in the hope that he would accept the offering and come to His Holy House.

Yet, the Temples were built for man that he would be able to partake of the ordinances that formed such an important part of the relationship of man with his God. The sacrifices that were laid upon the altars of the temples and upon the mountain tops when no Temple existed, were tributes to God yet the ordinances and history of the Children of Israel have always been a schoolmaster's lesson to His pupils. Has not the whole history of the Israelites and more specifically the religious history of the Jewish nation served as a series of examples to them? Was not Isaac prepared to submit as a sacrifice to God at the hand of his father, Abraham? Has not the sacrifice of a lamb without blemish been offered throughout the Jewish history as an acceptable sacrifice? On the Day of Atonement, were not two goats prepared to bear the sins of the nation; the one being allowed to go free and the other to be sacrificed? Was not Jonah restored after three days within a whale? Isaiah and other prophets spoke clearly of the great sacrifice that was to come. Christianity owes most of its scriptures to the Jewish nation, without which we would have little religious heritage and very little of the Bible.

One of the problems with this saga is that it has so many profound implications that one is wary of plunging in, out of one's depth. The Masons and of course, the Templars have always held that they have preserved many of the features surrounding the sacred ordinances of the Temple of Jerusalem. One aspect of this story hinges upon this theme, revolving around the requirement that the Jewish Priesthood and nation should have their temple vessels restored to them, that they might again make an offering in righteousness. There presently exists a hundred and twenty Christian temples throughout the World using many of the original temple ordinances on a regular basis. The temples have been operating with full probity and authority since the middle of the nineteenth century. No secret combination or deep mystery was ever required to establish them so perhaps we must view the subject in its true perspective. Returning to *Les Bergers d'Arcadie*, the same principle of superimposing the skull image upon the cross should apply.

However, when prophecy was fulfiled with Christ's death on the cross, many were unable to recognise this great event and inestimable gift for what it was. Many there are who would use the mysteries surrounding the treasures of Rennes-le-Château to weave a web of doubt around the death of Christ and his resurrection. Wondrous hypotheses have gone forth from the void created by questions left unanswered. The only way to penetrate the veil of darkness that shrouds the vaults of Rennes, where a web of intrigue is spun in a nest of mystery, is to open up the vaults. When the light of day shines upon the hidden things that have lurked for too long in the minds of men then the veil of darkness will be rent and the true contents will be revealed.

Such is the power of this mystery that many have followed trails, which lead them away from the standard Judeo-Christian beliefs into strange paths of mysticism. If we can but dispel the illusions, then truth will stand in its own right. The closer we can come to truth the more the mind will be enlightened and we will gain greater understanding of things as they are.

Sir Isaac Newton dedicated his life studies in many spheres yet in every case he was driven by an overwhelming search for truth wherever it might be found. His great work in the study of light was not simply research into the various properties and composition of white light, and how its rays could be divided into various colour components. It was part of his lifelong journey into the light of truth and his quest for Deity. In science, he sought that great engineer and scientist of the universe who controls all by wonderful forces working together in what we regard as nature. In the seventeenth century our comprehension of the laws of physics and chemistry was awakening. Not least of these studies were geometry and the laws of mathematics. Sir Isaac made many exciting discoveries in his lifetime and delved deep into what then were mysteries in order to find truth. There has never been a discovery from that day to this in the field of invention, where the desire for knowledge was not the prevailing force in working upon the mind of the searcher to aid his choice between truth and error. Nor do the fruits of success depend on the suitability of the searcher but rather upon his diligence, or even on pure chance; or perhaps some divine plan intervenes to bring the light of knowledge to his understanding. The pliable mind of man can be turned in certain directions to accomplish ends that we cannot always foresee.

On the other hand, the mind that becomes obsessed with myths and fantasies sees through a glass, darkly. The way before lies down twisted paths into a forest of confusion that numbs the desire to escape. False trails of flawed logic lead us on into a deep morass of error. Sir Isaac Newton is famous for his thoughts on gravity. A visit to his resting place in Westminster Abbey will throw a new light on his passing if we view his resting place, key in hand. There are other places of interest that may be viewed in relationship to our Rennes-le-Château discoveries. The complexity of the key would seem to indicate that the Knight Templars used this method of concealment in several other locations where security was paramount. Such other sites might be Templar Commanderies, where wealth and even treasures might be stored. The Knights Templar are reputed to have excavated under and around Herod's Temple during their occupancy of Jerusalem and later they became the bankers of Europe. They learned to conceal their wealth with great cunning.

To gain an insight into the ascent of the Knight Templars, the following passage from the archives of the Commanderie of Coulommiers provides a glimpse into the fortunes of the Knight Templars at the end of the thirteenth and opening of the fourteenth centuries. The treasures acquired by the Templars were founded upon the donations of the faithful, but finally led to the downfall of that order.

In November 1294, Philippe le Bel (who was at that time, generously disposed towards the Temple...) and his wife, Jeanne, queen of France and of Navarre, Countess of Champagne, grants to The Templars of Brie the right of possessing, with amortisation and exemption from all other dues, several possessions belonging to them by acquisition.

In 1301, Madame Lore, of the Grange-Justain barn, makes faith offerings and homage of three arpents of woodland called le Buisson de la Grange (the Bush of the Barn), situated in the cultural centre of Essette and this homage is received at Coulommiers by Raoul, the brother of Giry, Commander of the baillie of Brie.

In October 1306, Daisy, widow of Jean Brisecolet, gives, bestows and leaves for perpetuity to the brothers of the Knighthood of the Temple of Coulommiers and to their successors the half of a house that she possessed, located near the mill of Osche, which was situated in the census district of the Knights.

Thus, the possessions accumulated by the Templars of Coulommiers until the time of their arrest in 1307 were considerable. The grants often were very modest; gifts of lesser people (four muids of wheat in 1201) and there were from time to time donations of greater importance (the four hundred arpents of Thibaut of Champagne). Ernest Dessaint recalls for us elsewhere in his history of

Coulommiers 'The possessions of the Templars were very important.' The domain of those of Coulommiers spread to Aulnoy, Montanglaust, le Theil, and comprised even the actual area of the entrance to Meaux. Thibaut IV, Count of Champagne and of Brie, became alarmed by such power wielded by those who could, at any moment, challenge his authority. He carried this complaint before King Louis IX, who decided that the Templars would not henceforth be permitted to make further acquisitions in Champagne and in Brie without the authorisation of the Count. 'We will mention confirmation of this fact farther, where directly concerning the commanderie of Coulommiers', according to the interrogations of certain 'legal process' of some Templars. In fact the domains of the commanderie of the Temple of Coulommiers spread throughout an area of about ten to fifteen kilometres around the commanderie, all on the right bank of the Grand Morin. The Templar possessions situated on the left bank (to the south of the river) belonged to the commanderie of Chevru. Probably this geographical distribution is due to the fact that the right bank of the Grand Morin came under the jurisdiction of the Bishopric of Meaux, while the left bank of the river was dependant upon that of Sens. The Hospitaliers were to continue with this distribution of the properties later on, even after the modifications to limit the powers of some bishoprics. The land of the commanderie of Coulommiers then extended as far as beyond La Ferté-sous-Jouarre.

As the Templars achieved increased power and financial control, King Philip the Fair of France was experiencing some difficult times and was thwarted by the power wielded by the Templars. Even in 1306, he and Queen Blanche had been kindly disposed towards the Knight Templars and had made bequests. It suited his purpose to arrest the Templars and falsely charge them with a number of crimes. To achieve his ends, the King stooped to have the inquisition extract confessions from the Templars by torture after having coerced the Pope by threats of similar false accusations.

How precarious was it to live in medieval times? How much was a life really worth, particularly in the days of the inquisitions and purges when the powers in control felt threatened by the rapid rise in the influence of the Templars? Many noblemen and even kings owed money to the Templars, having borrowed to finance their ambitions and wars. They coveted the Templar castles, land and vassals, but more particularly they coveted the wealth and the power wielded by the Templars.

On that fateful Friday 13th October 1307 the Templars were arrested in their hundreds and forced to yield up their lands. Many were burnt and tortured to death to persuade them to repent of their heresies, or more particularly to force them, by any means, to reveal the key to the locations of their gold. Doubtless, a purge of this magnitude and cost had not been undertaken for purely high aesthetic reasons, for the welfare of the eternal soul of man alone.

Many souls departed this life enduring varying degrees of discomfort at that time, bearing with them their secrets and their oaths. It is likely that the knowledge of the key could have passed to the perpetrators and eventually to the Holy See or to King Philip the Fair. Such is the frailty of mankind, particularly for those being hung, drawn and quartered;

eviscerated (sounds painful) while their wives and children were forced to watch. The inquisitors, who had clearly earned their reward in heaven, could then congratulate themselves on having dispatched a large consignment of souls and suitably mortified flesh back to their maker for further processing.

Perhaps the King's real objective for the purge was known to a very few, whereas the Inquisition was concerned with questions relating to the transgressions of the Templars, so that they might gain absolution by repenting of their wicked ways. Doubtless King Philip the Fair would have concentrated on more apposite questions, such as,

"Where have you hidden the treasure?"

Few there were in France who escaped the Inquisition and the purges. Many fled to Scotland and other safe havens and possibly some sailed to the Americas with the maritime wing of the Templars. Much was lost yet there was much that was preserved. The key by which the Templars marked their hoards was complicated and not easily understood. Confusion could arise when information is extracted under duress as one's body is being torn limb from limb and it is not the bowels of compassion that can be seen glistening in the cheery glow of branding irons in a brazier of hot coals. A key is a great device, yet without a keyhole or door, it loses much of its usefulness. Thus many an over-zealous inquisitor was robbed of what he might regard as his just reward — at least until he too met his maker.

Overwhelmed by an urge to win absolution from the insistence and powerful persuasion of the inquisitive prelates, the luckless Templars perhaps revealed all. And on discovering that one leg had suddenly become longer than its partner and racked with remorse, who could blame any one of them?

As a small gesture of gratitude and as an additional *aide memoire* from those zealous seekers after truth and light, the torturers would perhaps adjust the other leg to match, before dispatching another soul to join that great majority. We know not whether the inquisition would have granted absolution for these tortured spirits and then released their troubled minds from the burden of hidden treasure and dreadful oaths or whether this would only come as they drank the final libation from the bitter cup of death. How else could this great secret survive within the realms of the Holy See?

Who can lay claim to such treasures? Many there were who sailed under the flag associated with the maritime arm of the Templars. The privateers or pirates sailed under the Jolly Roger at the command of kings and queens to wage maritime warfare. Under this flag, much destruction was wrought upon the enemy and much bloody murder, rape, pillaging and the sacking of whole towns took place. The Jolly Roger, so familiar to the Templars, bore the skull and cross that appear on many Templar graves. This familiar Masonic symbol requires the keys to be but placed upon its macabre form to reveal it for what it is!

What is the significance of the name Jolly Roger, if it was indeed used extensively as a Templar symbol? The ways of Rennes would suggest 'EGO' reversed with an 'R' at each end as in 'REGOR'. Naturally, the key will fit perfectly upon a correctly designed set of skull and cross bones. It does wreck one fine quotation to say,

"Egos are like onions; they have layers."

*   *   *

Let us peel some of the layers from the Knight Templars of that era. Elaborate designs such as those depicting a fully sculpted effigy of the knight, were the prerogative of more prominent members of the order. These more detailed carvings show that the knights were buried in an unusual position, with one leg crossed behind the other. This has given rise to speculation that this position made the deceased's legs form the letter 'X', which is the last letter of the Hebrew alphabet, (Tau), which symbolises death. The urge to generate mysticism from mystery seems practically irresistible to the human mind. Mysticism has ever been a source of wealth and power. There are those who will seek a connection with the esoteric in everything. In mediaeval times where knowledge was limited, this may have had more justification.

Many Templars managed to escape the great purge of Friday the thirteenth and by no means all the Templars were arrested. Among those who avoided arrest was the St Clair family. They settled in Scotland and built the Rosslyn Chapel adjacent to Rosslyn Castle near Edinburgh at Roslin.

The building is well preserved, having escaped the destruction that befell many churches. The Chapel has been constructed on a similar layout to the plans of the Temple of Jerusalem as understood by the Knights Templar. The style of architecture is heavily accented to the Templar symbolic style and uses the dimensions and ratios known to them in the fourteenth century. Many of those ancient crafts have now dwindled into obscurity and have been replaced by the new style of Masonry developed in the eighteenth century.

Not only is Rosslyn Chapel constructed in true Templar architectural style but also it is claimed that within those ancient walls lie relics taken from Herod's Temple that were carried back to where the Rosslyn chapel was to be built to house those sacred relics.

During their occupancy of Jerusalem, the Knights Templar took more than a passing interest in the ancient ruins of the Temple in the city that they had fought so hard to win. During this period when the Knights Templar had control of the site of the ancient Temple of Jerusalem, they carried out excavations in an attempt to locate a tunnel that might lead to the repositories and to the sacred areas. If the Temple were to be attacked, those officiating in the holy places of the Temple would have to remove themselves with great haste from the sacred area. For this purpose, a special passageway was required. This has been located and remains sealed now. The Templars' exploration reputedly met with some success and they undertook extensive excavations into the foundations. The St. Clair family are the descendants of one of the original thirteen Knights and now this family are the custodians of Rosslyn Chapel a few miles outside Edinburgh, Scotland.

It appears likely that during their explorations in Jerusalem they did find certain emblems and artefacts that had been concealed by the Priests of Levi during or before the sacking of the Temple by the Romans. What would the Priests need to hide? One can imagine the scenes of panic as the High Priest received the news of the attack. He would have experienced feeling of despair that the judgements of The Almighty had once more fallen upon the nation. However, the well-rehearsed emergency plan would swing into action and delaying tactics would be adopted whilst the High Priest would purify himself before his entering the Holy of Holies with fear and trepidation to retrieve the sacred emblems.

Perhaps the sacred areas of the Temple would require it to be de-sanctified to permit removal of the contents of this sacred place. This routine must have been undertaken on a regular basis as the Children of Israel travelled for forty

Fig. 12. 1. The dramatic architecture has a story to tell.

years in the wilderness with their mobile temple.

Streams of Levites would transfer everything sacred to secret vaults. To satisfy a greedy army intent on destruction and desecration, gold and silver would be carried to selected points together with strategically placed replica artefacts. The secret vaults would then be sealed in the most cunning manner to delude the foe.

Such sacred objects, thought to comprise, amongst other things, a copper scroll must surely be preserved in a special way befitting their status. Sir William St Clair, last Prince of Orkney, conceived the design of Rosslyn Chapel in 1446. The construction is based on the Knight Templar concepts of design current during that era. Some of the descendants of those original thirteen knights hold the title deeds to the Rosslyn Templar chapel. It remains part of the tradition of the St. Clair family, who now preside over the chapel, that some of the sacred artefacts from that original Knights Templar dig found their way into the possession of Sir William St Clair. He had gone to great pains in the fifteenth century to design and build the chapel in order to replicate Herod's Temple, including a replica of some of the temple ruins. The purpose of this is supposedly to provide a secure resting place for those precious relics retrieved from beneath Herod's Temple. The architecture of Rosslyn Chapel is rich in Templar symbolism and the layout, based on the original Temple design, provides a fitting repository for the sacred artefacts. On the floor plan of Rosslyn, the two pillars that figure so prominently in Masonic ritual are shown. These two pillars named Jacinth and Boaz are richly decorated with complex designs and symbolism.

The tradition remains that one of the copper scrolls, of great religious significance in the Judeo-Christian religions, is concealed somewhere in or near the Chapel. The secret of its location is supposed to be concealed and revealed in the elaborate architecture.

It is reasonable to suppose that the system of concealment would be the Knight Templar method. If the Templar key related to the floor plan of Herod's Temple then it should still fit Rosslyn Chapel.

There is within the Masonic Royal Arch Degree, the Companion Jewel, which is in the form of a double triangle. This jewel bears certain relevant inscriptions, including the following:

Nil nisi clavis deest; Nothing is wanting but the key. Also there is written:

Si tatlia jungere possis sit tibi scire posse, translated as: If thou canst comprehend these things, thou knowest enough.

Should the key be related to the Knights Templar, then it should prove effective to resolve the location of the main reported item that is claimed to be lodged at the Chapel.

In this research into this jewel, I am indebted to the authors of *The Hiram Key* by Christopher Knight and Robert Lomas. Having an interest in the literature on this general subject I was reading about this jewel and I came to the plan of the Rosslyn Chapel upon which Christopher Knight had superimposed the Solomon's seal, Star of David as shown on the Companion Jewel. Knowing the strong similarity the key has to some aspects of the Royal Arch symbolism and the inclusion of the parts of the lesser seal of Solomon, I decided

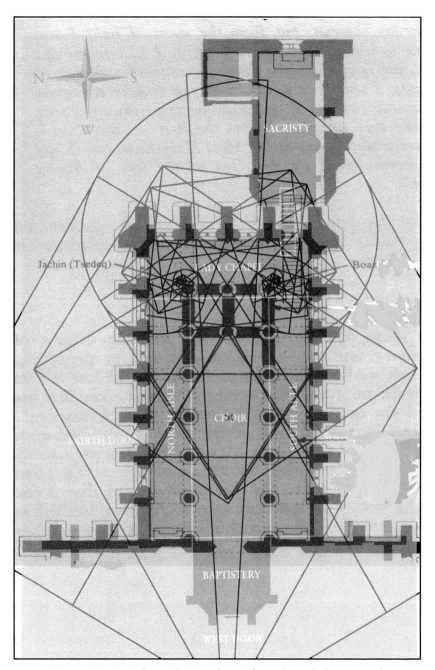

Fig. 12. 2. Plan of Rosslyn Chapel with key overlay.

to try the fit of the key onto the Solomon's seal that Christopher Knight had constructed on the Rosslyn Chapel floor plan. I used the two columns, Boaz and Jacinth to locate the two eyes of the key on the plan. After some adjustments to scale and position, to my pleasure, I was able to obtain a perfect fit. Dependant upon what interpretation was applied to this, it was extremely likely that one location of particular importance might be pinpointed

I saw, superimposed on the plan before me a perfect arch, which course lies through the side door of the sacristy and the small door to the hermit's room. I believe St. Anthony never resided in that small cell in person, though it would have been most apt. The two sides of the arch meet within the hermit's room and one would expect to see at least some significant feature on floor or ceiling at that point, together with an appropriate Templar symbol inscribed upon the adjacent wall, or perhaps a keystone at that exact point. We have to be exact as Templar geometry tends to be precise.

This was still purely another hypothesis, just speculation admittedly based on other sites and on experience so far achieved. It had to be put to the test to be worthy of any serious consideration. This would require a visit to Rosslyn Chapel, to the southwest of Edinburgh. Yet, what would be the purpose of pursuing this hypothesis? To me, the prime objective would be to confirm that this versatile key could provide access to vaults containing relics concealed with the aid of the key. The Knights Templar certainly made use of the key in their symbolism and in their monumental masonry. I must confess that I was gripped with enthusiasm to follow through this train of thought to its conclusion. The quest for answers outweighs the fever of the treasure seeker. For me, the glint of gold in the prospecting pan or on the concentrating tables of a mine gives a greater sense of achievement than processed gold. Gold fever is something that will influence people as this project proceeds and must not be taken lightly.

To follow in the footsteps of Bérenger Saunière in the practical application of the key we would also tread the path taken by Anton Bigou and the murdered Priests Gélis and Boudet. Once the secret was passed to Saunière, he could have used it to advantage in delivering from their resting place, sufficient resources to cover his exploits. This logical source of his funds required proof that the key could be used in such a manner. The Rosslyn Chapel experiment was worth pursuing to establish its validity, and to provide some further provenance for the key. To estimate the size of the target location was crucial. A potential hoard could well comprise artefacts that the Levitical Priesthood considered important enough to conceal from marauders under the Temple of their God in Jerusalem. In all probability, this would include the copper scroll, which might lead to listing the locations of other artefacts concealed in or near Rosslyn Chapel. On that basis, the target area might be something as small as a single Templar grave.

Until excavations are carried out at Rennes, we can only speculate on the contents of that particular hoard. However, with Rosslyn it is fairly certain that if anything is discovered it will be something held sacred by the Judeo-Christian religions. These religious traditions claim that the Sons of Levi, the Levitical Priesthood will again make an offering in righteousness to their God. In order to achieve this, the requirement for a temple is essential. Various other items need to be in place, such as the sacrificial red bulls and the religious paraphernalia and regalia for the ordinances, duly sanctified. The question arises as to who would be required to officiate in such a sacrifice. This is dependent on the selection of a suitably purified and authorised member of the lineage of the Cohen clan to administer in the Temple ordinances, as required under Mosaic Law. The Jewish Nation has endeavoured to remain faithful to the Law of Moses over the centuries despite scattering and persecution. Yet, they are condemned for their part in the one act that fulfiled that law and without which Christianity would not stand. The restoration of artefacts from Herod's Temple would accentuate and accelerate the undoubted progress to achieve these worthy objectives and aspirations of the Jewish Nation; a significant member of the traditional Tribes of Israel. The political and religious implications contained in these few sentences cannot be lightly dismissed.

The hoard of Rennes may also have similar implications though there is no evidence yet to support this. However, if the coffers of Rennes do contain Levitical treasures it seems reasonable that those items should also be restored to their traditional owners. Truth must stand in its own sphere as a worthy goal in retrieving these artefacts. Nothing should stand in the way of the fullest knowledge and understanding of truth, which must go towards dispelling the layers of ignorance and mystery that enslaves the mind. This restricts our comprehension of God. For God surely exists, despite varied interpretations by innumerable religions and sects.

These ever presume to convert The Lord their God to their philosophies and beliefs, and then purport to send Him forth to battle against those who would dissemble. All too quickly, do they discover that their new master has lead them into contention by a silken thread until they become bound in a web of error and corruption.

After some more research, having read *The Templars* by Piers Paul Reid and watched the Rosslyn video obtained through the Rosslyn Trust website, I decided that I had done sufficient preparation to justify a trip to Edinburgh to verify my hypothesis. I believed that the Key could be used to locate previously unsuspected features of Rosslyn Chapel. I took the train to Scotland. The key itself I did not take, as I prefer to keep it in my mind and in a safe place.

When the train pulled into Edinburgh, Waverly station, I found myself in familiar surroundings having worked in Princes Street in the fifties doing Scottish genealogy. I took the bus to Roslin and found a room in an attractive bed and breakfast establishment furnished in the Old Dutch style. The room was comfortable and the next morning an ample breakfast prepared me for the cold and blustery weather. I arrived at the Chapel a little after nine thirty — half an hour before it was open. This gave me an opportunity to walk down the steep path past the graveyard to the ruins of the ancient castle, which clings precariously to the edge of a gorge through which the stream flowed peacefully. Returning to the crest of the hill, I found the entrance to the Chapel grounds and paid my admission fee within the cosy souvenirs shop that I had first seen in the video. Leaving through a door, which gave on to the Chapel grounds, I was immediately encouraged by the intricate structure of the tall arched stained glass windows. Of course, originally, these were not glazed, but the stonework looked ancient and impressive. The ravages of the Scottish weather had taken their toll over the centuries, yet Templar Chapels had been lucky having escaped much of the religious persecution, which had destroyed many other monasteries and churches.

As I pushed open the heavy Chapel door and found the temperature within about the same as outside. There was a crowd of tourist there already and I wandered around to identify the two main pillars, Boaz and Jacinth, distinguished by the elaborate Templar stonework for which they are so famous. I spent an hour photographing the two pillars, Jacinth and Boaz, along with some of the other Templar architecture while most of the multi-national crowd of tourists moved on to warmer parts such as the shop and the reception area.

The approach to the sacristy was guarded by a heavy, iron-studded door, which stood at the head of the broad flight of stone stairs. As I heaved it open, the wind moaned through the widening gap. I was met by an icy blast of fresh Scottish air. This whistled up the stairs from the gloomy sacristy below and I could see why the door was kept shut. The ambience of the building was irresistible and drew my mind straight back into the past when the constant tread of faithful worshippers, in that harsh climate, had worn away these steps. In the chill wind, I imagined a monk drawing his heavy cowl over his tonsured head against the cold. The steps were well worn by countless faithful feet over six centuries. They had trodden their path over the years for what purpose? They may have descended these stone steps into the sacristy to stand in awe before the secret location of that sacred emblem from the Temple.

As I crossed the flagstones of the sacristy, I saw the design curves etched into the wall on my left. This was probably where the first design and construction work took place and it would have been appropriate to secure a resting place for the copper scroll at the first opportunity. Above the entrance to the hermit's cell was the St. Clair crest that depicts a scroll. The floor of the cell should have contained at least a Templar gravestone bearing an effigy of a Templar in full armour or an engraved tombstone with Templar markings on the wall. There was nothing there except a bowl to catch the drips from the ceiling! In the gloom, I was able to make out one Templar mark on the wall near the entrance passage.

The flagstones were cracked and the empty cell showed all the signs of neglect. St Anthony, tempted by rising damp, would certainly have moved cells long ago. The small barred window permitted only a little light. Practically no glimmer filtered through the passage from the sacristy, as this was quite long. I had difficulty in photographing anything apart from the cracked floor and water bowl. I needed a new camera for this sort of work. The beauty of an hypothesis is that it can be discarded at any time. This was the time and place to discard the hypothesis and concentrate on the many issues relating to Rennes. Outside the cell, I photographed the St Clair crest and found a drainage channel, which runs from the wall across the width of the Sacristy at a point near to door to the hermit's cell.

Once outside the Chapel, I visited the strange, unfinished wall at one end of the building. To preserve the stonework, a coat of lime wash had been applied. Yet, unfortunately this had tended to lock in the moisture to the detriment of the stonework. An ambitious plan was well under way to build a shell around the entire building. The scaffolding stood out in stark contrast to the elegant gothic lines of the Chapel.

The steps that lead up to the scaffolding walkway gave access to the roof where I could admire every detail of its gargoyles and flying buttresses. The ragged stonewall, at the far end of the building stood out stark against the clouds. Nothing was built here without a purpose. The high arched window, visible from the walkway caught my attention and I levelled my camera at the triple Tau design of the intricate stonework of the window. It struck me that other windows bore specific designs to guide the ardent observer in his search for enlightenment. It was cold and windy up there but the view was spectacular. Below me the land fell away to form a steep ravine where flowed the river overlooked by the castle ruins perched precariously on the hillside. A line squall burst upon me, with icy rain hammering at my face. Surely, the protective shell was essential to preserve the structure of the Chapel against the Scottish climate.

Returning to the warmth of the reception area and the shop, I had a good look round at the books and bought a guidebook. I returned to Edinburgh on the bus and took the train back to London. On the train, I settled down with the guidebook, which contained some interesting tales. There has recently been quite a lot of drilling and exploration with high hopes of success.

Fig. 12. 3. Through a narrow passage from the sacristy.

When I came to examine the floor plan shown in the
guidebook, I was more than surprised to see that it differed
from the plan in the *Hiram Key* that showed the hermit's cell
wall to be less than two feet thick. In reality, the entrance
to the cell passes through a wall of several feet in thickness
as I had noticed while examining the room. Thus the passage
way had restricted the light available for photography. This
meant that instead of the exact location that I sought being
in the room, it actually lay in the thickness of the wall where
I had seen the Templar marking. The St Clair crest and scroll
were exactly on the other side of the wall just to the right of
the passage in the sacristy, as was the drainage channel. The
hypothesis was given a new lease of life on the spot, more
particularly as the drainage channel followed the tangential
side of the square on the key (Fig. 12.2.).

The Rosslyn Trust had recently built shelves against the wall of the cell to convert it to a store room. On the walls there are several very significant Templar marking, which have not been obscured and these are shown in Fig. 12.4. The design curves marked on the Sacristy wall are also of interest. The complex layout of Rosslyn Chapel would depend on a set of accurate curves if based on one key using a particular base unit of measurement and suggests that the sacristy was built in the early phase of the construction work. Any valuable artefacts were likely to be concealed in that area of the chapel rather than be left at risk, perhaps for years, awaiting completion. The prerogative to explore this further must now rest with the St Clair family and the Trust.

Fig. 12. 4. Interesting Templar marks in the hermit's closet.

The current hypothesis was now gaining credence. The implication was that Sir William St Clair could well have used the key when designing the Rosslyn Chapel and employed it in the concealment of artefacts. This has great relevance in establishing the source of the wealth so evident at Rennes, and points towards the key being used to conceal the remaining hoard of Rennes-le-Château. Present day Masonry may express more than a passing interest in the restoration of their ancient system with its symbolism. The secrets of the Templars are many and not limited to the hoard of Rennes but may reveal the code by which many treasures have been concealed. To lay bare this mystery opens up the possibility of disclosing the whereabouts of the Templar caches that have lain hidden since the great purge of 1307. Surely many sites have already been pillaged and the wealth restored to circulation. This has proved to be a task fraught with danger when surrounded by the greed and the chicanery that has existed in the minds of some. Yet, for Saunière much good came of his efforts and much good would have been possible if he had survived the grim reaper to liberate more funds. However, he succeeded well in his efforts to preserve his heritage for this generation.

Over the centuries, this subject has engaged the mind of Masonry and religionists when contemplating the true nature of God and the purpose of His Holy Temples. The paths of religious history have become so clouded that it seems that only by direct revelation we will ever be able to fully comprehend God and the meaning behind the rituals of His temples.

CHAPTER THIRTEEN

DEATH'S HEAD AT POMPEII

Golgotha had added a macabre touch of mystery to the tale. The first time that I caught sight of two empty eye sockets staring at me from the past came as quite a shock all those years ago. Over time I had become familiar with the random occurrence of skulls and the story had moved forward. But suddenly my heart sank into my boots as, once again, I saw, a grotesque and unexpected skull staring up at me with those sightless eyes. No! I really did not need another twist in this tale of romance and treasure that has intrigued us all over a quarter of a century. However, there it was and had been, since 1894. No! This had been there since long before then. Better by far that it had been buried forever in the depths, or perhaps, that a burning mountain had flowed down and covered it with ashes and lava. History seems to repeat itself. I was now confronted by those empty eye sockets; this time they glared up at me from a mosaic that had remained hidden since the catastrophic volcanic eruption that occurred on the 24th August 79 A.D. Now it had returned to the light of day and had been removed from the dangerous shadow of Vesuvius to the safety of the National Archaeological Museum at Naples. The mosaic of the skull is now on display on the mezzanine floor with many other fine mosaics, frescos, statues and artefacts. from the past.

Though it had lain hidden amongst the ruins of Pompeii for centuries, I had become so familiar with the same cipher key that I could not miss it, even when it emerged in the most unexpected places. The mosaic contained the usual elements including the tilted cross; depicted as a withered branch, like the one Saunière had painted in his Church at Rennes-le-Château. Discovery of this ancient occurrence of the cipher key meant that I could not avoid following up this lead. Of course I could have excluded it from this book and included it in *Keys of Antiquity*, which is shortly to follow. However this would leave the tale incomplete.

The subtleties of concealment in Saunière's great artistry do not appear to exist in this blatant work of the Greeks or Romans. This indicates that the cipher was established before the eruption of Vesuvius when that poisonous cloud of ashes and lava swept down from the mountain of fire to engulf the city. Pliny the Younger described this scene of devastation so it is certain that the mosaic lay undiscovered from that era. Romans or the Greeks must have been well aware of the geometry, which could not be described as sacred. We may never know what purpose it served or who it was that ordered its execution, the artist who designed the layout or the craftsman who fitted each coloured cube of stone to bring the picture to life.

Fig. 13. 1. The *Memento Mori* from Pompeii.

It is there and it is most certainly a death's head, *Il est là, mort*. I remember the impression imprinted on my brain by a picture in my Latin Primer text book at school. It showed a bas-relief that the famous Celt, Vercingetorix, chief of the Mandubii tribe, had etched on his cell wall while awaiting his execution. The Romans had captured him and he was sentenced to languish in a Roman dungeon before being put to death. However, to this day the bas-relief he carved in his cell wall remains in Rome, in my mind. What was it that he wished to leave to posterity that was so important to him? One day I would need to make a visit to Rome to find this.

But now I would need to visit Pompeii before the book could be completed. Either destination could shed some light on the past. My last visit to Rome was as a guest of Alitalia and the Italian Tourist Board many years ago in the days of the song *Volare* and the film *Three Coins in a Fountain* leaving me with fond memories of Italy. A year spent in Tripoli, Libya had given me a fair grasp of the language and the prospect of returning to Italy filled me with nostalgia.

Naples was one part of Italy that I had never before visited and I was already looking forward to using my rusty Italian. The objective of the visit was to verify the shape, size and colouring of the mosaic together with its location and to check any other associated mosaics or artwork. These factors could be relevant in fully understanding its usage and background in ancient times.

Verification of the early existence of the cipher seemed important from an archaeological standpoint but the format depicting the cross as used by David Teniers, Leonardo da

Vinci in his *Yarnwinder* also Saunière, in his painting central to his church architecture, depicting the maiden with the book and skull, demonstrates the adaptation of art styles. The symbolism of the cross is almost exclusively associated with christianity since the crucifixion. The presence of a cross in the cipher has resulted in an ideal adaptatation of the displays to include christian religious themes in the later art-work, many examples of which depict Christ.

It required only a minor leap of logic to err, and include Christ in the solution to a conundrum that had defied any clear resolution. The association of the themes of death, Christ and the tomb, linked with an undefined treasure that must be preserved at all costs by nobles and clerics alike enhances the image of a sacred tomb containing some relic of vast religious significance. Many are reluctant to accept the writings of ancient Prophets of the Old Testament such as Isaiah and the New Testament accounts of the crucifixion and resurrection of Christ. The theme has developed by the association of Christ's crucifixion at Golgotha, the Place of the Skull with the references to Golgotha in connection with the cipher at Rennes.

When we consider the Templars, their cross and the Templar links with excavations beneath the Jerusalem Temple, together with their requirement to guard their treasures by a secure method, then this association is greatly reinforced. It is little wonder that some rumours of the Templars using a skull in their worship was seized upon by the inquisition. Certainly the skull and crossed bones are associated with their burial memorials and other rituals.

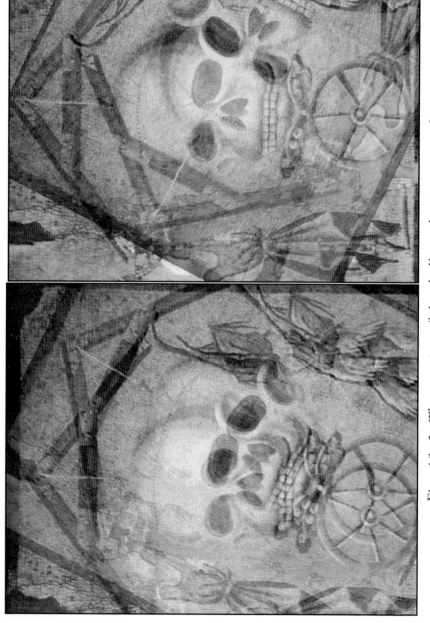

Fig. 13. 2. The rotation of the skull overlapping eye and ear.

Undoubtedly preserving the key did require their using the skull symbolism and this may have assumed a quasi-religious significance. Or thus it may have appeared to those with a score to settle and an axe to grind. Many an unsettled score was owed to the Templars by those in power and many blades were sharpened to settle the debts with blood and the inquisition rather than with their gold.

Thus the development of such notions as these could lead the unwary to reach a conclusion that somehow the tomb of Christ had figured in the early use of the cipher key. Though such an hypothesis could not be substantiated or proven by archaeological research, yet it could never be refuted except by resorting to the Judeo-Christian writings and by the exercise of faith. Now that the mountain on the slopes of Vesuvius has been partially moved there remains but little evidence to support this association of idea. Yet the actual contents of the vaults of Rennes still await some meaningful archaeological excavations and Saunière certainly did employ christian symbolism to conceal and reveal his message, as did the Templars.

Though the mosaic I sought was not to be found at Pompeii, I spent a day there marvelling at the rich heritage that had been preserved in that former Roman port in the Bay of Naples. The town had been a flourishing Roman coastal centre with all the infrastructure such as villas for the wealthy and houses and shops, theatres, administrative buildings and temples built for the worship of a variety of deities. The Hellenistic influence features many of the gods of Greek mythology.

Some years prior to the main eruption a Roman geologist of that period advised the authorities that Vesuvius had already produced a significant quantity of ash and lava. The farms surrounding Pompeii yielded excellent crops in great abundance due to the fertile volcanic soil and supported a rich economy. The possibility of any further eruptions was disregarded for 'it would never happen again'. However, in 64 A.D. there occurred a series of earthquakes that damaged much of the town of Pompeii.

Reconstruction was well under way. Further extension work to the town had progressed when the violent eruption of Vesuvius covered the area in volcanic ash, mud flows and lava to a depth of more than twenty metres. Some made their escape early by sea or by road. But, all too soon, the volcanic outpouring of flying rocks and ash mingled with the poisonous fumes that penetrated to the remotest parts of their dwellings showing no mercy for humans or beasts. Pliny the Younger wrote his eye-witness account of the carnage and though ships were dispatched they could avail but little. The crews could only watch the scene of destruction in horror from ships some distance from the shore.

Many of the more precious artefacts are preserved in the National Archaeological museum in Naples and on the morning following our trip to Pompeii we visited the museum. On the mezzanine floor, among a fine collection of beautiful frescoes and more attractive mosaics, resides the *Memento Mori* mosaic proclaiming its sombre message.

While standing before the mosaic we were surrounded by a party of tourists lead by a French speaking guide. As I moved from the heart of the throng the guide started to talk about the *Memento Mori*, as the mosaic had been dubbed. He described it in detail, ascribing human attributes to the various elements. The *Memento Mori* served as a grim reminder of our own mortal state. The skull, with its empty eye sockets and deaf ear represented the human state, unwilling to see or give ear to the message. The cart wheel at the base represented the world, implying the universal nature of the message while the oblique cross on the right, draped with rags represented the poor contrasted with the colourful dress hanging on the opposite side. Here we may see that the message is the same regardless of our wealth or status.

How could we fail to recognise the haunting whisper, *Et in Arcadia ego* echoing down through the centuries? Yet more startling was the similarity to the two large skulls sharing three eyes, or was one really an ear, as depicted in the *Arcadian shepherds* of the Devonshire collection?

After leaving the museum with its wonders, a lighter touch was called for. A train ride through the hills and coastal scenery to Sorrento with its picturesque shops and buildings prepared us for the gastronomic delights at one of the open air restaurants in the town centre. After lunch a gentle stroll provided an opportunity for some photography before tackling the steep winding road down to the harbour. Relaxing in the sun, the mind was no longer clouded with the foreboding of death, even against the backdrop of Vesuvius. I was filled with feelings of gratitude for the beauty that surrounded us and for our very existence. Later, the World and his wife seemed to mingle in a babble of

Fig. 13. 3. Swinging skulls.

voices as we strolled though the narrow streets of Sorrento. Here the charming shops and boutiques were filled with the intoxicating aromas of the Mediterranean and the vision of a myriad treasures delighted our eyes.

On the Saturday we visited Herculaneum, once a Roman port, that suffered a similar fate to that which befell Pompeii. Those exposed to the onslaught of hot volcanic gases were instantly destroyed. However, the state of preservation of the buildings is remarkable. Like Pompeii, there are still parts to excavate including the ancient library at Herculaneum, as yet unlocated.

On returning to England, it was possible to analyse the images of the *Memento Mori*. Where exactly would one start? There was nothing subtle about the grotesque ear as it hung there begging to be married to an empty eye socket, most likely the adjacent one. The ear had that look about it with the long curved section at one side that just pleaded to be rotated.

To discover some of the secrets of the *Memento Mori* the first superimposing move was to align the eye with the ear by sliding one image in a clockwise rotation through the usual 26.565 degrees such that the right eye moves into alignment with the ear of the other image, reminiscent of the strange arrangement of skulls in *The Arcadian Shepherds*.

This action pinpoints the axis of rotation at the centre of the bow tie. This is the device beneath the skull's jaw with it double row of gleaming teeth that any Roman, slave or freeman, would be proud to own. This centre point of the baseline of a square, being set at an angle, is also located at the highest point of the wheel. The length of a side of the original square was thus the bow tie centre to the eye socket. The exact dimension of this could be confirmed only when the rotation of the ear was completed, revealing its precise axis. The moment of truth came as the ear was rotated, as is immediately apparent when ones own ear is twisted. However no grimace appeared on the long-dead features of Fred or perhaps, using the Templar's *nom de guerre* for the skull, 'Simon'. The mosaic leant itself to this sliding movement and the subtle outline of the ear matched the contour of the eye blending the finely set mosaic pattern perfectly.

On looking at what this exercise had done I discovered that I had not replicated the rotation of the Poussin painting as previously defined. The mosaic layout has induced me to continue the rotation until I had actually rotated the one copy of the mosaic through an additional 180 degree half circle. This provides the same geometric figure but with the rotated skull being head down. The limit of rotation was clearly defined as the two patterns merged to lock in on the angled bar, the outline of the skull and other features.

Perhaps the more obvious lure to induce the unwary to become gripped by this new aspect of the antiquities is the thread of yarn by which the skull is suspended from the wooden frame. The cord is attached to the skull by a blue chip of azurite in the familiar shape formed by the diagonal of the half square to remind the searcher of the angle to use. When the mosaic is rotated clockwise through this usual 26.565 degrees, pivoted upon the suspension point of the thread, would not the skull remain vertical, notionally motionless, suspended by its cord such that the top of the ear comes into perfect alignment with the curved stick? One cannot fail to feel a variety of emotions; surprise, wonder and a deep sense of antiquity. We have been thrust back in the first century A.D., not a mere three hundred and fifty years ago.

By establishing the first and second steps, as shown in the illustration, the dimension of one of the Tau squares can be determined relative to the scale of the mosaic. There is much contained in that one mosaic and the subject of the cipher could not be covered fully in this book without diverting from the main theme. The intricacies of the cipher in its various forms and applications extend far beyond the scope of Rennes and its treasures. Suffice it to demonstrate the correlation between the St Madeleine murals of the fourteen stations of the cross in the angle of a staff.

However as we visited the various excavation sights, we entered the Villa of Mysteries and I was struck by the murals. So familiar in their design, the murals leapt from the walls, redolent with the cipher key. It was everywhere; the curve of a Dionysian buttock and the tilt of a head, the staff, the face with the staring eyes – it was all there with the familiar red and green colours!

The interesting use of the keys as shown in Fig.13.6.

demonstrates the way the two curves intersect on the lady's buttock at the exact point of the *midi pommes bleues* of the next dexter key. The lines tally satisfactorily with the rod and other features. The complexity of the overlays can be seen it is sufficient for this book to be aware that the origins of the key extend back through the centuries. But the way that the curved lines intersect does have some importance and has been employed in the Rosslyn Chapel solution that is proposed as described in Chapter 12.

Yet the most elegant application of the cipher is in the house of two wealthy merchants, Aulo Vettio Restituto and Aulo Vettio Conviva, where again Dionysus is depicted in one of the wall paintings. The murals are believed to have been executed in the restoration period after the severe earthquakes of 62 A.D. and of particular excellence in one of the smaller rooms is a scene from the myths of the Theban cycle depicting the infant Hercules strangling a snake sent by Juno.

The golden helis next to the winged figure matches the key perfectly with the stone plinth upon which it stands. The angles of the various rods are typical and relate to the straight lines of stool, plinth and doric columns. The curves of the snakes wrestled by the infant Hercules tie in with the rods to eliminate any possibility of the design being purely by chance. The design and balance of this work is strongly reminiscent of the perfection achieved by Nicolas Poussin. The basic geometry is factual but its application, by virtue of its aura of secrecy and mystery has led many to spin a web of fantasy around what is, after all, the precise application of a

Fig. 13. 4. The Villa of Mysteries well deserves its title.

The ruins of Pompeii may yet hold answers to the many questions raised by these ancient colourful images. Where will this trail of mystery lead, as historians peel the layers from this azure onion?

Fig. 13. 5. Keys of antiquity.

Fig. 13. 6. The curve of a Dionysian buttock.

complex geometric pattern in graphic design.

Hidden meanings, geographic locations and text, may be portrayed in secrecy by use of the system. It can be employed just to achieve the aesthetic perfection of artistic design. Study of the weird and devious ideas that these secret combinations have attracted over the centuries has contributed little to provide a resolution to the mystery and has led those who have sought answers therein to wrestle with the spider. Yet, now the pattern is defined with its interlinking movement of sliding squares and sliding arcs there are various methods of using arrays of mirrored letters or numbers in sliding boxes. Codes exist, linked to the alphabet based on the position in the key itself related to its occurrence in the artwork. But what was the usage in the days of Pompeii and before? What numbering system and alphabets did the ancients use?

In summing up the application of the key in the death's head mosaic and in other paintings at Pompeii, there are some salient points worth mentioning. Matching halves of sliding equal squares determines the usage of the mirror images of the key. The concept of using the ear as the point of rotation, or in the geometry at the centre of the Tau oblique cross, has been applied. The linguistic contortions of Boudet's in this respect have been mentioned previously.

The large skull is the main feature of the image rather than just an ancillary feature. The image of the oblique Tau cross, as depicted by Saunière, is employed in the mosaic and the curved end to the staff idea is present, reminiscent of the lower end of the staff in *Les Bergers d'Arcadie*.

Pompeii, with its archaeological and art treasures has provided an interesting diversion but we must return to the theme of this book, which must be the resolution of the mystery surrounding the Rennes hoard. This must take preference over my boiling enthusiasm to include more information in these pages rather than afford the subject the coverage it deserves in *Keys of Antiquity*.

Reaching back into the past to find early occurrences of the key, there is a prime example, which has recently been acquired by the Victoria and Albert Museum. This is the work of the French illuminated manuscript illustrator, Jean Bourdichon (circa 1457 — 1521). *The Nativity* was once contained in a Book of Hours, now known as *The Hours of Henry VII and* was due to be sold to the Getty Museum in California. Because of its artistic importance, government intervened to retain this work in the UK. The Victoria and Albert Museum has now acquired this tempera on vellum illustration after raising £187,000 from the National Memorial Fund, £25,000 from the Friends of the V.A. and £30,000 from the leading British arts charity, the National Art Collections Fund. Negotiations were opened after its recent purchase by a London art dealer who recognised it as the work of Jean Bourdichon, a talented illuminator of manuscripts enjoying royal patronage in his day.

The illustration is an excellent example of the system used to achieve perfect balance in his painting by employing the geometry to incorporate the golden mean. Though the Book of Hours page is only 29.3 x 17 cm the geometry is explicitly visible and is worthy of study.

Fig 13. 7. *The Nativity*. by Jean Bourdichon (c. 1457 - 1521).
V&A Picture Library.

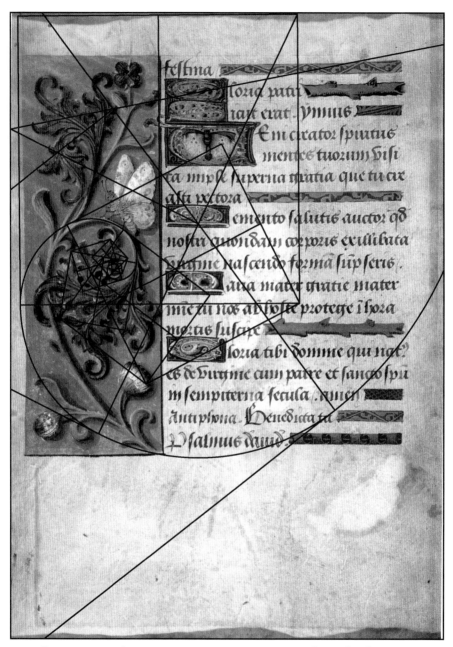

Fig. 13. 8. The verso containing text employs the key.

Of particular interest, in addition to the obvious use of the key, is the illuminated text on the verso, which also appears to employ the key. The exactitude of the match to the spiral design and specific points such as the blue flower suggests that the designer had an intimate knowledge of the key. The adherence to this discipline at least gave elegance and balance to the masterpiece if nothing else.

The widespread usage of the key in the world of art opens out a whole new field in art studies generally and this could prove to be as important as the discoveries to be made at Rennes. A little experimentation using other paintings might provide an interesting diversion. *The blue boy* Pre-Raphaelite painting demonstrates the extent to which this knowledge has filtered down through the years.

Neither does this preclude investigations into other Templar sites with their associated artwork treasures and their relevance to Templar hoards both land and maritime. Like the artifacts of Pompeii the *Book of Hours* has survived the centuries that have ravaged many a lesser work. There seems to be no end to the threads of antiquity woven into this tale. It opens new corridors of investigation and there is much to learn from the work of the Old Masters, often including those of royal patronage and, of course, Leonardo da Vinci with his *Yarnwinder* painting.

CHAPTER FOURTEEN

THE HERITAGE OF RENNES

Only in the last few hours of her life did Marie Denarnaud breathe a word of the great secret that dominated her life. Gérard de Sède wrote that Marie had intended to pass on what she held locked in her mind for over thirty years. The irony was that, smitten by a stroke, the words she breathed were meaningless to Noel Corbu and no sound escaped her blanched lips as she approached her end.

Just as Bérenger Saunière was unable to complete his new tower to preserve his heritage so Marie was unable to pass this vital information to posterity. Now we struggle to draw some meaning from the host of clues we find on every side.

Returning to the cipher contained within Manuscript I of the parchments, found on page 101 of *The Accursed Treasure...* Gérard de Sède divulged information that defined the method of breaking the code. This code was derived from the extraction of 140 letters that had been inserted into the text taken from the first eleven verses of Chapter 12, St John's Gospel. The parchment ends with two lines that are separated from the main text. This may be translated thus:

Jesus' heart is wounded. One hope. Penitence. Through the tears of Magdalene. Our sins are washed away.

The heart or *pommes bleues* is certainly pierced. The tears of Magdalene fall constantly on the hillside. Our sins may be forgiven by the atonement of Christ and his death on the cross at Golgotha, should we choose repentance. In the context of the known location of the Golgotha site, already identified, immediately below the Church, the text becomes significant.

Rumour strikes at the very heart of Christian beliefs and this is perhaps the most powerful tool working upon the mind of man. It has been claimed, ever since the time of His crucifixion that Christ had not died on the cross at Calvary but there is certainly no evidence of this at Rennes. The rumour that He was rescued by his confederates and escaped to France is without foundation. On His demise, it has been suggested that His remains were entombed somewhere in the Languedoc region together with documentary evidence to substantiate this conjecture. More prevalent is the idea that Mary Magdalene was espoused to The Saviour and that His direct line formed the Merovingian dynasty, the rightful heirs to the throne of France. The validity of this suggestion is somewhat diminished by blatant manipulation of suspect genealogies. Much has been written on this subject. Though it lacks the lure of gold, it contains the intrigue of religion and mystery.

Anyone may lay claim to the gold of Rennes, now as in the past. If it has lain hidden since the early Visigothic times any group who happened upon some clue to its existence, could conveniently adopt it and claim it as their own. Even if the exact location of the hoard were not known, this minor consideration would be of little consequence in any attempt to ensnare the fervent minds of the masses.

A knowledge of the original ancient system of the markers used to define the location of the treasures is crucial to an understanding of its history. We have looked closely at the cipher and have found the key. The precise location of the treasure has been defined. We have also seen the direct alignment from the Tour Magdala to the exact spot on the ground. There still remains many strands in the web. Nevertheless, how was the web spun in those distant times when the spider first drew the golden fly into the centre of its web?

It was precisely in that manner. From the key, we have learned that there is a spiral emerging from a central core, just like a spider's web. As the exact location of the main hoard has been defined by Saunière, thereby verifying the hypothesis, then the key can be applied to the landscape in relation to ancient markers that remain visible to this day.

Along the curvature there are placed nodes on the ever widening arcs. Each node should figure on the landscape. There are two shepherd's huts on the hillside to the north of the village, below the ancient château. One of these huts is situated near to the pathway from the old well and the other lies further to the west adjacent to a small wall built in the shape of an arc. In the middle of the wall is a hole that might have held something of interest in ancient times.

Both of these huts, which resembled those across the Sals River above Coustaussa, may have been constructed as markers that would stand the test of time and the attentions of a zealous Priest. These huts have not moved in a long time, neither has the treasure location. If the node at the centre of the key's arc is placed on the treasure in the same way as on the hand in Les Bergers d'Arcadie one might expect that two other nodes would match precisely the two huts with the curve coinciding with the adjacent curved wall.

The first requirement to establish this principle was to map out the list of GPS locations at Rennes that I had recorded on my Garmin E-Trex. The software is designed to downloads data from the hand held GPS straight onto my computer. Taking an electronic image of the map and also the aerial photo it is possible to identify two GPS points on the ground, which can be identified on the map. It is best if these two 'ground control' points are some distance apart as their relative positions establish the link between all the other GPS locations and the digital map at the correct scale and orientation.

Armed with this digital map it was not long before I had matched the key to all three of the locations; the treasure and two of the nodes along the spiral represented by the two stone huts. It was obvious that another node along the arc lay at a point somewhere between the treasure hoard and the more westerly of the shepherd's huts. The calculations give the position of where this additional node would be placed on the landscape. This new node was located at the foot of Roque Fumade at N 42⁰ 55' 59" E 02⁰ 15' 38.3". Referring to the map and to photos of the area such as in Fig.14.1. this point seems to coincide with the dark entrance to a cave. This will be the subject of some further exploration work that could prove of great interest.

From *The Accursed Treasure of Rennes-le-Château*, it appears that our diligent Priest may have excavated a few of these way-points in the early days of his travail. It seems more probable that he addressed other Templar sites rather than interfere with those associated with the main hoard.

To investigate this third node point, it would be necessary to spend time in the near future to check this on the ground to verify the type of marker and to check whether the spot is undisturbed. There are several interesting features on the ground there, including the dark entrance to a cave. The precise spot is to be confirmed against the GPS location. The slightly raised arcs of stone at either side of the drystone wall suggest that a further set of markers swinging in from the north are a distinct possibility; there remains so much more to do.

This has been a story of treasure lost, treasure found and treasure yet to be revealed. There has been much about a cipher to conceal and reveal the gold and jewels of the ancients. There will be another tale; of the moment when

Fig. 14. 1. The eastern slopes of Roc Fumade.

Fig. 14. 2. The rugged terrain north of Rennes-le-Château.

the first shafts of daylight strike upon the ancient treasure hoard of Rennes-le-Château. This could be a grisly event if the cadavers of those who carried the treasure to its resting place, perhaps in the dead of night, are entombed with the hoard to preserve the secret. First, we must explore the contents of that vaulted cavern on a lonely hillside overlooked by the crumbling ruins of the châteaux of both Coustaussa and Rennes. Yes, these ruins have watched over this hoard but what others do they yet guard?

The story so far tells of the journey to the point where a treasure must be excavated as it is too much at risk now to let it rest where is has lain for so long. This book will stir up a nest of spiders that can be quelled only with swift blows from both pick and shovel by the responsible authorities. What will be revealed is subject to speculation. We may each set out on a flight of fantasy and imagine the best or the worst outcome according to our own desires or ambitions. Can this cipher really reveal text by simply following the convolutions within a painting?

There is still much work to do. There are three more treasure locations at Rennes. Some must be revealed and one will remain hidden for future generations. It seems a never-ending task, not without its excitement and intrigue as we tread warily, as *Bergers, pas de tentation.*

* * *

Before leaving Rennes-le-Château, we must pause, once more, to look at Bérenger Saunière's domain as we try to appreciate the work of those hands that held the secret almost too well. But, still, we see it through a glass darkly,

in part only. Let us take a key to his workmanship. The layout of his domain contains many secrets but to savour the
delights and intrigue that were his life's work we must place
the key where it rightly fits. He has meticulously laid out his
tower, gardens, Church and so many other details that we
might pass by without a single glance.

The belvedere with its sweeping arc and the graceful
curve of the flight of steps invites the key to a perfect fit.
However, that is not all. We are now familiar with that north
south line from the hoard to the *échauguette* on his tower. By
placing the key upon this line we find that everything falls
into place but a full site plan is needed. So much precision
and preparation has been invested for just this moment. As
we follow the sweep of the arcs across the landscape he
watched over for so many years, the intersection falls
exactly upon a certain piece of land covered in bright yellow
broom, which belies the thorns that guard it so well. By
now the English oak tree will be in its third year and will
provide welcome shade to the many visitors who will flock
here. Alternatively, there will be a massive archaeological
dig in 2004 when the tree will be uprooted.

Perhaps we will all share in the feeling of Marie
Denarnaud as we shoulder a portion of the burden carried
by Abbé Bérenger Saunière who once held a secret in his
hand and kept it for this generation to discover. There are
many things that are not revealed in this book. There remain
more treasures here, so investigations will continue for
many years, perhaps forever.

* * *

As this book draws to a close, now that we have been inundated with ciphers, calculations, images and mystery yet the crucial question that dominates the mind of the reader remains unanswered! What became of Myfanwy and indeed of her sister Glynis? Never mind the treasures. They can all await their turn.

As a result of the wide circulation of the previous book Glynis did make contact and better still, both she and her sister, Myf came to a party we held to celebrate the last stages of completion of the book. So, this moment of deep nostalgia will not go unrecorded. The twin ladies, facing each other chatting, looked identical after all the years had flown by. The only way I could tell the difference was that Myf stood a few inches taller than her sister. They were both early guests that evening. Both were accompanied by their husbands, having left the grown children in Merther Tydvil where they all now live. Glynis married a South African so we were able to reminisce about those balmy days in Rhodesia and South Africa and Myf had married one of the CAA pilots. We all had plenty to talk about. Myf was as spiky as ever and ribbed me about my hair having turned white and speaking with a certain jargon I had picked up. This was mainly due to my rubbing shoulders with all the puns and particular language associated with Rennes.

"Why did you have to put so many complicated diagrams and all those calculations in the book? I suppose you still expect me to read it all some time."

"Well you can always look at the pictures. Perhaps I just put them in just for you," I retorted.

"Well you needn't have bothered because I don't like those either, especially the shepherd one. I had a nightmare imagining the back to back images sliding across each other with all those arms and legs looking just like some giant ugly spider."

"If you were any good at ciphers you should have written it all on a microdot hidden on a twenty pence stamp and posted it to me in Wales. At least it would have saved me the bother of coming all this way just to be insulted."

Her accent now was pure Welsh mingled with just a faint tinge of South African.

"Perhaps it could be on a stamp, but with a few changes," I replied.

"Any stamp will do, look you." she said, tossing her head so that the silver and gold of her hair shimmered in the light.

Fig. 14. 3. An oak tree grows amidst the broom.

"It would have to be a twenty centimes stamp in the colours of the French tricolore. That famous maid of the French Revolution, Marianne would have to have her head on it, with her hair all swept back not flowing all over the place like yours."

"Anyway its lovely to see you again and if you send me a copy of your next book I promise to look at all the pictures."

"Glynis let me into a little secret, Myf. She told me you read every page of the draft and wouldn't put it down, even at meal times and that you complained that the last chapter had not been finished."

"I have to admit that I am still just as much a bookworm as I was when we first met in the castle library at Cardiff. So I promise to read every word of your last chapter. But don't make it too long."

With that she opened her bag and pulled out a much thumbed copy of *The Accursed Treasure...* Again those green pools of her eyes met mine as I felt the gentle touch of her hand.

"Anyway its lovely to see you again after all these years and that trip out to Rhodesia really did change my life."

I could no mistake the tears welling up in her eyes as she quickly brushed them away with her free hand, which still held the book, so once again the *Accursed Treasure* was splashed with tears. I glanced down and noted that she still wore the curious celtic ring but now there was another matching Celtic gold band on her wedding finger.

With a gentle squeeze and a tearful smile she withdrew her hand from mine and swept away to rejoin her husband across the room leaving me murmuring to myself,

"Tears so soon, yet this book has barely started to peel the many layers from this onion."

There remains so much yet unsaid yet line upon line the story will unfold. Perhaps a whisper of it could be painted on the wall of a church in Covent Garden? Did not the artist say,

"As I paint I write."

The seals have been broken yet we have hardly rippled the surface of what is harboured in the unfathomable depths. The seal on the first cavern, which lay under the shadow cast at midday by Rennes, will be rent forever in the next few weeks. However, this is only the start of the mystery of Rennes-le-Château.

One seal will never be broken — the link that unites two souls that lie at the heart of this great story. The treasures of the Temple may yet be revealed to the light of day. Yet, the bond that exists between François Bérenger Saunière, that man of mystery and Marie Denarnaud, the maker of hats, will surely outlast the grave. The linked hearts that appear over the entrance to the villa Bethania symbolise the eternal bond between two souls laid to rest in a little graveyard overlooking a rugged hillside.

But look again! While half dozing in the midday sun at Rennes one might spy, on the belvedere, a tall man draped in a red robe, that is now devoid of tassels, his left arm rests gently on the shoulders of the slight figure of a young girl as she gazes up at his chiselled features. His right arm is extended due north, pointing down the sloping hillside, as if indicating some priceless treasure lost beneath the bright yellow carpet of broom. Surely, their memory will remain here in the Razes forever, as may also remain a portion of a Visigothic hoard.

He and Marie, Saunière's Madonna, now more than ever, would be watching over the treasure from his domain. Perhaps they would see the shade of a painter, with his easel set out on the Poussin seat, gazing earnestly at a tomb. The rank odour of decay tweaking his nostrils as the front swings open to reveal the blackened head of a dead man, or, in the dim sepulchral glow might it be just the outline of an ancient ruined castle?

By the entrance to a stone hut there stands the ancient guardian, a Knight Templar in full regalia, his head tilted slightly to the right and his right foot placed upon his left. Covered by his shield, his hand rest upon a skull set upon the cross of his sword hilt, the converging outlines of the sword, straight as an arrow,draw to the point now set firmly in the ground.

"*Mort Epée*", he whispers from the past; the cross and the skull.

"*Il est là, mort.*". This stone he knows but cannot see, for it remains concealed behind an impenetrable mass of bushes.

Many other players will be there with Marie de Nègre gazing from the upper window of the château to guard over her three remaining treasures, one arched roof collapsed under its own weight.

However, in the next few weeks, the first part of the treasure of Rennes-le-Château should see the light of day after many centuries; for none may rest until the hoard is secured. When the clamour has ceased and the spoils returned to the Nation of France, or to those who have a rightful claim to them, peace will descend on the village. This tranquillity will be broken by the continued steady stream of visitors to the museum, the bookshop and the church where, for the searcher, so much of the mystery will ever remain. How can we fully interpret the many signs and symbols concealed yet revealed for the world to fathom?

What yarn still spins the spider in the cobwebs of the past? There will be tales of Visigoths, of Vercingetorix, of Dagobert and of the Albigensian and Knight Templars, some of whose coffers were pillaged yet many remain stuffed with the treasures of Europe and the Orient. There are pirate treasures sealed with the key of the skull and crossbones. But all this will still be subject to misinterpretation and human foibles. Much of what will be told will be packed with falsehoods and misguided hopes and fears, yet it will be filled with excitement and intrigue. The blood courses through the brain and the pulse races as we gain an insight to the lives and aspirations of those long dead, our ancestors, captive to the same hopes and fears that we feel today.

There is so much more to tell yet this must wait until *Keys of Antiquity* is completed ready for publication. To cram even more into these pages would detract from the purpose of this book, which is to facilitate the controlled excavation of sites of archaeological interest. Whatever happens, the ruins of Coustaussa across the Sals River will continue to stand guard over the ancient city of Aeredae and its treasures. Yet

there is sufficient contained within these pages to solve the
mystery of the cipher.

THE BEGINNING

APPENDICES

APPENDIX A

STEREOSCOPIC IMAGES.

The Mirror Stereoscope serves for the viewing of stereoscopic pairs. In conjunction with the Tracing Stereometer stereoscopic measurement can be made on the stereo-pair, simultaneously with the planimetric evaluation of image details. The principal scope of application for the Mirror Stereoscope and the Tracing Stereometer is in the interpretation of aerial photographs. The instrument can however be used with success also for a range of special problems.

Demands on the stereograms

Suitable for stereoscopic observation are all image pairs the component photographs of which have been taken of the same object from different camera stations. The type of camera used, focal length and extent of overlap is of no importance.

When taking measurements on the photographs the following should be noted;

a) A prerequisite for any satisfactory measurement is a representation of the relevant object obtained by means of perspective projection. The latter will be falsified where the photographic lens has pronounced distortion errors or where a camera with a focal plane shutter is used. These shutters will inevitably lead to images of insufficient fidelity when taking photographs whilst the camera or objects are in motion. With paper prints, the disproportionate shrinkage of the photographic paper will likewise often cause some distortion. For the purpose of measurement, one should therefore not use prints with a high gloss finish. Measurement from the original film or plate will always give the most accurate results.

An essential to the accuracy of evaluation is adherence to an arrangement of the survey, which owing to the design of the Stereoscope should conform to the normal case of stereo-photogrammetry. Applied to aerial photography this means that the photographs shall be taken with cameras of equal focal length at the same flying height, and vertically downward. Photographs of larger tilt and from different heights must be rectified before being evaluated.

b) Graphical evaluation is effected by the transfer of the picture details of the left-hand photograph onto the drawing surface. Large-scale photographs as for instance those taken with a camera of long focal length offer a higher evaluation accuracy. Large differences in the elevation of the terrain cause local perspective displacements of picture detail and differences in the image scale, which factors are bound to lead to noticeable errors in plan.

c) The errors in stereoscopic measurement are directly proportional to the image scale coefficient and the 'base ratio' (object distance: base length). For aerial photographs with the usual 66% overlap, the base ratio, when using a standard-angle camera, is approximately 3:1 and, when using a wide-angle camera, approximates the value one.

Noncompliance with the normal case of stereo-photogrammetry will influence the stereoscopic measurement in particular. Large convergence errors of the camera axes produce excessive warping of the model, which in aerial photographs mainly appear as errors in elevation. By the application of a suitable evaluation method these errors can be eliminated approximately.

Therefore the best measuring and mapping results are obtained if the arrangement of the survey corresponds to the normal case of stereo-photogrammetry and the depth of the object does not exceed 10% of the object distance.

Refs: Extracts from Carl Zeiss Jena *Instruction Manual, Mirror Stereoscope with Tracing Stereometer, Brochure No. 14-GB351b-2.*

1) Rzymkowski, J.: Die stereophotographische und stereophotogrammetrische Wiedergobe der Sklera des lebenden Auges nach der Methode Denks-Rzymkowski. 1 (1953).

2) Keyserling, H. v.: Die Auswertung stereoskopischer Schadel-Rontgenaufnahmen mit dem Spiegelstereoskop.

Dt. Gesundheitswes. 11 (1954).

Aerial Photography of the Terrain: Distortion of the Image.

Once the Site position has been defined on the map, it is interesting to identify it in an aerial photograph. Distances should be proportional for the two presentations, but the perspective effects, foreshortening and large variations in the height of the terrain might lead to erroneous estimation of distances and angles in a photograph.

A summary of these well-known effects is available, for example, from Nottingham University, on web-site www.geog.nottingham.ac.uk/~dee/rs/photo. It is concluded that, under normal conditions of aerial photography, distortions only become significant, for our purposes, for points on the terrain more than half a kilometre or so from the point on the ground directly below the camera, known as the 'nadir'. In particular, if the nadir is at the position of the base of the supposed 'marker' tower, radial distances from the image of the tower, for example in our aerial photograph (Fig .2.2.), will appear to be diminished. Because of the approximately 100 metre drop to the Site, this amounts to a 2 mm diminution of the (65 mm) radial distance when measured on the photograph to the north of the tower. This corresponds to 12 metres on the ground. If necessary, some correction can be applied to nullify this discrepancy. There will, of course, be no such distortion effect in the transverse direction. Therefore, features in the neighbourhood of the village and shown on the map, may readily be identified in the photograph, and measurements of distance and angle reliably made to sufficient accuracy.

APPENDIX B
REMOTE AND DIRECT SENSING METHODS FOR LOCATING NON-METALLIC BURIED PIPES.

INTRODUCTION

1. Applicability

One of the principal fixed assets of a gas or oil supply company is its pipelines and associated equipment. But for sound commercial and ecological reasons these assets must be buried, rendered inaccessible and completely hidden. Even maps loose their efficacy as the face of the land changes, or they may not be of sufficient accuracy to avoid costly trial excavations to again trace the pipeline route.

There is a certainly a need for an efficient, low-cost breakthrough in technology to determine accurately the position and depth of these lines, also to identify existing services in proposed new routes. This would facilitate the timely establishment of crossover points well in advance so avoiding costly repairs and interruption to services with the resulting claims for damages.

SCOPE

The use of aerial photography and satellite imagery is discussed together with walk-over direct sensing methods with particular reference to the location of pipelines that fail to respond to the commonly used detection methods.

AERIAL PHOTOGRAPHY

An outline of the essentials of aerial photography is included in Appendix A. The following techniques are of particular use in tracing lineaments relating to trenching where associated with the burial of pipelines:-

1. As many parts of Europe have been aerial surveyed by different organisations at different times it may now be possible to obtain photography flown within one or two years of the actual pipe laying operation and float from the excavation will usually show up particularly in areas of chalk or quartz which have high light reflectivity.

2. The change in the vegetation pattern will persist for many years, either as a line of denudation or as a line of increased growth due to the turning of the soil resulting in a change of soil chemistry or drainage, either favourably or adversely. This is a very durable and is a useful indicative feature persisting for decades.

Lineaments due to other secondary causes such as path patterns may serve indicators to the skilled observer. For example, the tyre tracks of earth moving vehicles and heavy excavation equipment may be easily detected from aerial photographs some years after they were formed.

Colour photography reveals changes in tone and colour and serve as an additional source of information used in the location of buried features.

DEGREE OF PRECISION

The accuracy of determining the position of ground features may be in the region of three metres dependent on the identification of ground objects. One problem is that some indicators seen clearly on a stereo pair of photographs are difficult to identify when on the actual ground.

SATELLITE SENSING TECHNIQUES.

Satellite remote sensing has now achieved a high degree

of precision and definition and is used to produce maps with great accuracy. Identification is down to about a 3-metre square. At the present state of the art, the greatest benefit is derived in mapping the progress and route of new pipelines. Lineaments indicated by remote infra-red heat sensing would probably be of little assistance due to the low specific heat of gases and the diffusion of heat despite the pipeline often being close to the ambient earth temperature.

DIRECT SENSING

The effects of multiple forces in the earth's electro-magnetic field are determined by the vector addition of the individual fields. Where differences are locally generated in the earth field caused by geological or other changes, where, for example, a current is passed down a metal pipeline, the resultant vector will change. These changes may be detected by use of a magnetometer. There is also another detectable signal, which is found to lie in the same vector as that detected by a magnetometer when an electric current has been set up.

Such features as geological faults also generate this additional signal, which is not dependent on any external current input, particularly where sulphide decay creates an electrical potential. However, the vector may be detected even when generated by local changes, particularly of a lin-ear nature, such as found in pipelines and associated earth-works. There appears to be no decay in the signal strength of the vector with time.

INSTRUMENTATION

There are various instruments, which are sensitive to

forces generated by changes to these fields. The two most practical instruments being the 'L' rods, which consist in two metal rods bent in an ' L' shape and the Stressed Wye, which is normally made of some springy wood. At the time of writing, technology has not so far perfected a more sophisticated instrument, which can equal the reliability and cost criteria of these basic designs.

SENSITIVITY

The rods are often useful in detecting the existence of a vector when in the immediate vicinity but these are non-directional, which reduces the information, which may be derived and may only indicate the existence of a vector. The Wye is far more useful and gives an accurate indication as to the strength of the vector signal and the direction, both in the horizontal and vertical planes.

This means that the origin of the vector may be determined accurately together with estimation as to the depth as later described. The relative signal strength derived from different vectors is also evident.

For pipelines, the vector, being the resultant of all fields present, including the background, will diminish in strength within about 10 metres either side, which gives a 20 metre detectable band, under normal conditions.

ACCURACY

The direction of the vector is vertical when over the centre of pipe taken in a direction normal to the pipe and associated excavations. The angle of dip may be determined to within 15 degrees, dependent on the signal originating from the disturbed trenching. The signal from a similar set of circumstances gives a pipeline under investigation a distinctive signature which, in the hands of an experienced operator enables a distinction to be made between the pipeline, crossovers, wye junctions or spurs or non relevant vectors which are often present in the surroundings.

DEPTH

The depth of burial is not a limiting factor in locating the existence of a pipeline. As the vector, normal to the pipe is vertical, and radiates from the centre, by moving away at right angles to the pipe, the vector angle will then change accordingly. When the angle indicated is 45 degrees, the centre of the vector will be equal to the horizontal distance from the point of the vertical indication. Using this feature, estimation may be made as to the depth of the pipe, which is usually the vector centre plus one third. For example, if the distance moved from the centre line of the pipe is three metres and the angle of dip is 45 degrees then the depth of the pipeline is estimated to be three metres plus one third, four metres.

SEARCH METHOD

The most effective method of operation if searching an area is to start from an existing known section of the pipeline, but this is not normally a requirement. A search may commence at right angles to the suspected pipeline route and some distance from it to avoid having to backtrack after starting on the wrong side. When a typical vector is encountered, the rods will swing from the search position, pointing forwards to cross. The Wye will move from the search position pointing forwards to align with the plane of the vector.

The pipeline is followed in the required direction by walking slightly at an angle to the route of the pipeline so to leave the vector every 20 metres and then turn slightly towards it and traversing across whilst moving along the pipe at a fast walk. In this manner, the speed is limited only by the speed of mapping. To this end, a mapper should be present to ensure an accurate record is kept. If desired, red road works tape can be reeled out for later mapping with blue to indicate crossovers. Where the route is thought to be straight searches may be made at various points using a vehicle to move from one point to the next.

EXPERTISE

Success is dependent on a high level of skill and practice coupled with good geotechnical knowledge. Interpretation is the salient point. As with all geophysical methods, however sophisticated, success is dependent on sound working practice linked with technical knowledge and backed by some years of practical work in the field. A high success rate may be expected as all pipelines normally generate a clearly detectable characteristic signal.

Extract from *Piping Guide* HOC archives 1994.

APPENDIX C

THE GOLDEN MEAN

In the sixth century B.C., the Pythagorean philosophers of Greece developed their view that the natural world was, at its most fundamental level, a unified system constructed from geometric and arithmetic relationships. On this rather abstract principle, they were able to construct a consistent system linking morality, justice and liberal education, and to make lasting contributions to mathematics and the theory of musical harmony.

One of their first discoveries was that every number, be it a fraction or an integer, could apparently be represented by a 'ratio', or fraction, involving two other quantities, both whole numbers. Take, for example, the number that we write in our modern decimal notation as 0.2857142857... (this one happens to go on for ever, and repeats every six decimal places, being a recurring decimal). It may be expressed simply as the fraction $^2/_7$, the ratio of 2 to 7. This concept of number might appear quite abstruse and even valueless, but the Greeks took such things very seriously. The concept of 'ratio', a relationship between the eternal whole numbers, offered to them the possibility of freeing mathematics, and indeed, philosophy, from the yoke of mundane things, such as man-made measuring-sticks. Number relationships became basic to their philosophy of life: their approach to intellectual reasoning was founded henceforth upon the pure, dimensionless quantities that were ratios.

Imagine, then, the horror of the Greeks when it was incontrovertibly proved, by none other than Pythagoras himself, that there existed an infinite multitude of numbers that could not be expressed as a ratio. Such numbers include the length of the diagonal of a square, which is $\sqrt{2}$ ($= 1.414213...$ etc.) times the length of a side. The list also contains the famous number π ($= 3.14159...$ etc.), which is involved in the classical problem of the 'squaring of the circle'; that is, evaluating the area enclosed by a circle of any precisely given diameter. Pythagoras showed that such a calculation is impossible, unlike the analogous task of 'squaring the triangle', because it involves the quantity π.

The foundations of Pythagorean philosophy seemed to have been fatally undermined, as more numbers were discovered that could not be expressed as a ratio. Numbers possessing this unwelcome property were dubbed 'irrational' to signify the fact, and an echo from that Grecian trauma has come down to us in our use of 'irrational' to describe that which is devoid of reason or possessing no ratio.

One particular irrational number turned out to be of especial interest to philosophers, mathematicians, architects and graphic artists alike. This was known variously as 'The Golden Mean', 'The Golden Section', 'The Golden Ratio', 'The Divine Proportion', 'and 'The Division of a Line in Extreme and Mean Ratio'.

Suppose we are given a straight line drawn between two points A and B, as in Fig.Ap.1. We are asked to cut the line at some point P, to generate the three line-segments AP,

PB and AB (= AP+PB). What 'interesting' ratios can be formed from these three segments?

The result depends on where we choose to make the cut P. If, for example, we choose to place P half-way between A and B, we can form the ratios AP/PB (=1), or AP/AB (= ½), or other obvious combinations and inverses of these. Such a choice is of no great interest neither to the mathematician, nor to the graphic designer, who is seeking a more 'artistic' position for P: a ratio of lengths on which he may base a composition that does not suffer from the banality of relentless one-to-one symmetry.

Another possibility is to place P close to one end or the other, of line AB. Then, for example, AP/PB and AP/AB become very small, while PB/AB is nearly equal to 1, and PB/AP is enormous by comparison. A basis such as this for pictorial composition would not appeal to an artist, who would find that the important features of his subject were being forced into the corners of his picture. Neither does this particular cut provide much scope for mathematical development. The precise position of P remains undefined, and interesting relations between near-infinite numbers and near-zero numbers, are sparse.

So where would the average artist place the point? It is found that the most favoured position is a little short of ⅔ of the way along AB. Such a cut seems to appeal to human artistic sensibility by defining a pleasing harmony between the lengths AP, PB and the given length AB, of length 1 unit. If, in fact, we make

Fig. Ap. 1. Division of a line.

AP/BP equal to AB/AP, we have extracted two meaningful ratios from the figure and have defined a precise relation between them. This represents the maximum amount of information that can be derived from the positions of the three collinear points. The human brain spontaneously recognises that there is something special about this P-position, hence its universal artistic appeal.

The feeling of balanced design seems to stem from the relation AP/PB = AB/AP. If we designate AP/PB by the Greek letter T (tau), which is the initial letter of the word meaning 'cut', this 'Golden' relation can be written : $T/(1-T) = 1/T$. Solving the quadratic equation for T, we arrive at $T = \frac{1}{2}(1 \pm \sqrt{5})$, which, taking the negative square root, evaluates to 0.618... etc., which is the sought-after distance of P along the unit line AB. It is rather less than the perfectly rational number $\frac{2}{3}$ and contains the irrational number $\sqrt{5}$, which is why it can never be written down as an exact decimal or fractional quantity.

The expression for T allows us to take the positive square root if we so desire, reminding us that we may achieve just as elegant a design by cutting AB at a point beyond B that satisfies the same 'Golden' criterion. This yields a T value of 1.618.. .etc, which, being greater than one, is useful in expanding distances within a picture-frame, while retaining the desired geometric relations.

Nevertheless, the mathematical properties of the number allow easy conversion of one solution into the other:

1/1 .618 = 0.618, while two consecutive enlargements of a given distance involve multiplication by (1.618...) and by $(1.618...)^2$, the latter quantity being just 2.168....

We have a method for extracting square roots, so we can calculate $\mathcal{T}$ to any desired order of accuracy. It is now available on the Internet, printed out to ten million decimal places. This is, of course, a computer exercise: few artists would need more than 4-figure accuracy, which represents the ratio of a typical picture-width (say 1 metre) to the width of the thinnest line (perhaps 0.1 mm) that they might scribe upon the canvas. To seven decimal places, $\mathcal{T} = 1.6180339...$ etc. so, in fact, 1.618 represents something better than four figure precision, because of the low-value digits immediately following the 8.

Nevertheless, mere numerical precision did not entirely satisfy the Pythagoreans. Geometry represented their highest ideal of spiritual purity, and even that discipline should not be contaminated by being dependent on man-contrived standards such as scales of measurement. So geometers sought, and eventually found, a method of draw-ing figures involving the Golden Mean, that relied only on using compasses and a straight-edge, and no gradu-ated ruler was required. The method advocated by Euclid (Elements, Book VI, Proposition 30) seems to have fallen rather short of this ideal, but another technique was discovered that fulfilled

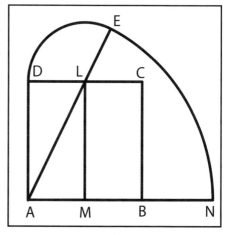

Fig. Ap. 2. Take a square.

all the criteria of practicality, accuracy and purity.

Referring to Fig. Ap.2, and using only the compass and straight-edge, we erect a square ABCD on a given horizontal line AB whose length we may take as 1 unit. Now we cut the square in half, by drawing the vertical line LM. Next, by joining A to L, we form a right-angled triangle ALM. Pythagoras' theorem enables us to analyse this triangle, and that the length AL is the square root of $(AM^2 + ML^2)$, or $\frac{1}{2} \surd 5$ units. Ignoring the awkwardness of this irrational quantity, we take our compasses, and with point L as centre, we draw the arc DE (radius $\frac{1}{2}$), where E is the point where the arc cuts the line AL, extended. We now have a straight line AE of length $(\frac{1}{2} + \frac{1}{2} \surd 5)$ units which, with the aid of the compasses, can be pivoted about point A so as to lie along AB, terminating at N. In this position, its length can be directly compared with the original line AB.

In our original derivation of $\mathcal{T}$ we considered three collinear points:

A, B and P, with AP/BP = AB/AP $=\mathcal{T} = (\frac{1}{2} + \frac{1}{2}.$ $\surd5)$. Now we have three collinear points A, B and N involving the ratios AB/BN and AN/AB.

Using a little arithmetic, we have:

AN/AB = $(\frac{1}{2} + \frac{1}{2} . \surd5) / 1 = \frac{1}{2} + \frac{1}{2}. \surd5$ $(=\mathcal{T})$ and AB/BN = AB/(AN -1) = $1/(\frac{1}{2} + \frac{1}{2}.\surd5 - 1) = 1/(-\frac{1}{2} + \frac{1}{2}.\surd5) = \frac{1}{2} + \frac{1}{2}.\surd5$ ($=\mathcal{T}$ also), so we have cut AN in the 'Golden Ratio'.

Since we are now able to introduce $\mathcal{T}$ into a pictorial design, let us follow the procedure of constructing a picture incorporating this ratio. Take, for example, a seascape. First, we need to decide upon the shape of the rectangular picture-frame. Immediately, we can bring in $\mathcal{T}$ by making one pair of sides approximately 1.618 times as long as the other pair. Already, the shape looks more interesting than, for instance, would an exact square. As regards orientation, we shall choose the longer sides to be the vertical ones (what is known as 'portrait' orientation). To assist in our description of the design process, we may take the height of our picture to be 1 metre. Now we have to draw a horizontal line right across the canvas, to represent the skyline. Its length will be 61.8 cm. Let us place it at a height such that the ratio of sky-area to sea-area is $\mathcal{T}$; that is, the horizon is drawn at a distance of $1/\mathcal{T} = 61.8$ cm from the top of the picture.

We now notice that we have constructed a perfect square in the region above the horizon line. Moreover, the area below it is a rectangle, again of 'Golden' proportions, since $61.8 \div (100-61.8) = 1.618$. Suppose, now, that we wish to introduce a strong vertical line, such as the mast of a ship. This can be placed to cut the horizon in the Golden ratio, i.e., at a distance of $61.8/\mathcal{T} = 38.2$ cm from the left-hand edge of the picture. Let the mast-height be 61.8 cm, then the mast-head can be 38.2 cm above the horizon,

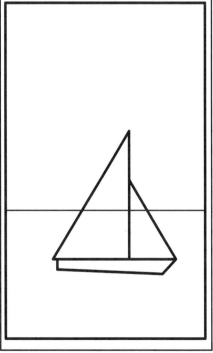

Fig. Ap. 3. A Golden painting.

while deck-level would be 23.6 cm below the horizon. Continuation of this process by the introduction of new features into the composition, leads to ever more detailed subdivision of the picture into squares and Golden rectangles. Even the positions of seagulls can be given a Golden significance! But all this may be accomplished with the aid of the straight-edge and compasses alone: no pocket-calculator is required.

It may be noted from Fig. Ap.2 that a certain angle becomes evident in the construction: the acute angle that AN makes with AB. This angle, so closely associated with the Golden Mean, has the value of arctan(2), or 63.434... degrees (1.1071... radians). Classical painters such as Poussin and Teniers, who made extensive use of the τ ratio, incorporated this 'Golden Angle' into their compositions, in various subtle ways, both for reasons of pictorial composition and as a means of making esoteric references for the benefit of the cognoscenti.

In any case, angular considerations were, and are, useful in artistic design, to introduce a note of dynamism into the picture. Slavish adherence to the τ ratio in the way just exemplified, although it might lead to a classically balanced design, leaves undefined the angle of any sloping lines that might be needed to bring a picture to life. Since the Golden Angle appears naturally in the construction leading to a τ ratio, it is often used to define oblique lines.

Classical painters believed there to be a further advantage in using a well-defined angle such as this. Part of their expertise rested in creating a visual path around their picture, so that the eye of the viewer will be drawn automatically, even sub-consciously, around the painting, passing from feature-to-feature in a sequence substantially determined by the painter. One way to achieve this is to arrange for points of interest to lie on a spiral track that traverses the picture in an ever-expanding orbit. Such a spiral may be derived naturally from the Golden construction of Fig. Ap.1, as follows:

We have a unit-length line AB, and have constructed the line AL, of length 1.618... units, at an angle of 63.434... degrees from it, rotated in the anti-clockwise sense. We may now use AL as the base of a second, larger square, and hence derive another line, say AL_2, analogous to AL, but of a length that is now $\mathcal{T}$ times AL, or $\mathcal{T}^2$ times AB, i.e. 2.618... units, and angled at twice 63.434... degrees from AB. Proceeding in this way, we progressively build up analogous points L_3, L_4, L_5, etc., at distances from the 'focal point' A, of T^3, T^4, T^5, etc. units. All such points, including the initial point B, lie on a 'Golden Spiral', of a type that is known to mathematicians as an equiangular spiral, and is frequently encountered in Nature, for example in Nautilus shells, in Sunflower heads and generally in phyllotaxis. Points on the spiral at distances less than 1 unit from A may be found similarly, by 'shrinking' the construction in the clockwise direction.

APPENDIX D

CALCULATION OF ANGLE OF THE SUN AT MID-DAY 17TH JANUARY AT RENNES-LE-CHÂTEAU.

Perhaps this crucial date is the one that Saunière had felt obliged to obliterate — the 17th of January. Is there anything remarkable about this date? Let us consider the astronomical aspects, well-known since antiquity.

The noonday Sun is at its lowest at the time of the Winter Solstice, 21st December. Its angular distance (say 'ø' degrees) from the zenith is then equal to the latitude of the observation point (42.9 degrees at Rennes-le-Chateau), plus the angle of tilt (23.5 degrees) of the Earth's axis. (In our winter, the N-pole is tilted away from the Sun, and the northern hemisphere is consequently colder).

Ninety days after mid-winter, at the time of the Vernal Equinox, 21st March, the tilt of the Earth's axis has no effect on the climate, since the N-pole is pointing neither towards nor away from the Sun. So the angular distance of the Sun from the zenith is just equal to the latitude. It so happens that the Earth has, during this ninety-day period, traversed 90 degrees of its approximately circular orbit around the Sun, so, apart from negligible variations in the Earth's orbital speed, it advances along its orbit by one degree per day.

What is the value of ø at some date in early spring, when the position of the Earth's axis is beginning to allow a little more sunlight to reach the northern hemisphere? Since the 17th of January has been the object of Saunière's attempts at effacement, let us focus on this date.

Students of trigonometry will realise that the fraction of the Earth's tilt that must be added to the latitude in order to calculate ø for any day of the year, has a sinusoidal dependence on the date. This is a consequence of projecting the direction of the Earth's axis onto the Sun's radial direction. Thus, 27 days (27 degrees) after Mid-Winter, we have:

ø = 42.9+23.5 cosine 27 = 63.8 degrees.

Since this is the angular distance of the Sun from the zenith at midday on 17th January, the elevation of the Sun above the horizon will be 90-63.8 = 26.2 degrees.

Notes

Notes